Successes in anti-poverty

Successes in anti-poverty

Michael Lipton
with assistance from Shahin Yaqub and Eliane Darbellay

Poverty Research Unit
University of Sussex

INTERNATIONAL LABOUR OFFICE GENEVA

Preface

For those with low incomes per person, the level of living depends almost entirely on the fruits of their labour. Even non-workers – children, old people, the chronically sick – rely mainly on the earnings of workers in their families, or on insurance or savings built up during periods of work. Public actions that are "successes in anti-poverty", therefore, have a large overlap with actions that, per unit of cost, are likeliest to achieve sustainable improvements in the level and stability of employment or self-employment, and of earnings, among low-income people.

In the 1960s the prevailing ideology in developing countries was that higher employment incomes for poorer people – and hence successes in anti-poverty – were best achieved by massive public-sector intervention in production, distribution and incentive structures, especially if it accelerated industrialization. The 1980s saw a strong, global reaction. The new ideology was that poverty is best reduced by economic growth, and that growth is best generated by states that maintain secure structures of law and property rights, avoid distorting incentives (especially those affecting foreign trade and exchange), and minimize controls and regulations.

Yet both the 1960s and the "market-friendly" 1980s saw numerous direct interventions aimed at helping to increase the employment of the poor. These actions were widely accepted, though they often strongly opposed the main ideology. Even in the state-friendly and industrialization-besotted 1960s, they were mostly rural, and aimed to increase incomes from private employment or self-employment. Even in the market-besotted 1980s, most direct anti-poverty actions ignored profit maximization and involved substantial selective subsidy.

This study asks two questions. Does growth suffice to help the poor, so such actions are superfluous? If not, are there rules for making them work?

Chapter 3 asks: is economic growth overwhelmingly the main engine of poverty reduction, and do growth and poverty reduction together suffice to enhance health and educational capabilities? Depending on definitions, the level (growth) of average GDP or private consumption appears to be linked to some 30-50 per cent of international variation in the level (decline) of poverty, in the narrow sense of consumption below a fixed absolute poverty line. Similarly, the level (change) of average GDP or private consumption *and* of poverty are linked to some 30-50 per cent of variance in the level (decline) of illiteracy and infant mortality.

Thus growth, as a rule, is very important to a country's successes in reducing poverty, and dissociating it from illiteracy and illness. However, 30-50 per cent is not 100 per cent. Moreover, poverty – and its "bite" into the health and illiteracy of the poor – are causes, as well as effects, of economic growth. So there is plenty of scope for other explanations than slow growth, both for poverty and for its bite. This creates the prospect that direct state actions might reduce or "de-fang" poverty by means other than increasing economic growth.

In evaluating these direct interventions, we cannot undertake the sort of statistical comparisons used in the above analysis, because there are too few internationally comparable micro-level data. However, there have been many studies of particular schemes. In Chapter 4, we collate their findings to derive "rules for success" in the design, location and implementation of schemes aiming to increase or improve incomes from self-employment, among low-income groups, through micro-enterprise credit. In Chapter 5, we ask whether analogous principles apply to schemes for hired employment, through public works or employment guarantees. More briefly, Chapter 6 examines other approaches to poverty reduction by direct interventions thought likely to lead to increased or improved work.

The extent to which principles emerge for each type of scheme, and the similarity of these principles across schemes of different types is very surprising (see table 4). Several of the principles are "market-friendly". They embody ways in which a scheme can be made more compatible with pre-existing markets (e.g. for private loans, or for hired employment) and can allow for the response to the scheme, and to the new incentives it creates, by people acting in these markets. Other principles recognize the actions of people in the political arena rather than the market-place. Other principles are rules of good administration – rules that ideologists claim are secured by the "bottom line" of market profitability or public rules, but rules that in practice often need other means of support, e.g. vigilance in civil society.

The principles of success in anti-poverty illustrate the need, not for bland compromise between statist and marketist ideologies, but for new policy approaches recognizing and sometimes transcending them. Civil society is paramount to overseeing both state and market, and in deterring the agents of each from corrupting the other. However, as Hegel emphasized, even civil society is unlikely to provide a level playing-field for the poor.

Samir Radwan
Director
Development Policies Department

Acknowledgements

Arjan de Haan and Shahin Yaqub have made a substantial input to revising this document for publication. Valuable and careful help with the bibliography was given by Sumir Hinduja and Saurabh Sinha. Statistical analysis was provided by Shahin Yaqub. Melanie Farlow translated various messy drafts up to the final stages of publication.

Contents

List of Diagrams

1. The problem and the approach

On a world scale, the risk, intensity and severity of poverty have fallen more sharply in the past fifty years than in the preceding thousand years [Lipton 1995]. So has the risk that poverty will force its victims into illiteracy, illness or death [UNDP 1994].

Yet in large parts of the world the proportion of people who are too poor to afford enough food regularly, and the intensity of their poverty, are no less – and in some cases more – in 1995 than in 1945. These areas include almost all sub-Saharan Africa. The question naturally arises: under what circumstances can policies or projects, successful in reducing poverty in much of the developing world, work elsewhere? A related question is: what are the features of policies and projects that have been successful in reducing poverty in countries that have in general failed in this endeavour?

In that spirit, this book explores the features of "successful" policies and projects to reduce poverty. It enquires whether any of these features, policies or projects can be imported into environments where poverty has not yet declined significantly. The fact that vast areas of Asia and Latin America, and some of Africa, have so greatly accelerated poverty reduction in the past 50 years strongly suggests that other areas can do so too. There are three more specific reasons for hope.

First, *in almost every country or region, some projects or policies have succeeded.* That is true even for some extremely "difficult" environments for poverty reduction – with very harsh initial poverty, severe inequality, few obvious developmental opportunities or resources, governments that are weak or dominated by local elites, overstretched administrations, and/or little functioning civil society (including NGOs). Such "successes under pressure" range from land redistribution and pro-poor farm extension in Northeast Brazil [Tendler 1993], through famine management in Cape Verde [Drèze and Sen 1989: 133-8], to the Integrated Child Development Service, and even locally successful land reform in parts of Bihar State in India [Heaver 1989; Gopal Iyer 1993: 105-14].

Second, *a few successful schemes appear to be replicable.* Some of the few examples of clear and widespread anti-poverty success tend to be discussed, after the event, as if they had taken place under relatively favourable conditions. Every advantage enjoyed by such schemes is stressed; the huge obstacles that they overcame are forgotten. Yet such obstacles suggest that the "success stories" carry lessons transferable, in part and with suitable adaptation, to areas where similar obstacles have so far frustrated efforts to reduce poverty.

For example, the Grameen Bank in Bangladesh has achieved substantial outreach to poor rural borrowers, very good repayment rates, and a motivated and effective staff. It has indeed enjoyed special advantages: outstanding leadership, substantial and concessional aid finance, and a combination of NGO-style independence and public-sector support. Yet Grameen also faced enormous obstacles in Bangladesh: exceptionally severe poverty and climatic risk; hierarchical rural societies; low levels of education; and in all these and other respects severe discrimination against women, who comprise over 90 per cent of Grameen borrowers. All this was in a country that, until its birth in 1971, had been damaged, bled, and in part corrupted by colonialism and war, with resultant loss of administrative capacity (and to some extent integrity), and of powers of overview by civil society, which even since 1971 remained subject to intermittent but severe political repression. In such difficult circumstances, many credit (and other) NGO-based credit activities in Bangladesh – although sharing Grameen's advantages of charismatic leadership, NGO independence, and external support from government and donors – had failed, either to get off the ground or to survive replication.[1]

Yet Grameen, like other experiments in Bangladesh such as BRAC [Chowdhury and Mahmood 1991] and Proshika [Wood 1984], has *partly* overcome these obstacles, reached the poor, and "gone to scale". Today, Grameen has 1.4 million borrowers; extends over $14 million per month in loans; and enjoys a 97 per cent repayment rate [World Bank 1994a: 54]. This has been achieved in circumstances where several other NGOs, as well as government initiatives, had

1. For example, according to their brilliant designer and implementer, the Comilla-based experiments of the Bangladesh Academy for Rural Development, while locally successful, missed the poorest and were non-replicable [Khan 1974].

failed [McGregor 1988]. Hence Grameen approaches have been successfully adapted to rural poverty reduction from Amanar Ikhtiar in Malaysia, Project Dungganon in the Philippines, and Savecred in Sri Lanka [World Bank 1994a: 55] to Malawi [Hulme 1989] and from urban Dhaka, Bangladesh, to the ghettos of Chicago.

Another example is the Employment Guarantee Scheme for rural public works in the Indian State of Maharashtra. The EGS indeed began with big advantages: a long period of prior preparation of works for construction, a big source of urban financing (taxes on Bombay) and relatively representative and efficient local government and administration. Yet, as with Grameen, so with EGS: it is too often forgotten, by those who seek to explain (or explain away) a scheme's successful efforts to reduce poverty sustainably, that it had faced grave obstacles. It operated in drought-prone and desperately poor places that had resisted earlier efforts at poverty reduction. So it is not surprising that some or all of the EGS principles have proved relevant in other "difficult" areas, from Bolivia to Botswana.

The third reason for a "bias for hope" [Hirschman 1971] about poverty reduction is that *even projects and policies that are oceans of failure often contain islands of success.* So there are lessons to be learned from comparisons within programmes and policy-sets, not just across them. That appears to run counter to the preference of analysts, and resource allocators, for findings that this or that type of project or policy (or agency, incentive, rule, or task specification) is clearly better designed to reduce poverty than the alternatives – at least for many, and precisely bounded, circumstances. Three sorts of evidence suggest that this natural preference may be less "scientific" than it seems:

- Some large programmes – such as India's Integrated Rural Development Programme (IRDP) of subsidized credit for the rural poor to purchase non-farm assets – persistently attract widely different evaluations at roughly the same time, in different places [e.g. Drèze 1988; Paul 1991]. Even allowing for different goals, preferences, and perhaps biases among the evaluators, we cannot escape the conclusion that this programme (like many others[2]) is persistently doing much

2. Indeed, the same evaluator often locates large, not obviously explicable differences in performance of the same scheme. See Heaver [1989] on the blockwise performance of the Indian Child Development Service (ICDS).

better in some cases than in others, despite apparent similarity of rules, circumstances and tasks.

- There are huge fluctuations in the anti-poverty performance of particular agencies. These fluctuations are not obviously related to changes in tasks, personnel, finance, incentives, briefing, or rules [Tendler 1993].

- Perhaps most intriguingly, there is a pattern, clearest in India, in which successful poverty-reducing agencies decline and are replaced by new successes, which then decline in turn. For example, there has been a succession of coordinating agencies responsible for a set of rural anti-poverty activities. From the days of Community Development in the 1950s, these have ranged from the Drought-prone Areas Programme, through the Marginal Farmers' and Landless Labourers' Programme, to IRDP and the employment-oriented JRY today. Most of these big programmes started well. However, each gradually succumbs to rent-seeking by non-poor clients or administrators, or to rivalry from line ministries. Some programmes live on in attenuated form, but usually they are replaced by new schemes, also *initially* successful. New schemes attract public scrutiny; old schemes accumulate clients.

These big differences in programme success, across space and time, leave a sense of discomfort with most standard explanations for success against poverty. Social scientists seek generalizations, applicable over broad swathes of phenomena and conditions. This is indeed essential for useful results. However, we shall not get far if we have the wrong principles of differentiation. For example, success or failure in identifying and helping the poor may depend more upon how *local* managers of an anti-poverty project have been selected, trained, and reassigned, than on their tasks, careers, incentives and rules.

The evidence in this book suggests a general principle for anti-poverty work that applies to the situation and the task design jointly. It is not just a set of rules for selecting project or policy set X in circumstances like A, set Y in circumstances like B, etc. This might be called the **Principle of Joint Requirements**. Poor people are unlikely to achieve durable progress in capabilities and functionings [Sen 1985], and may be unable even to achieve lasting one-off welfare gains, unless they can meet several requirements jointly. They need to be adequately fed. They need sufficient water, clean enough not to make them ill. They need control of infection (and some other primary health care) sufficient to transform adequate nutritional intakes into decent health, for adult work and child growth. They need either physical assets or job access, sufficient to turn their improved physical condition into income. In many cases, they also need access to education, if their improved health, nutrition, and physical assets or job access are to generate levels of income secure against poverty.

The principle of joint requirements is clearest among inputs of human capital. A celebrated finding from the "Narangwal study" [Taylor et al. 1978] is that, given the amount of resources per beneficiary available for *primary health care* and for *food supplementation*, a much greater gain in child health is achieved if those resources are divided between those two uses than if the resources are concentrated on either one of the uses. Similar links have been found between education, especially female education, and the returns to resources used for health improvement, or for family planning.

The non-poor already have access to adequate primary education and preventive health care in most cases. So it is the poor who are likeliest .to gain, if resources for these uses are increased – especially if (for example) primary schooling, preventive health care, sanitation, and screening expand in proportions that satisfy the principle of joint requirements. Moreover, the principle goes beyond social-sector inputs. Health, education and food will raise welfare even if productive opportunity is unchanged; but the high "rates of return to education" and other social-sector inputs, so much emphasized in the literature (e.g. [Psacharopoulos 1981]), will be realized only (1) for those who have the productive capital, or the job access, to turn their mental and physical "capabilities" into income-earning "functionings", and (2) in conditions where the demand for such functionings then grows to match the expanding supply.

Joint requirements need not imply **complementarity**. This, in turn, need not imply a particular pattern of **optimal shared spending** among types of activity, such as a project to expand effective demand for food (e.g. by increasing employment opportunities) and another project to provide extra nutrition and health care:

- Poor people need adequate food and adequate health provision. In the Narangwal case, as in many others, they lack both, so that "joint requirements" for the two goods may well imply "complementarity" between uses of resources to improve them both; and the returns to resources happen to be such that it is best to share extra spending between them.

- But complementarity can exist without optimal joint spending, if one deficiency is very much more serious than the other. For example, if the poor are only slightly and rarely deficient in dietary energy intake, but are subject to serious and frequent malaria, it might make sense to spend the available resources entirely on meeting the graver threat. In Sri Lanka in the 1960s and 1970s, extra public expenditure on primary health care was apparently more than 30 times as cost-effective, in reducing infant mortality, as was extra private consumption (of which over half typically went to obtain food).[3]

- In extreme cases, people's joint requirements need not even imply complementarity (let alone joint spending) on projects or policies to meet such requirements. In rural Sierra Leone, with ample land and (usually) water, seriously deficient calorie intake is rare, but child mortality is terribly high as a result of a near-absence of primary health care in a disease-ridden environment. There, the poverty-reducing return to resources for "poor people's health" might well not be increased at all by spending on nutrition.

- Nevertheless, consumers are usually rational, and the very poor are under special pressure to "ration" their scarce means sensibly. When they find themselves "near the margin" of adequacy – or, in unlucky times or places or circumstances, within that margin – they will not cut right back on *one* key

---

3. The special nature of this striking result [Anand and Kanbur 1991] should be clearly understood. In Sri Lanka about 8 per cent of consumption expenditure accrues to the poorest quintile of persons [World Bank 1994: Table 30], who spend over two-thirds of it on food. Hence, of every extra 100 rupees of private consumption, some 6 rupees may have directly enhanced the nutrition of the quintile at joint health/nutrition risk of increased infant mortality. The Anand-Kanbur result is saying that about 3 rupees spent on primary health care (largely benefiting the health/nutrition situation of the at-risk quintile) could have had the same impact on infant mortality as 100 rupees spent on private consumption (of which little more than 6 rupees may have affected that situation). Furthermore, the disparate effects in Sri Lanka owe much to the availability of free or subsidized rice to the poor.

item such as food. Instead, they will "rationally" choose to cut back to some extent on several items: food, education, health care, etc. These are joint requirements for the decent life. In such circumstances, many of the poor will be unable to meet several such requirements. Often, it will then be best to divide extra public projects or policies between (say) health, education, and employment schemes. There will be optimal joint (shared) spending, as well as complementarity and joint requirements.

If so, there are two main policy implications. The first arises from the administrative shortages, and the high costs of coordination, that have discredited "integrated development programmes" in many countries. If many things must be done, then it may often not be feasible for the public sector to do even those things for which it has a comparative advantage in the field of poverty reduction, in all areas at once.[4] Yet these things are complementary. So poverty reduction may require strong concentration of public actions, in several complementary sectors, on a few regions of greatest need, or where such actions are most cost-effective. This may be needed even at the cost of neglecting some "needy" areas for some time: to be effective the public sector may need to do several things in one region, or for one group, until it becomes able to fend for itself. Indeed, that region or group – once over the poverty threshold – can begin to contribute to the tax revenues needed for the public sector to help in the required many-pronged attack on poverty affecting *other* regions or groups.[5]

The second policy implication of the "principle of joint requirements" relates to instruments. Attempts to rely on just one half of the over-simple dichotomies between paths to policy goals – between states and markets, prices and infrastructure, growth and distribution, productive instruments and welfare instruments, private goods and social services – are likely to be fatal to effective poverty reduction. To meet its joint requirements all the tools are likely to be

---

4. It is also wrong to conclude that the public sector, let alone one "integrated" public agency, needs to do all or most of the job. However, persistent poverty implies that existing public and private agencies had failed to eliminate it.
5. Note that this provides a rationale for concentrating some resources on helping to push people near the poverty line over that threshold – and into the position of net tax payers. However, *most* anti-poverty policy should (but does not) concentrate on the poorest, rather than on those just below the poverty line.

needed, working together, if a poor country is to reduce poverty substantially over much of its terrain.

Apart from the principle of joint requirements, another principle affects the assessment of anti-poverty policies and projects: the **Principle of Total Effect**. It is obvious that we wish to assess the effect of a policy or project on whichever poverty indicator is judged appropriate. Yet those effects are usually evaluated by looking only at the *overt* effects signified by its label. For instance, we often ask only whether an employment guarantee scheme is a cost-effective way to increase employment (in its region of application or even nationwide); or whether a food subsidy cost-effectively improves the nutrition of the poor. In fact, both a food subsidy and an employment guarantee scheme can well affect the poor by changing the level, or the variability, of (1) the wage for unskilled labour, (2) the demand for unskilled labour (i.e. the ease of finding employment), (3) non-labour, or labour-enhancing, sources of earned income – land, health, literacy; (4) social safety nets; and (5) the price of necessities, especially the main food staple. All five depend on (6) the rate of growth of total income, (7) changes in the composition of demand induced by changing incomes and relative prices, (8) similarly induced changes in the factor-mix, and (9) changes in income and asset distribution.[6] Guaranteed employment will not help the poor if it raises their working time by 20 per cent, reduces their average wage rate by 10 per cent, and bids up the price of food by 10 per cent.[7]

"Quick and dirty" checks on the impact of (say) employment guarantees, credit programmes, or food distribution upon total unskilled employment and wage rates, prices of main food staples, and social safety nets usually suffice to trace such effects. Only very large anti-poverty projects and policies justify impact assessment through computable general equilibrium models. These are expensive, hard to interpret, and often dubious because of their simplifications.[8]

---

6. Both distribution and growth are responsible for changing poverty indicators in several developing countries.
7. Many people have a confused understanding of Tinbergen's famous demonstration that, in lower economic systems, there need to be exactly as many policy instruments as there are goals of policy. Even if we lived in a linear economic system, the Tinbergen theorem in no way implies a one-to-one relationship between an instrument and a policy goal.
8. Most CGE models lack a specified capital market, and some – including one that has been widely used to assess alternative anti-poverty programmes in India – lack a market-clearing rule in the labour market as well.

---

2. Outline

An account of all the many types of anti-poverty policy, with examples of success and failure, would be long and themeless. This book, therefore – after examining national performances in turning growth into poverty reduction, and both into better outcomes for the poor – seeks common principles underlying success against poverty in two main policy areas: programmes to enhance the capital (credit) and the labour (employment) resources of the poor. Next, we briefly discuss land-related and other sorts of public policies relevant to poverty. Finally, we ask if any *overall* rules of success in poverty reduction emerge.

First, Chapter 3 examines the evidence about the relationship between growth and poverty, and between the two jointly and two indicators of human misery: illiteracy and infant mortality. This chapter confines itself largely to evidence from the 37 developing and three transitional economies with reliable household surveys. It also explores the evidence about which sorts of country have achieved better anti-poverty outcomes, or less human misery from a given anti-poverty outcome, than would have been expected from their levels of output or growth. Appendix E explores more recent evidence, using new international GDP comparisons (Penn World Tables 5.6); our results are not significantly changed by this new evidence.

Second, Chapter 4 identifies 13 rules that appear to underlie success in programmes to get *credit* to the poor, and thereby to help them to escape poverty by building up *income-yielding physical capital*.

Third, Chapter 5 applies 13 closely parallel "rules" to explain the determinants of success (and failure) in enhancing poor people's *labour income* via programmes of *works to create employment* for the poor. Chapters 4 and 5 comprise the bulk of the work, and are an attempt to summarize what has been learned about how to succeed in anti-poverty policy in two of the most important fields where progress has been made. However, we still need to look at other sources of income enhancement for the poor. Chapter 6 attempts this. Each income source is treated more briefly than was done in the preceding two chapters, and mainly in order to enable readers to assess, in the context of other sorts of anti-poverty programme, the usefulness of the "13 rules" of success that have been illustrated for programmes of credit to enhance poor people's income from physical capital, and of public works to enhance their labour incomes. Among policies to enhance the *land income* of the poor, we look at land reform and at policies affecting agricultural growth and the paths of technical change. We next examine policies to bring social services to the poor, so as to build up their *income from "human capital"* through health or education improvements, or so as to stabilize or increase *social-security income* for persons, times or circumstances that offer no good prospect of earning incomes from land, labour or capital. We next touch on the efforts to create specific *commodity income* for the poor via food subsidization or distribution, and the special difficulties of urban anti-poverty policy.

The discussions in Chapter 6 are brief. Given the constraints of time and space, it seemed better to give a fairly full account of "rules of success" in two types of pro-poor policy (Chapters 4-5) and to use other types to indicate whether these rules were applicable elsewhere, rather than to attempt a skimpy review of all the types. In a fuller review, one would need to assess, for each main type of reform, three issues dealt with by us only for credit and employment schemes. The first issue is the role of price incentives vis-à-vis institutional considerations; thus we look at the role of interest rates and sizes of lending groups in our discussion of credit, and at the wage rate and the political organization of beneficiaries for rural public works, but do not discuss in any detail the compensation price or tenancy rules in land reforms. Second, a fuller review also needs to evaluate, for each main type of anti-poverty measure, the relative importance of raising the income and expenditure of the poor, vis-à-vis transforming a given income-and-expenditure into well-being. Third, one should review the relative benefits to the poor from income transfer as compared with income stabilization; this is discussed only in Chapter 5, in the context of public works employment, and briefly in Chapter 6 in the discussion on human capital. Policy success here requires a sensible balance of goals and outlays, as between improving poor people's average outcomes vis-à-vis reducing their risks of downward fluctuations.

The book raises, but deliberately leaves open, the question of the extent to which similar rules of success indeed apply to all the various types of anti-poverty policy: to macro-policy or food distribution as well as public works programmes, to land reform as well as primary schooling or credit policy. Chapters 4 and 5 suggest, and Chapter 6 to a considerable extent confirms, that there may well be *administrative* rules, especially regarding the degree of decentralization, the use of performance incentives, and the role of NGOs. There are probably *political* rules, for building a strong lobby for an anti-poverty programme by allowing some (but not too many) benefits to accrue to the powerful, and/or for helping the programme to generate lobbies of the poor who, in their own interest, will agitate for more effective use of programme money to benefit them. Finally there may be some common *economic* rules for anti-poverty policies, affecting design, targeting and incentive. *To develop and test common rules of success that cut across programmes, and to specify the regional circumstances – physical, political and economic – where each rule applies in particular ways, is a massive research project of high priority which cannot be attempted here; hence the deliberately open-ended ending.*

The search for common rules, across different types of anti-poverty policy, should in any case not be pushed too far. We should expect to find somewhat different rules for success in macro-policy; in highly political interventions like land reform; and in public works, social services, and food-based and credit-based programmes to reduce poverty. However, the last four types of programme share many "rules" for good performance. One test of these rules will be their relevance to understanding a major mystery of development policy: why, despite the pervasiveness of urban bias and the substantial amount of urban poverty, almost all the success stories of anti-poverty policy are rural.

Three principles may underlie any "rules of success" that we can discover. We proposed earlier a **principle of joint requirements** that applies to the *relationship* among anti-poverty activities and outlays. We also added a **principle of total effect** for *evaluating* each of them. It may be useful to close this outline by proposing a single, though complex, overriding "principle of success" for *designing and implementing* specific anti-poverty activities and outlays. A **Principle**

of Joint Planning does seem to apply to almost every anti-poverty programme – despite their diversity of scale, location, timing, and type. The principle is that an anti-poverty programme's (1) targeting and (2) sustainability need to be planned jointly with (3) income-yielding quality and (4) usability by the poor of acquisitions (whether of capital, education, land, food or whatever) under the programme, and with (5) ways to graduate people out of the programme as they move out of poverty.[9]

The need for *joint* planning of these five features of a poverty programme arises because they *interact*, in ways dependent on the detailed content of the programme, to make it succeed or collapse. Whether an anti-poverty programme of rural credit, or of public employment, is politically sustainable, for example, depends in part on its capacity to enthuse sufficient powerful people (e.g. by producing assets that benefit their farms), or to mobilize poor people in sufficiently powerful political groupings. Whether a programme is economically sustainable depends in part on the accuracy of its targeting, the returns to the projects contained in it – and the extent to which beneficiaries move on and up, into a situation where they can keep themselves out of poverty and contribute to taxes for moving the next cohort of beneficiaries onwards and upwards.

Joint advance planning does not contradict participation and flexibility. Indeed, a programme to get credit, food, or public works jobs to the poor will soon contain nothing to participate in or to be flexible about, unless joint advance planning has secured three things. The first is a shelf of projects, properly pre-assessed or at least with principles for reasonably swift and reliable assessment as new projects are added to the shelf, together with means of implementation and monitoring. The second requirement is that the set of projects is, by and large, of (more or less) known political sustainability, poverty-focus, and benefit/cost ratio. The third requirement, like the others unlikely to be met without joint advance planning, is a means to ensure that net beneficiaries from a programme do not constantly increase, relative to net contributors to its costs.

---

9. This principle, of course, does not imply comprehensive, top-down, centralized planning, but does imply the sort of prediction of likely outcomes, and putting in place of incentives and institutions to make them more likely, that a competent private firm, NGO, or arm of government undertakes before using money for a complex programme or purpose.

3. Anti-poverty success: National-level performance

(i) Assessing performance: Poverty, damage, and the level of resources

Which countries have done better at keeping down, or reducing, the burden of poverty? We look at two sorts of measures of success: direct *poverty* indicators, and indicators of *damage* associated with poverty. Next:

- We establish values of both indicators to be expected at that country's *level of resources*, measured by per capita private consumption or GNP (both adjusted for purchasing power parity). This confirms, of course, that poverty and damage are related to a nation's level of resources; less obviously, it shows that other factors greatly affect success in fighting poverty.

- We compare each country's indicators of poverty and damage with values expected at its level of resources. This identifies aggregate national "success stories" – countries that, by policy or good fortune, have kept poverty or damage below what would be predicted from their resource endowments.[10]

The poverty measure we use is private consumption poverty (PCP) incidence.[11] PCP occurs when private consumption (including imputed value of consumption of own produce, but excluding durables) falls below a "poverty line".

---

10. Other ways of assessing success could have been used; see Appendix A.
11. PCP *incidence* simply counts heads in households with *average private* consumption below the poverty line, as a proportion of the total population. Other indicators are in principle preferable. (a) PCP *incidence* ignores average depth ("intensity") of poverty. Some indicators, e.g. the Foster-Greer-Thorbecke alpha-2, combine incidence, intensity, and maldistribution among the poor to estimate "severity" of poverty [Ravallion 1994; Lipton and Ravallion 1995; Kakwani 1993]. Sometimes, for example in Bangladesh in the 1970s, poverty incidence falls but severity increases [Khan 1977]. Here, we seek to rank countries, areas or projects by performance against poverty or damage; this ranking is seldom affected by measuring poverty incidence rather than severity. (b) *Private* consumption poverty ignores consumption out of common property; out of the subsidy value of public services like education; and sometimes out of some subsistence production. (c) *Average* PCP ignores intra-household maldistribution and fluctuations in circumstance and vulnerability; both may greatly affect poverty and damage.

For international and inter-temporal comparison, this line has to be constant (absolute and fixed, across and within countries). We use the two World Bank [1990] poverty lines: $30 per person per month of private consumption, and a harsher "ultra-poverty line" of $21, both at 1985 prices and purchasing power parities. At $21, the recipient's harshly constrained private consumption choices typically leave barely enough to purchase sufficient food.[12]

As indicators of the damage done by PCP, we choose infant mortality and over-15 illiteracy. Even in poor countries, these events are much rarer among non-poor people, and can be regarded as being largely a consequence of poverty. We avoid composite indicators of damage, such as low values of the "physical quality of life indicator" [Morris and McAlpin 1982] or the "Human Development Index" [UNDP 1991, 1994]. Such indicators have value, but for our purposes they are too arbitrary in respect of (1) what they leave out, (2) what they put in, and (3) the relative valuations (weights) it assigned to the items they put in (e.g. life expectancy and adult literacy). Moreover, (4) all composite indices lose crucial information. We want to know which countries, regions or groups have avoided particular sorts of damage – have attained high life expectancy *and/or* high literacy – despite low average income and/or high PCP; we would learn less from an indicator arbitrarily *amalgamating* literacy and life-expectancy. The HDI, in particular, is based on a magnificent data-gathering effort, from which this paper has benefited; but it has special problems.[13]

---

12. Based on Indian food consumption bundles. This "food energy method" defines the ultra-poverty line as the private consumption level at which a person's dietary energy intake, on average, just meets (rigidly defined) minimum expected needs. This assumes that households optimally select among and between foods and non-foods, and optimally allocate them among members, to maximize satisfaction of needs.
13. The HDI until 1994 was so defined that improvement in the performance of highest-HDI countries appears to worsen the performance of others [Kanbur 1990]. In response to this and other criticisms it has been subjected to several changes, in part impeding year-to-year comparisons [UNDP 1994: 92, 95]. Most seriously for our purposes, the HDI is a weighted sum of several items, including GNP per person – so that it cannot be used to measure (absence of) damage at given levels of GNP per person.

We thus look at two kinds of aggregate "success" at national level against poverty. A country, given its resources and problems, may achieve low levels, or high downtrends, of private consumption poverty (for the $21 and $30 lines), and/or of damage to humans from such poverty. Section (ii) asks: to what extent is PCP associated with lack of real national product, or consumption per person – with lack of resources, rather than of good policies for their allocation and distribution? Which countries seem especially good at avoiding PCP despite small resources? Section (iii) asks: to what extent is "damage" (high illiteracy, high infant mortality) associated with low resources and/or high poverty? Which countries seem especially good at keeping damage low, despite high poverty and/or low resources?

Our work builds on earlier studies at the World Bank by Anand, Chen, Datt and Ravallion (see Bibliography). Our sample of countries rests on their careful selection of household surveys from which reliable and comparable national PCP can be estimated. Chen et al. [1993] report, for the period 1981-91, point estimates of PCP in 40 low-income and middle-income countries (three in Eastern Europe and 37 in the developing world, and including more than 80 per cent of the population of the latter). For two Eastern European and 16 developing countries (over two-thirds of the population of developing countries), data at two time-points are available.[14] For the damage indicators, in order to compare the harm done by poverty, one would ideally seek indicators of health, literacy, etc. among groups in each population below the PCP line. National-level (or at best urban, rural and regional) indicators are usually all we have. However, it is safe to assume that the non-poor can much more often buy into health and education than the poor. If so, higher literacy or life expectancy reflects, to a substantial extent, better access by the poor, probably via public provision.

---

14. The countries listed in Chen et al. [1993] are: in East Asia, China, Indonesia, Malaysia, Philippines (all with two data points), and Thailand; in South Asia, Bangladesh and India (two data points each), plus Nepal, Pakistan and Sri Lanka; in sub-Saharan Africa, Ghana (two data points), plus Kenya, Lesotho, Rwanda, the United Republic of Tanzania, Uganda and Zimbabwe; in Latin America/Caribbean, Brazil, Colombia, Costa Rica, Guatemala, Jamaica, Venezuela (all two data points), plus Chile, Dominican Republic, Honduras, Mexico, Panama and Peru; in the Middle East and North Africa, Morocco and Tunisia (two data points), plus Jordan and Algeria; in Eastern Europe, Poland, and Yugoslavia (each with two data points) plus Hungary. Yugoslav data were incomplete and are omitted in our regressions.

Table 1. Survey-based poverty and related indicators

Country	Household survey year	Country labels in scatter diagrams	In 1985 US purchasing power parity				Infant mortality (per 1000 live births)	Illiteracy (% of persons 15 yrs+)
			Private consumption		Average per person			
			% of population below:		Pvt consmp	GNP		
			US$21/month	US$30/month	US$/month	% of USA 1987		
Algeria	88	Algeria88	0.5	1.5	145	25.9	73	42.6
Bangladesh	85/86	Bangla85/86	2.2	17.0	53	5.0	121	67.8
	88/89	Bangla88/89	7.8	28.5	46	5.1	116	64.7
Bolivia	90	Boliv90	6.7	17.8	86	10.0	102	22.5
Botswana	85/86	Botswa85/86	42.6	54.0	58	16.3	69	30.0
Brazil	85	Brazil85	16.4	26.7	123	23.8	67	21.5
	89	Brazil89	20.6	31.1	124	25.9	61	18.9
Chile	89	Chile89	6.1	15.6	133	32.0	20	6.6
China	85	China85	2.6	11.1	74	5.6	36	31.8
	90	China90	4.7	13.5	82	7.5	30	26.7
Colombia	88	Colomba88	4.6	9.1	205	24.6	46	13.3
	91	Colomba91	2.9	6.6	223	25.5	39	13.0
Costa Rica	81	CRica81	22.7	33.9	65	23.3	27	38.2
	89	CRica89	11.0	18.8	97	23.2	18	7.2
Côte d'Ivoire	85	Ivoire85	5.4	14.3	9	10.0	105	51.3
	88	Ivoire88	4.9	15.7	970	8.9	95	46.2
Dominican Republic	89	DomRep89	11.2	22.3	96	15.8	63	16.7
Ethiopia	81/82	Ethop81/82	9.1	31.6	47	2.0	140	75.7
Ghana	87/88	Ghana87/88	4.7	15.3	73	8.2	89	47.2
	88/89	Ghana88/89	4.5	15.1	73	8.4	87	39.7
Guatemala	86/87	Guate86/87	45.4	60.0	44	14.0	60	48.1
	89	Guate89	38.8	51.6	56	514.8	56	44.9
Honduras	89	Hond89	46.2	60.5	45	8.8	66	26.9
Hungary	89	Hung89	0.1	0.1	159	30.1	16	1.1
India	83	India83	46.8	73.5	27	4.2	120	55.9
	89/90	India88/90	43.3	70.9	28	5.3	94	51.8
Indonesia	84	Indon84	15.8	38.7	45	9.7	79	28.2
	90	Indon90	5.4	21.7	56	12.2	71	23.0
Jamaica	88	Jama88	2.3	6.5	128	15.0	18	1.6
	90	Jama90	0.0	1.9	143	417.0	16	1.6
Jordan	91	Jordan91	5.0	18.3	75	17.2	40	19.9
Kenya	81/83	Kenya81/83	748.7	63.0	40	5.9	80	35.0
Lesotho	86/87	Lestho86/87	35.5	52.3	58	6.6	101	n.a.
Malaysia	84	Malay84	4.6	12.4	138	26.9	28	26.0
	89	Malay89	0.9	6.4	154	30.3	23	21.6
Mexico	84	Mex84	11.4	22.9	97	32.9	50	15.3
Morocco	84/85	Moroc84/85	2.3	7.0	95	13.7	90	58.3
	90/91	Moroc90/91	0.2	11.8	131	15.4	75	50.5
Nepal	84/85	Nepal84/85	17.5	44.3	40	4.2	134	77.6
Pakistan	91	Pak91	2.9	11.4	66	8.9	104	65.2
Panama	89	Panma89	19.2	27.4	109	19.8	23	11.9
Peru	85/86	Peru85/86	11.9	23.9	78	18.6	91	18.0
Philippines	85	Phil85	17.2	34.8	5	10.4	48	12.3
	88	Phil88	12.3	29.7	561	11.4	44	10.3
Poland	85	Pol85	0.6	2.7	79	24.6	19	1.2
	89	Pol89	0.7	3.2	84	26.6	16	1.2
Rwanda	83/85	Rwnda83/85	26.4	57.5	34	4.0	127	54.6

Table 1. Survey-based poverty and related indicators *(cont.)*

Country	Household survey year	Country labels in scatter diagrams	In 1985 US purchasing power parity				Infant mortality (per 1000 live births)	Illiteracy (% of persons 15 yrs+)
			Private consumption		Average per person			
			% of population below:		Pvt consmp	GNP		
			US$21/month	US$30/month	US$/month	% of USA 1987		
Sri Lanka	85	SLank85	26.2	46.6	53	10.8	36	13.3
Thailand	88	Thai88	0.4	10.4	101	19.2	38	7.0
Tunisia	85	Tunis85	1.0	4.6	13	20.4	78	42.4
	90	Tunis90	0.8	2.9	6150	21.6	48	34.7
Uganda	89/90	Uganda89/90	46.9	72.3	28	4.9	99	51.7
U.R. Tanzania	91	Tanzn91	30.5	42.6	73	2.8	102	n.a.
Venezuela	87	Venez87	2.2	6.6	151	36.5	36	14.3
	89	Venez89	10.4	20.5	83	33.1	35	11.9
Yugoslavia	85	Yugo85	3.6	12.1	76	n.a.	23	9.2
	89	Yugo89	10.7	19.8	76	n.a.	24	7.3
Zimbabwe	90	Zimb90	23.3	39.7	78	9.7	61	33.1

Sources and Notes:

Poverty incidence and real mean consumption: Chen, Datt and Ravallion [1993]: Table A3. For those observations where the household survey spans a two- or three-year period, the year of conclusion is used to identify the appropriate annual value of those variables not found in Table A3.

Estimated GNP PPP per capita (as proportion of USA):   GNP at PPP is available for all 40 countries (except Yugoslavia) in Table 30 of WDR 94. However, estimates are provided only for the years 1987 and 1992. These have been extrapolated to the year of household survey for each of the 56 observations. Extrapolation has been based on per capita GNP growth for each country (constant prices, local currency) and mid-year population estimates (World Bank, World Tables 1994)

Infant mortality (per thousand live births):   Table 1 in The State of the World's Children UNICEF (1984, 1985, 1987, 1988, 1990, 1991, 1992). For nine of the 56 observations IM estimates for the year in question were unavailable, and estimates for the immediately preceding or succeeding year were used.

Adult literacy (proportion of those 15 years and older not literate):   For 50 of the 56 observations (as Yugoslavia is excluded from regression), data are from Table 4 of Compendium of Statistics on Illiteracy – 1990 Edition, UNESCO (1990). Data for two of the remaining observations (Lesotho and Tanzania) were unavailable and were excluded. For Ethiopia, Hungary and Poland, we used Statistical Yearbook – 1993 (UNESCO). Of the 54 observations used for the regression the year of illiteracy estimate is separated by no more than two years from the year of household survey. the 7-11 year gap in the remaining cases (two for Poland and one for Hungary) is unimportant since their illiteracy rates were under 2% (by UNESCO in 1980) and could not have fallen much subsequently.

Table 1 reports, for each country and year,[15] two indicators of "resources" (viz. average per-person real consumption and GNP); two indicators of the incidence of PCP (at the $21 line and at the $30 line);[16] and two indicators of damage (viz. infant mortality and illiteracy). These data are shown *for the same year as that for which PCP is given* in each of the 58 nation-wide household surveys in [Chen et al. 1993]; all the years lie between 1981 and 1991. Infant mortality and illiteracy are also extrapolated to the year of survey. Detailed methods are given in the notes to Table 1. Further issues on poverty measurement are taken up in Appendix A. Appendix E reviews a recent revision of the PCP estimates, and shows that this new evidence supports the main conclusions of Chapter 3.

(ii) *Poverty, GNP, consumption: Links and positive deviants*

Table 2 reports eight (2x2x2) simple relationships between the two PCP incidence measures and the two national resource measures, tested for two functional forms: a direct linear regression, and a double-log transformation[17] (implying rectangular-hyperbola relationships between the untransformed variables). The results reveal:

● the strength and shape of the relationship between poverty and per-person resources;[18] and

---

15. The figures in Appendix 3 show that although observations for the same country at two different times are generally fairly close to each other, so are many observations for different countries. Therefore, in preparing the regressions, we have taken all the observations in Table 1 as separate "countries" (i.e. we pool the 40 first-point observations with the 16 second-point observations). Elsewhere we average first and second observations for the eight countries with both [Eastwood, Lipton and Yaqub, work in progress]; results (available from authors on request) are very little affected.

16. The PCP cut-off lines (and hence PCP estimates from the household surveys) are measured in 1985 US purchasing-power-parity dollars, as is average real consumption per person. Average GNP per person is reported [using the World Bank's *World Tables* to extrapolate data from World Bank 1994] as a percentage of the *1987* US per-person PPP-GNP, because 1985 data are available only for GDP – sometimes very different, and a less good measure of resources available to nationals.

17. The double-log functional form is sometimes preferred [e.g. in Chen et al. 1993], because it prevents poverty incidence from taking on negative values on the best-fit line, and embodies an intuitive notion of diminishing returns to resources in reducing poverty (i.e. it is harder to cut PCP (i) from 1 per cent to 0 per cent than from 70 per cent to 69 per cent at a given level of resources-per-person, and (ii) by 1 per cent for each of several successive rises in resources-per-person). Below, we prevent the linear form from predicting negative poverty at high resources-per-person by constraining expected incidence not to fall below zero.

18. See Table 2 for strength, and scatter diagrams 9 – 12 in Appendix B for shape.

Table 2. Poverty regressions (selected years 1981-91)

		Dependent variables	
		Surveyed % of persons with private consumption in 1985 PPP US$, less than:	
		$21 (% below = P1)	$30 (% below = P2)

Explanatory Variables, monthly/capita average	Private Consumption (=C), US$ 1985_PPP	(1) P1= 31.8 − 0.203 C
		
		    (8.7) (-5.5)
		adj. r-sqr.= 0.34 F = 29.8
		
		(2) ln_P1= 11.0 − 2.116 ln_C
		
		    (7.5) (-6.3)
		adj. r-sqr.= 0.40 F = 39.5
			(5) P2= 54.8 − 0.333 C
			
			    (12.7) (-7.6)
			adj. r-sqr.= 0.50 F = 57.0
			
			(6) ln_P2= 10.3 − 1.715 ln_C
			
			    (10.3) (-7.5)
			adj. r-sqr.= 0.50 F = 57.0

	GNP (=G) in PPP, US 1987=100	(3) P1= 24.6 − 0.662 G
		
		    (6.6) (-3.3)
		adj. r-sqr.= 0.15 F = 10.6
		
		(4) ln_P1= 4.3 − 0.968 ln_G
		
		    (-5.5) (-3.3)
		adj. r-sqr.= 0.15 F = 10.9
			(7) P2= 44.4 − 1.185 G
			
			    (9.6) (-4.6)
			adj. r-sqr.= 0.27 F = 21.4
			
			(8) ln_P2= 5.0 − 0.888 ln_G
			
			    (9.4) (-4.4)
			adj. r-sqr.= 0.25 F = 19.1

Source: Table 1.

Notes: Figures in brackets are t-statistics.
All F-statistics and t-statistics are significant at the 1% level.
There are 58 observations for eqns. 1 and 2, and 56 for eqns. 3 and 4
(Yugoslavia has no GNP PPP data).
Logs are to base e.

- the "positive deviants": country-year combinations with less poverty (*perhaps* signifying more success in reducing PCP via distributive or allocative policies) than each of the regressions would predict from national resources; we can examine progress over time in this respect, for 18 countries with data for two years.[19]

---

19. See Appendix B: Tables 1-6 for top performers, and scatter diagrams 5-12 for individual country performance in relation to the regression line; we include enlarged versions of "insets" for clarity.

The results in Table 2 suggest three policy conclusions:

1. *For effective PCP alleviation, countries should pay attention to policies which increase average national resources and to policies that improve the anti-poverty impact of a given level of resources.*

   Obviously, low PCP is harder to achieve with fewer resources per person. Higher averages of per-person real GNP and private consumption are both linked with lower PCP incidence, at both \$21 and \$30 per-month PCP lines. However, depending on choice of resource measure (GNP or consumption), poverty line and functional form, 50-85 per cent of the variance in PCP incidence among countries is not linked to differences in resources-per-person. Thus other things, almost certainly including policies, mediate between average resources and PCP. Most of this book examines the principles of success in specific types of anti-poverty intervention.

   Substantial "space for policy" appears to exist whatever the level of resources per person. The four pairwise comparisons of equations (1) and (2), (3) and (4), (5) and (6), and (7) and (8), provide almost no evidence that resource-poorer countries will find it easier than resource-richer countries to decrease poverty, with an extra dollar of resource. In other words, the double-log relationship between poverty and resource variables is not systematically stronger than the linear relationship (in terms of r^2, F-statistic and t-statistic) except for the regression of PCP below the \$21 line on private consumption per person – admittedly the more "serious" poverty measure, regressed on the more plausible direct explanator.

2. *Private consumption predicts PCP better than GNP. GNP is available for several purposes other than cutting PCP. Nations with high shares of GNP comprising investment, export surplus, and public outlay are somewhat worse (other things equal) at reducing current PCP.*

   The four pairwise comparisons, of equations (1) and (3), (2) and (4), (5) and (7), and (6) and (8), show that average private consumption predicts private *consumption* poverty better than average GNP (all differences were significant at 5 per cent):

more so for the double-log form, and much more so for poverty below the "more serious" $21-line. Of PCP variance,[20] 18-28 per cent more was linked to variance in private consumption per person than to variance in GNP per person, thus at least doubling the r².

The differences between countries in distribution between poor and non-poor are thus more for gains from GNP (including private consumption) than for gains from private consumption itself. It follows that countries with higher private consumption per person are much likelier than others to have lower PCP; countries with higher per-person GNP apart from private consumption are only somewhat likelier. Among countries, the non-private-consumption components of GNP are distributionally regressive (compared to private consumption). This overall result tells us only that for the sampled countries *as a whole*, the *total* value of *all* forms of government expenditure plus private investment does much less than *total* private consumption to reduce the *incidence* (and almost certainly the severity) of *PCP*. The result does not deny that specific types of government expenditure or private investment may be better at reducing PCP than some or all types of private consumption; nor even that public spending or private investment as a whole may be better at reducing non-PCP components of poverty, and/or the "damage" from poverty. Also, this is still just a bivariate result, and there is no causal structure. Nevertheless, especially at the $21 line, the result is very suggestive.

3. *If a country has more resources, this is linked to less improvement in "trickle-down" to the very poor than to the moderately poor.*

The four pairwise comparisons (1) and (5), (2) and (6), (3) and (7), and (4) and (8) show that variance in resources-per-head variables is linked to 9-16 per cent more of the variance in PCP below a poverty line of $30 (US 1985 PPP) per month, than of the variance below a $21 line.[21] This implies that trickle-down effects reducing extreme PCP (below $21) differ much more

---

20. Attempts to regress PCP on both GNP per person and private consumption per person proved unfruitful on grounds of collinearity.
21. The improvement in r² was more for the linear than for the double-log regressions, and for GNP-per-person than for private consumption per person.

among countries with similar resources – GNP or consumption per head – than do similar effects reducing moderate PCP ($21-30). Circumstances (including policy) *other than* resources make more difference to national success in targeting on the very poor, than on the moderately poor.

The above three results are all bivariate, other-things-equal – and have no proven causal structure. They are at best suggestive.[22] Taken together, they suggest that differences in PCP among countries are linked to differences in:

- absolute average resources, and (more importantly, since r^2 for 6 of the 8 equations is well below 0.5) circumstances and policy affecting

- (a) anti-poverty impact of non-private-consumption elements of GNP,

- (b) access of the very poor to national resources.

The next step is to identify the positive residuals from the above equations – the countries with better poverty outcomes than are predicted by the equations. These are the "positive deviants" in the scatter diagrams (Appendix B). Table 2A ranks the top 30 best observations (countries and dates), in decreasing order of "positive deviance" between private consumption poverty, i.e. *rank* in terms of (percentage predicted below poverty line from regression) minus (percentage actually below line). Entries next to country-years show the *value of* this difference, instead of absolute ranking.

---

22. Like all the regressions in Table 2, these three results may be vulnerable to data error. PCP estimates are all from reliable nationwide household surveys [Chen et al. 1993]. Yet problems remain, such as the long Indian controversy about the 10-20 per cent gaps between household-survey (National Sample Survey) and national-accounts private-consumption data. We use *average private consumption* from the same household surveys that provide poverty incidence, but must use PPP conversions (of both consumption and GNP) based on national accounts data; and these are the only sources for *GNP-per-head* numbers. So there may be some non-commensurability between dependent and independent variables. Furthermore, some numbers in Table 1 seem counter-intuitive. One notes the low poverty incidence for Bangladesh (absolutely and as compared to India), and the high incidence, especially in 1981, for Costa Rica. Almost nobody with knowledge of these countries would have expected them to emerge as, respectively, a "good" and a "bad" deviant from worldwide relationships predicting poverty from the resource base. On the contrary, Bangladesh is a byword for severe poverty and hierarchy, and Costa Rica for social arrangements that reduce PCP even when incomes overall are low. However, we are wary of rejecting data such as those in Table 1 – selected to cover all and only countries with good recent consumption surveys – because of preconceptions about poverty (or anything else). We need to look at the residuals with open minds, though not minds emptied of *known* facts about specific countries.

The pattern of the residuals is only briefly touched upon here. First, we note the general pattern of "presences and absences" from the list of apparently successful anti-poverty contenders in Table 2A. The Eastern European countries did somewhat better than predicted in keeping PCP down, though poverty worsened more than resources – slightly for Poland, sharply for Yugoslavia – between the 1985 and 1989 surveys. Indonesia's performance in 1990 – like its sharp improvement on earlier levels – reflects the reported facts [World Bank 1994] of an adjustment programme unusually geared towards improving the position of the poor. But some, perhaps most, of the "good guys and bad guys" implicit in Table 2A are surprising. By 1990, China had ceased to show significant positive deviance on several of the relevant comparisons. Sri Lanka and Costa Rica, normally commended for their anti-poverty performance, are not positive deviants – rather the contrary (see Appendix B, Tables 1-6). On the other hand, few would have predicted that Ethiopia (1981-2), Bangladesh, Pakistan and Morocco – and to a lesser extent Jamaica and Nepal – would emerge as consistently good at turning limited resources into above-expected anti-poverty outcomes.

Probably, the reason for these surprises is twofold:

- Some countries often cited as positive deviants but not so shown in Table 2A – Botswana and the United Republic of Tanzania in Africa; Chile in Latin America – appear to owe their success to a real (PPP) level of income and consumption per person that is higher, relative to other countries in their respective regions, than is indicated by the values at official exchange rates: these countries are not so resource-poor as had been thought.

- For other anecdotally agreed success stories not so shown in Table 2A, positive deviance probably consists mainly, not in turning scant resources into good PCP outcomes, but in preventing serious PCP from inducing very low levels of life expectancy, literacy, or other aspects of human development among the poor. This is confirmed in sub-section (iii) below, for Sri Lanka and Costa Rica. Conversely, some "Table 2A positive deviants" such as Algeria and Pakistan may have kept PCP low, yet done badly for the human capital, or welfare, of the poor or near-poor.

Table 2A. Positive deviants: Private consumption poverty

Entries indicate ranks of top 30 "scorers" (country and year), by "positive deviance" between private consumption poverty, i.e. [rank in terms of (percentage predicted below poverty line from regression) minus (percentage actually below line)]
Entries in brackets show value of this difference instead of absolute ranking.

Rank	PCP incidence: US$21/month poverty line							
	Resource: Pvt consumption/ capita				Resource: GNP/ capita			
	Direct		Log-log		Direct		Log-log	
1	Bangla85/6	18.9	Bangla85/6	11.5	Bangla85/6	19.0	Ethop81/2	26.1
2	Pak91	15.5	Bangla88/9	10.7	China85	18.2	Bangla85/6	12.3
3	Pol85	15.2	India83	10.2	Pak91	15.8	China85	10.4
4	Indon90	15.0	India89/90	9.5	China90	14.9	Bangla88/9	6.7
5	Bangla88/9	14.7	Rwnda83/5	8.6	Ghana88/9	14.5	Pak91	5.5
6	China85	14.2	Ethop81/2	8.5	Ghana 87/8	14.4	Moroc90/1	4.9
7	Pol89	14.1	Nepal84/5	7.3	Ethop81/2	14.1	China90	4.8
8	Ethop81/2	13.2	Indon90	6.8	Moroc90/1	14.1	Jama90	4.6
9	Yugo85	12.8	Uganda89/90	5.9	Ivoire88	13.8	Ghana88/9	4.4
10	Ivoire88	12.7	Pak91	5.7	Bangla88/9	13.3	Ghana 87/8	4.4
11	Ghana88/9	12.5	Pol85	5.3	Jama90	13.3	Thai88	3.6
12	Ghana 87/8	12.3	Pol89	4.5	Moroc84/5	13.2	Ivoire88	3.5
13	Thai88	10.9	China85	4.2	Ivoire85	12.5	Moroc84/5	3.3
14	Jordan91	10.9	Indon84	3.5	Jama88	12.1	Tunis90	2.9
15	China90	10.5	Thai88	3.1	Thai88	11.4	Tunis85	2.8
16	Moroc84/5	10.2	Yugo85	2.8	Boliv90	11.2	Jama88	2.7
17	Boliv90	7.7	Ivoire88	2.7	Indon90	11.1	Pol85	2.6
18	Phil88	7.1	Ghana88/9	2.5	Tunis85	10.1	Algeria88	2.5
19	Indon84	6.9	Ghana 87/8	2.3	Tunis90	9.5	Hung89	2.5
20	Ivoire85	6.3	Moroc90/1	1.8	Pol85	7.6	Pol89	2.2
21	Nepal84/5	6.2	Moroc84/5	1.7	Jordan91	7.4	Ivoire85	2.1
22	Yugo89	5.7	Jama90	1.6	Algeria88	6.9	Malay89	1.7
23	Moroc90/1	5.0	Hung89	1.2	Pol89	6.2	Boliv90	1.3
24	Venez89	4.6	Algeria88	1.1	Colmba91	4.7	Indon90	1.1
25	Peru85/6	4.1	Jordan91	0.9	Phil88	4.7	Colmba91	0.3
26	Jama88	3.5	Tunis85	0.9	Hung89	4.5	Venez87	0.0
27	Phil85	3.4	China90	0.7	Nepal84/5	4.3	Nepal84/5	-0.2
28	Tunis85	3.2	Tunis90	0.7	Colmba88	3.7	Jordan91	-1.3
29	Jama90	2.7	Malay89	0.5	Malay89	3.6	Colmba88	-1.4
30	Algeria88	1.9	Jama88	-0.2	DomRep89	2.9	Malay84	-1.7

Source: Tables 1-6, Appendix B

Table 2A. Positive deviants: Private consumption poverty *(cont.)*

PCP incidence: US$30/month poverty line							
Resource: Pvt consumption/ capita				Resource: GNP/ capita			
Direct		Log-log		Direct		Log-log	
Pol85	25.8	India83	26.4	China85	26.6	Ethop81/2	50.8
Pol89	23.7	India89/90	23.0	Moroc90/1	24.3	China85	21.7
Pak91	21.5	Uganda89/90	21.6	Pak91	22.5	Bangla85/6	19.4
Bangla85/6	20.2	Bangla85/6	14.4	Jama90	22.4	Tanzn91	18.4
China85	19.1	Pol85	13.1	China90	22.1	Moroc90/1	12.2
Yugo85	17.4	Bangla88/9	11.6	Bangla85/6	21.5	China90	11.2
Moroc84/5	16.1	Pol89	11.1	Moroc84/5	21.1	Jama90	10.9
Ivoire88	15.8	Pak91	10.2	Jama88	19.7	Pak91	10.6
Ghana88/9	15.4	Rwnda83/5	9.8	Ghana88/9	19.4	Ghana 87/8	8.3
Ghana 87/8	15.2	Ethop81/2	7.0	Ghana 87/8	19.4	Ghana88/9	8.1
Indon90	14.5	Indon90	6.9	Ivoire85	18.3	Moroc84/5	7.9
China90	14.0	China85	6.6	Ivoire88	18.2	Bangla88/9	7.9
Jordan91	11.6	Nepal84/5	6.6	Tunis90	16.0	Tunis90	7.5
Bangla88/9	11.0	Moroc90/1	4.9	Tunis85	15.7	Hung89	7.4
Thai88	10.8	Yugo85	4.8	Boliv90	14.8	Algeria88	7.0
Yugo89	9.7	Hung89	4.7	Pol85	12.5	Jama88	7.0
Moroc90/1	9.4	Moroc84/5	4.4	Algeria88	12.2	Pol85	6.2
Boliv90	8.4	Algeria88	4.1	Thai88	11.3	Ivoire88	6.2
Ethop81/2	7.6	Jama90	3.8	Ethop81/2	10.5	Tunis85	6.0
Ivoire85	7.6	Ivoire88	3.8	Bangla88/9	9.8	Ivoire85	5.5
Venez89	6.7	Ghana88/9	3.0	Pol89	9.7	Pol89	5.1
Jama88	5.7	Indon84	2.9	Hung89	8.6	Boliv90	3.3
Jama90	5.3	Ghana 87/8	2.8	Indon90	8.2	Colmba91	2.5
Algeria88	5.1	Tunis90	2.4	Colmba91	7.6	Malay89	1.0
Tunis85	5.0	Tunis85	1.6	Colmba88	6.2	Thai88	0.7
Peru85/6	5.0	China90	1.4	Jordan91	5.7	Colmba88	-0.2
Phil88	4.8	Jama88	0.4	DomRep89	3.4	Venez87	-0.3
CRica89	3.7	Thai88	0.0	Malay89	2.1	Nepal84/5	-1.5
Tunis90	2.0	Jordan91	-1.0	Phil88	1.2	Malay84	-4.1
Hung89	1.8	Malay89	-1.4	Malay84	0.1	Indon90	-4.4

The rankings information in Table 2A may be analysed for each country in two complementary ways: first, by country case study, and second by analysis of changes in rank arising from the choice of poverty line, resource measure, functional form, and (for two-observation countries) changes in rank between two points in time. Country studies are not presented, but preliminary comments for Bangladesh, China, Indonesia, India, Ghana and Côte d'Ivoire are made in Appendix C. Analysis of ranks appears in Table 2B in Appendix C. To untangle the implications of the rankings requires deeper analysis (and more econometrics) than is feasible here. Our limited goal has been to show that residuals, and surprising ones, do exist: that anti-poverty success, *given* past growth, is feasible.

(iii) Delinking poverty and resource scarcity from damage and misery?

Table 3 gives linear and double-log regressions of infant mortality (Eqs. 9-12) and over-15 illiteracy (Eqs. 13-16), in the year of household consumption surveys, upon that year's:

(a)   GNP per person (as a proportion of US PPP GNP per person in 1987), and

(b)   PCP incidence below $21 or $30, per head/month.[23]

Table 3 is best read with Table 3A showing rankings of residuals, and with the scatter diagrams below. Table 3A and the diagrams are presented differently from Tables 2A and 2B. Table 3A shows the residuals, but only for the regression equations 10, 12, 14 and 16 in Table 3 where the dependent and independent variables were logged (partly because these alone give significant relationships to poverty; but mainly because there are, putting it mildly, serious

---

23. Again at 1985 PPP. We regressed on mean GNP rather than mean private consumption, because GNP proxies the capacity of a country to support both private consumption and social spending. Our results should be compared with those of (a) Anand and Ravallion [1993] for the relationships; they use double-logged regressions for 22 countries to relate life expectancy at birth and over-15 literacy to PPP public spending on, respectively, health and education per person, and in both cases also to PPP GNP per person and poverty incidence below the $30 PPP (1985) line; and (b) Sen [1980: 13] for the residuals; he compared the ranks of 34 developing countries by life expectancy, poverty incidence (but he had to use national, non-standardized poverty lines, partly because few household surveys were then available) and GNP per person, using Kravis's partial adjustments for PPP.

difficulties in interpreting residuals from the linear equations, which can predict negative or above-100 per cent illiteracy or infant mortality rates).

Table 3. Illiteracy and infant mortality regressions

		Dependent variables						
		Infant mortality (M, per 1000 live births)				Illiteracy (I, proportion of over 15s)		
Explanatory Variables	GNP_PPP/cap (US_1987=100) (=G) % below $21 1985_PPP pvt consumptn per month (=P1)	(9) M= 106 – 0.03 P1				(13) I=55 – 1.53 G – 0.03 P1		
			(11.8)	(-6.6)	(0.1)		(9.5)	(-5.9)	(0.2)
		adj. r-sqr.=	0.48	F = 26.3		adj. r-sqr.=	0.41	F = 19.7
		(10) log_M= 2.28 – 0.55 log_G + 0.07 log_P1				(14) log_I= 2.05 – 0.78 log_G + 0.18 log_P1		
			(18.3)	(-5.7)	(1.8)		(8.4)	(-4.1)	(2.3)
		adj. r-sqr.=	0.48	F = 26.5		adj. r-sqr.=	0.38	F = 17.4
	GNP_PPP/cap (US_1987=100) (=G) % below $30 1985_PPP pvt consumptn per month (=P2)	(11) M= 100 – 2.48 G + 0.14 P2				(15) I=54 – 1.50 G – 0.004 P2		
			(9.2)	(-5.8)	(0.8)		(7.7)	(-5.4)	(0.03)
		adj. r-sqr.=	0.48	F = 26.8		adj. r-sqr.=	0.41	F = 19.6
		(12) log_M= 2.20 – 0.53 log_G + 0.10 log_P2				(16) log_I= 1.80 – 0.71 log_G + 0.26 log_P2		
			(13.5)	(-5.2)	(1.7)		(5.7)	(-3.6)	(2.3)
		adj. r-sqr.=	0.48	F = 26.2		adj. r-sqr.=	0.38	F = 17.5

Source: Table 1.

Notes: There are 56 observations for eqns. 5 and 7 (Yugoslavia has no GNP PPP data), and 54 observations for eqns. 6 and 8.
Figures in brackets are t-statistics.
All F-statistics are significant at the 1% level.
All t-statistics on constants and CNP PPP per person are significant at 1%; t-statistics on P1 and P2 are not significant in linear equations; they are significant at 2.5% in the double-log form for illiteracy, and at 10% for infant mortality (actually 8% in eqn. 10, upon the harder $21 poverty line).
Logs are to base 10.

As was done for Tables 2, 2A and 2B, we now ask: what expectations of country performance are implied by Tables 3-3A? Which countries outperform them?

First, attaining favourable levels of illiteracy and infant mortality – indicators of both "misery" (disutility) and "damage" (reduced capability) [Sen 1985] – is harder for countries with (a) lower GNP per person given incidence of poverty, and (b) higher poverty incidence given GNP per person. This should be interpreted in the light of earlier results about the relationship of PCP to GNP per person.

Second, Table 3 shows that, regardless of choice of poverty line or functional form, *variance among observations (country x year) in PCP and in average real GNP is associated with about half the variance in infant mortality rates, and about 40 per cent of the variance in literacy among over-15s.* This suggests that successful policies have major scope to increase literacy and survival prospects, even with low GNP per person and severe PCP. PCP and per-person GNP are more closely linked to concurrent infant mortality rates than with concurrent over-15 illiteracy rates, because fluctuations in GNP – which, to some extent, captures fluctuations in social provision – affect infant survival prospects more immediately and directly than adult literacy.[24]

Third, a 10 per cent higher (real PPP) GNP per person seems to make a bigger, and more significant, difference to a country's expected illiteracy or infant mortality rate than does a 10 per cent lower incidence of poverty.[25] This result – even though mean GNP affects the risk of misery, and policy can improve this effect – should *not* be read as implying that poverty is unrelated to misery (nor,

---

24. This would make no difference, if the ratio between each pair of countries in terms of PPP GNP per person, and the corresponding ratios in terms of PCP at the relevant poverty line, were to stay still over long periods; however, this is not the case.

25. Using the logged regressions (which alone assign significant influence to the poverty variables), we find that Country A, with a 10 per cent higher real PPP GNP per person than Country B *but the same incidence of private consumption poverty*, can expect an illiteracy rate that is 7-8 per cent lower (e.g. 46-46.5 per cent rather than 50 per cent), and an over-15 illiteracy rate that is rather over 5 per cent lower. However, Country C, with *the same real GNP per person* as Country D but a 10 per cent lower PCP incidence (e.g. 18 per cent rather than 20 per cent of people below the PCP poverty line), can expect an illiteracy rate only 1.8-2.6 per cent lower, and (with only 90 per cent confidence) an infant mortality rate 7-10 per cent lower. Earlier, in Table 2 we showed that a 10 per cent higher real GNP per person was associated with about 9 per cent lower poverty incidence (e.g. 45.5 per cent rather than 50 per cent).

Table 3A. Residuals from logged-form regressions of infant mortality and illiteracy, upon per person GNP (PPP) and poverty incidence (at $21 and $30 lines), and rankings of countries by residuals

COUNTRY	Yr	IMR (GNP, $21) Residual	Rank	Illiteracy (GNP, $21) Residual	Rank	IMR (GNP, $30) Residual	Rank	Illiteracy (GNP, $30) Residual	Rank
Algeria	88	.37589	56	.73931	54	.39516	56	.79566	54
Bangladesh	86	.15901	44	.26929	45	.13261	43	.21453	40
Bangladesh	89	.10712	39	.16008	39	.09795	36	.14424	37
Bolivia	90	.21274	49	-.06281	21	.21392	49	-.05668	21
Botswana	86	.10124	37	.08566	32	.10847	40	.09533	32
Brazil	85	.20761	48	.14220	37	.21233	48	.14642	38
Brazil	89	.18014	47	.09784	34	.18471	47	.09996	33
Chile	89	-.21580	10	-.19341	12	-.22132	10	-.21386	12
China	85	-.34483	4	-.03252	25	-.34832	5	-.02966	25
China	90	-.37550	2	-.05821	23	-.37114	3	-.03990	24
Colombia	88	.09282	34	.04408	30	.10402	39	.07032	31
Colombia	91	.04447	30	.09236	33	.05480	31	.11804	36
Costa Rica	81	-.20206	11	-.30832	10	-.19732	11	-.30530	9
Costa Rica	89	-.35592	3	-.30961	9	-.34834	4	-.29606	11
Côte d'Ivoire	85	.23262	51	.31252	46	.23651	51	.32660	46
Côte d'Ivoire	88	.16488	45	.23546	41	.16257	45	.23486	42
Dominican Republic	89	.09619	36	-.07631	20	.10003	37	-.06932	20
Ethiopia	82	-.04188	22	-.10657	17	-.04292	22	-.09414	16
Ghana	88	.11813	42	.21977	40	.11630	42	.22130	41
Ghana	89	.11438	41	.15478	38	.11159	41	.15383	39
Guatemala	87	.01055	26	.24573	43	.01615	27	.25190	44
Guatemala	89	-.00894	25	.23589	42	-.00191	26	.24624	43
Honduras	89	-.06655	19	-.17666	14	-.05671	20	-.15546	15
Hungary	89	-.19682	12	-.67303	4	-.11155	16	-.43997	5
India	83	.01634	27	-.11217	16	.02416	29	-.09010	17
India	90	-.03128	24	-.05919	22	-.02627	24	-.04601	23
Indonesia	84	.06859	33	-.03991	24	.06322	32	-.05426	22
Indonesia	90	.11032	40	.03223	28	.09439	35	-.00669	26
Jamaica	88	-.40397	1	-.98097	1	-.39618	1	-.95666	1
Jamaica	90	-.29493	6	-.61169	5	-.37141	2	-.78760	4
Jordan	91	-.05892	20	.08196	31	-.06851	18	.05635	30
Kenya	83	-.07813	18	-.20008	11	-.06518	19	-.16779	14
Lesotho	87	.05801	32	—	—	.06823	33	—	—
Malaysia	84	-.10129	17	.36593	47	-.10432	17	.35456	47
Malaysia	89	-.10746	16	.45146	49	-.13415	13	.38493	48
Mexico	84	.16934	46	.13323	36	.16661	46	.11703	35
Morocco	85	.26671	52	.54012	50	.27162	52	.55797	50
Morocco	91	.29385	54	.70870	53	.28043	53	.68866	53
Nepal	85	.09432	35	.10504	35	.09317	34	.10819	34
Pakistan	91	.21994	50	.42453	48	.21504	50	.41953	49
Panama	89	-.30531	5	-.18925	13	-.29524	6	-.17034	13
Peru	86	.29301	53	.00737	27	.29441	54	.00640	27
Philippines	85	-.13350	15	-.38256	7	-.13214	14	-.38044	7
Philippines	88	-.13959	13	-.40346	6	-.14264	12	-.41204	6
Poland	85	-.22670	9	-.84258	2	-.22688	9	-.83697	2
Poland	89	-.28757	7	-.82788	3	-.29093	7	-.83182	3
Rwanda	85	.04845	31	-.09318	19	.04925	30	-.08644	18
Sri Lanka	85	-.26289	8	-.36857	8	-.26127	8	-.36791	8
Thailand	88	.02824	29	-.12947	15	-.04153	23	-.30029	10
Tunisia	85	.32540	55	.60152	52	.31967	55	.59213	52
Tunisia	90	.13531	43	.55139	51	.14218	44	.57511	51
Uganda	90	-.03217	23	-.09606	18	-.02478	25	-.07632	19
Un. Rep. Tanzania	91	-.13735	14	—	—	-.11596	15	—	—
Venezuela	87	.10307	38	.26627	44	.10176	38	.26006	45
Venezuela	89	.01825	28	.03250	29	.01741	28	.02157	29
Yugoslavia	85	—	—	—	—	—	—	—	—
Yugoslavia	89	—	—	—	—	—	—	—	—
Zimbabwe	90	-.05759	21	-.00273	26	-.05175	21	.01033	28

Source: Eqns. 9-16, Table 3.

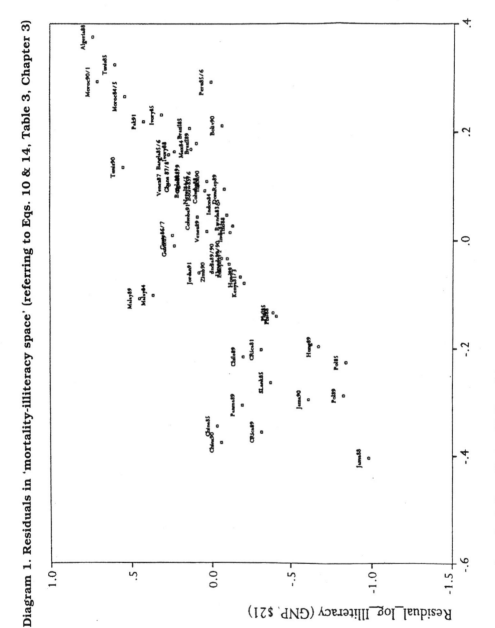

Diagram 1. Residuals in 'mortality-illiteracy space' (referring to Eqs. 10 & 14, Table 3, Chapter 3)

Diagram 1 (Inset) (Section enlarged from previous page)

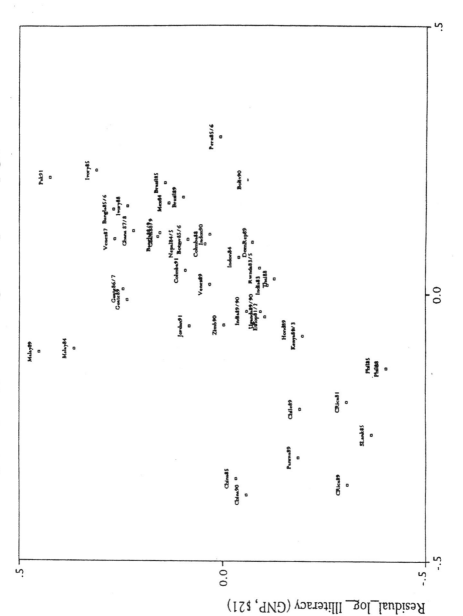

Residual_log_IMR (GNP, $21) (INSET 1)

Diagram 2. Residuals in 'mortality-illiteracy space' (referring to Eqs. 12 & 16, Table 3, Chapter 3)

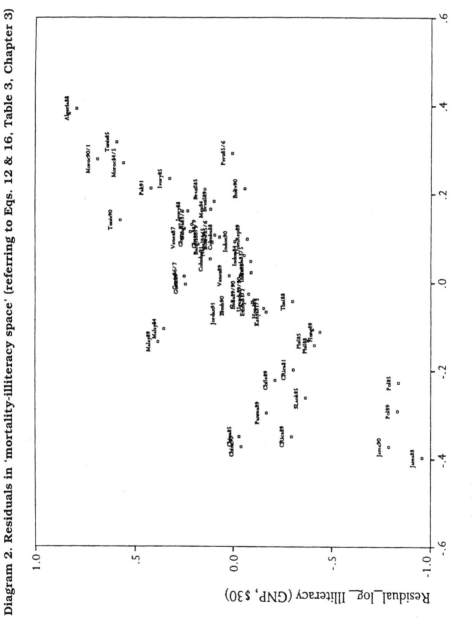

Diagram 2 (Inset) (Section enlarged from previous page)

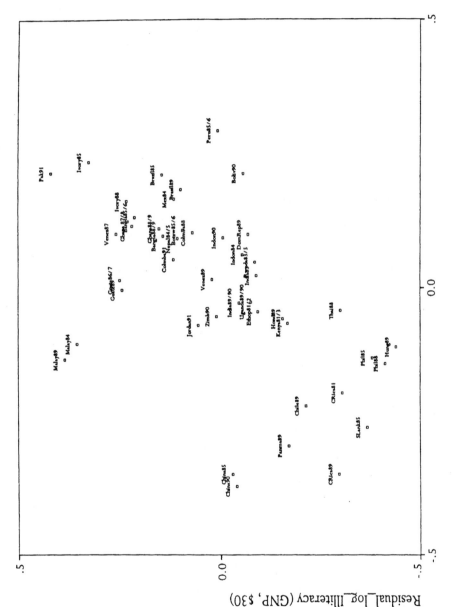

Residual_log_IMR (GNP, $30) (INSET 1)

Residual_log_Illiteracy (GNP, $30)

therefore, that policies against poverty, or delinking it from the misery variables, will do little to improve them). There is no such implication, for two reasons. First, correlation is not causation: Table 3 does not structure the causal links (or absence of links) among poverty, GNP per person, and the misery variables. Causal sequences to "misery" remain to be explored. Second, PCP is not the whole story even of consumption poverty; in particular, government spending (on health care and education) may reduce the components of "misery" considered here, especially among the poor (respectively, high infant mortality and over-15 illiteracy). Anand and Ravallion [1993] estimate the impact on these misery indicators of public spending in health and education; our results are compared in Appendix D.

Fourth, given GNP per person and PCP incidence below $30, there appears little scope for policy to reduce "misery" by altering the distribution *of consumption below the $30 PCP line.* This is in sharp distinction to the situation in Table 2. Pairwise comparison of equations (9 with 11, 10 with 12, 13 with 15, and 14 with 16) in Table 3 shows that the choice of PCP cut-off makes almost no difference to the predictive power (r² and F-statistic) of the regression equations.[26] The beta on G remains almost unchanged between the pairs indicating that, when assessing the impact of extra GNP per person in reducing infant mortality or illiteracy given the incidence of PCP, it makes no difference whether PCP is held constant with the poverty line at $21 or at $30.[27]

We might expect that it is a harder policy task to cut infant mortality or over-15 illiteracy (i) from 9 per cent to 8 per cent than from 25 per cent to 24 per cent at a given level of resources-per-person, or (ii) by 1 per cent for each of several successive 1 per cent rises in GNP-per-person, or in the proportion of persons not in PCP. Thus regressions with dependent and independent variables logged should outperform linear regressions. The impact of PCP on the

---

26. Given GNP, a 10 per cent fall in the incidence of "poverty below $30 per person per month" is associated with a 2.6 per cent fall in illiteracy; as against a 1.8 per cent fall in response to a decline in "poverty below $21". With the $30 PCP line (comparing betas in equation 16), the elasticity of illiteracy to PCP is 37 per cent of its elasticity to real GNP per head; with the $21 PCP line, 23 per cent (equation 14). A similar, though smaller, difference appears in elasticities of infant mortality (for which the betas on poverty are themselves less significant).

27. The t-statistics on the betas on G are somewhat higher for the $21 than for the $30 poverty cut-off, but since both indicate statistical significance at well below 0.1 per cent this hardly matters.

---

misery variables indeed seems to work like this; as noted above, PCP incidence (whether at $21 or $30) becomes significant only in the logged equations in Table 3. However the r^2's, F-statistics and t-statistic on GNP are the same or better for the linear fit than for the logged regression. As with Table 2, so here: the preference for a logarithmic fit lies in the theory (i.e. reduction of heteroscedasticity, or prevention of absurd results such as negative poverty or illiteracy), not in the explanatory performance.

The real need, in subsequent work, is to move on to causal modelling. The unlagged regressions alone suffice for the purpose of this book – to show that private consumption poverty and GNP are associated with much but not all the variation in misery variables, and to preface a look at the residuals, and at the story they may tell about macro-successes in uncoupling poverty from misery. But that is about all they can usefully do.

Success in reducing misery, given resources and PCP:[28] By plotting in the "mortality-illiteracy space" residuals from equations 10 against 14, and 12 against 16 (in Table 3), we identify the countries which have lower over-15 illiteracy and/or infant mortality than would have been expected from their GNP/capita and PCP incidence (below $21 per person per month in Diagram 1, and below $30 per person per month in Diagram 2). Each diagram is followed by an "inset", magnifying a section where the country/date names are too crowded to be read from the main diagram. The larger a *negative* residual, the better is a country performing in keeping the "misery variables" below the expected values; countries are ranked from best (= 1) to worst in Table 3A. Small deviations from the origin (0,0) are of little significance, both in the statistical sense and because of specification error.

Four categories of countries are illustrated in the diagrams. Group 1 comprises clear good performers (on both misery indicators) as compared to misery performance predicted from GNP-per-person and $21 PCP incidence. Group 2 contains good performers, and Group 3 under-achievers, in both cases on only one variable. Group 4

---

28. Note that in this section "successful" countries have large negative values (of actual minus predicted, infant mortality and/or over-15 illiteracy); in the discussion of "positive deviance" in PCP (cf. Tables 2 and 2A) "success" went with large positive values (predicted minus actual PCP).

consists of clear under-achievers (on both indicators). No countries perform significantly worse than expected on one misery indicator but significantly better on the other. In other words, circumstances (including policies), causing a country to perform well or badly as compared with expectations based on GNP and PCP, are linked as between education and health. This is consistent with the "principle of joint requirements", and hence the frequent complementarity of interventions in conditions where several requirements are unmet (Chapter 2). These groups are discussed below using Diagram 1. No major changes in residuals occur over time for the 17 countries with two observations,[29] nor by the choice of poverty line in the equations.[30]

The Group 1 countries, performing better than predicted on *both* literacy *and* infant survival, include some striking examples. Jamaica and Poland (each in two survey years) and Hungary do so well as to be "off the map", to the south-west of countries in Inset 1 related to Diagram 1. Somewhat less successful, but still achieving substantial residuals (especially since these are logarithmic) on both literacy and infant survival, are Costa Rica (in each of two years) and Sri Lanka,[31] and arguably Chile.

---

29. Table 3A and the scatter diagrams do not show really sharp changes in residuals over time, for the 17 countries with estimates for more than one year of illiteracy rates, infant mortality rates, GNP, *and* (from national household surveys) poverty. The years are often close together, leaving too little time for trends in illiteracy to emerge; but this is not the case for infant mortality, which can change quite quickly. The substantial recovery (in only two years) in the social indicators in Venezuela, as compared with expectations from the logged predictions from real GNP per person plus PCP incidence, is striking. The scatter diagrams tend to converge somewhat; the very weak performers on either or both social variables (as compared to the prediction) tend to become stronger, and the outstanding performers slightly less so.

30. Not a lot changes when the $30 PCP line is used (rather than the $21 line) in the equations. The country groupings are then as follows (cf. Diagram 2 and Inset): Jamaica, Poland, Costa Rica, Sri Lanka, and Chile remain in Group 1 (the last three less clearly so); but Hungary moves down to Group 2. China and (to a lesser extent) Panama remain in Group 2 for their performance on infant mortality (but their performance on literacy falls a little); also in Group 2 are Hungary, the Philippines and Thailand for their good performance on literacy. Honduras moves towards the origin. The Maghreb countries, Pakistan and Côte d'Ivoire remain in Group 4, but Bangladesh moves up to Group 3. Peru (especially), Brazil, Mexico and Bolivia remain in Group 3 for under-achievement in infant survival; while Malaysia and Guatemala remain in Group 3 for under-achievement in literacy.

31. This confirms our earlier hypothesis that these two countries' lack of positive deviance of PCP, given resource levels – while contrary to the general view – conceals success in keeping down "misery variables", given both the resource level and PCP; this success in fact underpins the "general view".

Of the Group 2 countries, some do significantly better *only* on infant mortality (China and Panama). Others do significantly better *only* on over-15 illiteracy (Philippines, Honduras and Kenya). The performance of these countries on the other misery indicator is much as predicted.

Of the Group 3 countries, some significantly under-achieve *only* on infant mortality (Peru, Bolivia, Brazil and Mexico). Others significantly under-achieve *only* on illiteracy (Malaysia and Guatemala). Again, the performance of these countries on the other misery indicator is as predicted. In both Group 2 and Group 3 countries, we need to understand what causes one of the social sectors to fall behind the other in respect of its ability to produce better-than-expected outcomes given the levels of poverty and national resources. These reasons may lie in circumstance – age-structure, locally specific health hazards, etc. – but may also lie in sector-specific policies.

Some Group 4 countries, such as Algeria and (in both survey years) Tunisia and Morocco, are so under-achieving on *both* misery variables as to be "off the map" on the inset. Pakistan, Côte d'Ivoire and Bangladesh are also under-performing. Possibly such countries have especially severe gender discrimination [UNDP 1995] in regard to access to health or education.

(iv) Poverty and damage: An assessment

How do the "success stories" on poverty overlap with those on the misery indicators? The really high achievers in *keeping PCP down*, given the resource base, were Bangladesh and China – in the first case with some concern that PCP may be understated, and in both cases with considerably less over-achievement in the later survey year. Other successes were Ethiopia, Ghana, Côte d'Ivoire (in 1988, not 1985), Poland (in 1985 much more than 1989), Morocco, Indonesia, Thailand and Jamaica. The outstanding successes in *keeping misery variables down*, given resources and PCP, were: for *both* illiteracy and infant mortality, Jamaica, Poland, Hungary, and less strongly Costa Rica, Sri Lanka and Chile; for *only* infant mortality China and perhaps Panama; and for *only* illiteracy the Philippines, Honduras, Kenya, and (on some measures) Thailand.

Except for a few countries (China, Poland in 1985, Jamaica, and to some extent Thailand), the two lists are mismatched. Countries such as Morocco, and to a lesser extent Bangladesh and Côte d'Ivoire, featured PCP below levels predicted from real GNP per person, but misery variables substantially *above* predictions from real GNP per person plus PCP incidence. And some countries that did better than predicted on the misery variables did no better, or worse, than predicted in turning GNP into low PCP (Costa Rica, Chile, Panama, Philippines, Sri Lanka).

A major thrust in development economics since the early 1970s – quite consistently across many changing fashions regarding "markets" and much else – has been to downgrade growth as an end in itself, and to upgrade "human development" or capabilities (while stressing that human development helps produce growth). Chapter 3 and new evidence (Appendix E) show that higher resources per person go with less poverty; that both go with more human development; but, above all, that there is much scope for circumstance and policy to enable a country to succeed in delinking either resource scarcity from poverty, or poverty from misery. The "mismatch" between the two sets of successfully delinking countries, just reported, does not downgrade stagnation as a correlate of poverty, or both as correlates of misery. Nor does it modify the finding that policy may weaken or break those links. Rather, it suggests more scope for such policy to reduce misery. Countries that could not weaken the link of resource scarcity to poverty have sometimes succeeded in weakening the link of both to low capability in health or literacy. We now turn to project-level, topic-specific successes against poverty and misery.

4. Credit: Rules for success in anti-poverty action[32]

(i) Measuring success

Usually the success of a credit programme is measured by the extent to which:

(a)   a larger proportion of programme credit goes to the poor than of other credit;

(b)   there is a good economic rate of return to the extra assets, or extra consumption, that beneficiaries obtain as a result of programme credit;

(c)   there is also a good private rate of return, so that poor recipients of programme credit are making more progress in escaping poverty (even after repaying loans) than are otherwise similar poor people who do not receive programme credit;

(d)   loans in the programme, plus interest at realistic (near-market) rates, are repaid to an extent sufficient to keep lenders viable; and

(e)   the programme is financially, administratively and environmentally sustainable.[33]

In assessing what makes credit programmes for the poor successful, let alone "policy-proof", we must confine ourselves mainly to the above indicators. However:

---

32. A recent study of the 3 million UK customers of the 1,200 moneylenders licensed under the Consumer Credit Act (who employ 27,000 house-to-house collectors) shows striking similarities to "rural credit" in the Third World: high interest (105-481 per cent per year – those who can borrow from a building society pay 10-22 per cent), because "lending to people with a high risk of default is very costly, [requiring] door-to-door collection" weekly; flexibility about missed payments, increasing that cost further; little lending to the poorest (on income support from the State), judged bad risks; and tiny loans [Rowlingson 1994].
33. These appear to be widely agreed goals. Exactly the same goals (and no others) are, respectively, (i), (iii), (iv), (ii) and (v) in Getubig [1993].

- Information even on these five dimensions of success is often confined to (a) and (d) above, plus some partial indicators of rates of return – (b) or (c), seldom both.

- The indicators are imperfect. For example (d), repayment, is often indicated by the proportion overdue, which is a very bad estimator of genuine bad debt.[34] On (a), the vast majority of studies fail to measure baseline, i.e. pre-programme, poverty levels of the recipients, and/or to show initial or current poverty levels for a control group of non-beneficiary persons or places. So we cannot know whether changes in the poverty level of credit receivers are associated with the credit programme (let alone the result of it).

- Even if good indicators of all five dimensions were available, there is no agreement on how to weight them. In India the economic returns to formal, state-backed bank credit in rural areas have been quite good if non-farm as well as farm effects are included [Binswanger and Khandker 1992], but how is this success on criterion (b) to be weighed against failure on (d) – the effect of the subsidized interest and poor repayment record in undermining financial viability, both of the formal lenders and of the competing informal lenders that they artificially undercut? Even with perfect and well-weighted indicators for all five "dimensions" (a) to (e), the measure of success of a credit programme for the poor can be misleading and incomplete, for several reasons. The first is fungibility (see subsection (iv) below). A poor person can honestly claim to use extra cash, provided by a programme loan, to buy fertilizer, although she would have bought the fertilizer even without the loan and is spending the extra cash on beer.[35] The second

---

34. See Wiggins and Rogaly [1989], who show that many so-called "overdues" in Tamil Nadu, South India, are backed by collateral (jewel loans). Often, repayment is expected by the agency on a fixed repayment date mistimed vis-à-vis the local farming year [Fernandez 1993: 4], and a secondary "industry" arises in making high-interest, short-term advances.

35. Rugarabamu [1993: 107] reports a common but incorrect suggestion that "in order to ensure that credit is used for the purpose for which it is given, e.g. food production, it may be worthwhile in many instances to deliver it in kind (fertilizer or equipment) and combine it with repayment in kind (paddy, wheat and maize)". This does not solve the fungibility problem; the borrower who had bought the fertilizer, etc., anyway (or who wants another fertilizer, or none at all) simply – or not so simply – sells the loan-in-kind in order to buy the beer. Loans and repayments in kind merely impose transactions costs on both agency and borrower, especially since there are numerous sorts of fertilizer and grades of grain.

problem is that externalities are unmeasured. A loan may reduce A's poverty, but cause A to take actions, e.g. as a consumer or a producer, that drive B, C,... into poverty and/or pull E, F,... out of it. Receivers of Grameen Bank credit in Bangladesh withdrew some labour from the hire market into self-employment, thus raising employment prospects, and income, for poor non-borrowers [Hossain 1988: 66-7]. Our concern is presumably to assess the total impact of a credit programme on the poor; the dimensions (a) to (e) examine only poor borrowers. Third, and especially problematic if it is a huge credit programme such as India's IRDP that is being assessed, the five indicators remain partial-equilibrium. Not only might the state or NGO, instead of providing credit, have used the same resources in alternative ways, perhaps with more anti-poverty effects, in the absence of the credit programme; also, both the programme and its alternatives have second-round effects well beyond the above externalities, and may improve or worsen poverty via prices, outlays, production, or demonstration.

Nevertheless, measurements on the above five dimensions, especially (a) and (d), together with a few hints on the issues considered above, do permit some consensus about what makes for success in anti-poverty efforts based on credit. It makes sense, for a start, to compare two extreme types of lender: the trader or moneylender, with a very localized clientele; and the big bank, whether privately or publicly owned.

(ii) Successful pro-poor credit: Towards synthesis – and some problems

Thirty years ago it was widely believed that the state could and should enrich the poor, at least the rural poor, by "freeing them from the moneylenders" through massive subsidized credit, provided either through state-run banks or by instructions or incentives to private banks. In the 1980s, the new conventional wisdom was that this was almost always disastrous. It was argued that moneylending rates correctly reflected costs and risks of lending; and that state-subsidized credit hardly ever reached the poor, but was drained into rent-seeking by bureaucrats and their rich clients. Perhaps most seriously, "financial repression" – it was argued – not only threatened to bankrupt official credit agencies as they were politically compelled to lend at unrealistic or even negative interest rates and to forgive debts (mainly to the non-poor); it also induced central banks to expand credit in a highly inflationary fashion so as to prevent such bankruptcies, while driving out private savers and lenders through subsidized competition. The state, it was concluded, should get out of direct credit support, and should instead concentrate on creating the environment of law and information that would underpin competitive private financial institutions, including NGOs and moneylenders as well as banks.

This critique contained much truth, but much grotesque exaggeration, especially when the worst excesses of formal credit systems, mostly in Latin America, were used as a basis for global generalizations. For example, expansion of formal-sector rural credit in India – especially provision of branch banks – had a substantial impact on non-farm rural growth, and appears to have earned an acceptable economic return [Binswanger and Khandker 1992]. Interest rates, while somewhat subsidized, have in recent decades hardly ever been negative. The formal-sector lenders, largely cooperatives and public-sector commercial banks, raised their share of rural household credit from 17 per cent in 1961 to 61 per cent in 1981, substantially at the cost of the moneylenders. Because of high transactions costs (and in some cases collateral requirements), these loans reached only a small proportion of the poor, and provided much smaller amounts *per person* than for the non-poor. But in respect of formal borrowing *per hectare* the poor were not discriminated against – rather the reverse. In June 1985, farmers operating less than 1 hectare received 33 per cent of Indian commercial bank loans, while farming only 12 per cent of operated area; small farmers (1-2 ha.) received 29 per cent of bank credit, while operating only 14 per cent of farmland [Dantwala 1989: 416-7; see Chadha 1994: 119, 124, for confirming micro-evidence]. These poorer farmers' share of cooperative and regional rural bank lending was even higher. The criticisms that such lending was not commercially viable, and (owing to debt forgiveness) constituted a huge and politicized drain on the state, are better justified [Reserve Bank of India 1989] – in India as elsewhere; but Indian levels of overdues on formal credit give a grossly exaggerated impression of the bad debts.

As regards the state role in credit for the poor, there is a developing "new synthesis" of the 1990s. It is much more firmly based in study and analysis of financial institutions than either the old populism of massive subsidized, directed credit, or the natural but extreme reaction against state involvement. The new synthesis recognizes that lending to the poor, while often competitive, is inevitably expensive. Transactions costs per loan, for both borrower and lender, are in part fixed, and thus form a high proportion of the very small loans that poor people often need. Big formal lenders, including banks, with thin local knowledge, face especially high costs due to adverse selection (people likely to abuse loans are also likely to seek them) and moral hazard (a person may take greater risks if they can be shared with a lender). Even localized moneylenders often face huge screening costs to reduce such dangers [Aleem 1989], and remote formal lenders tend to fare much worse. Moreover, such costs comprise an especially high proportion of the small, seasonally peaked, often consumption-oriented loans sought by the very poor. Banks also face greater problems in enforcing repayment in remote or dispersed areas, especially if there is no plausible collateral, as is usual for non-landowning poor borrowers. However, formal lenders have one huge advantage over localized lenders. Local loans, especially in agricultural areas, tend to go sour together; when the rains fail, many borrowers in the same village mostly have difficulty in paying – at the very time when very few local lenders are able or willing to refinance the local moneylender thus caught. Such covariance is much less for a big, multi-purpose, multi-sector lender.

The upshot of all this is threefold.

- Formal lenders face even higher costs than local informal lenders in reaching and screening dispersed rural poor borrowers, and in following up loans to them. Indeed, the poor often cannot get the loans they need by offering higher interest rates: the lender will find these may be a self-defeating way to recoup the cost of supervision, since they will induce borrowers to invest in riskier prospects (moral hazard) [Stiglitz and Weiss 1981].

- Therefore, the real problem of the very poor is often not that they face very high interest rates, let alone that they are caught in a debt trap, but that (unless they have collateral, or better-off relatives) they cannot borrow at all.

- Informational and other features of Third World credit markets, especially in remoter rural areas, normally prevent the achievement of a desirable equilibrium (or even a Pareto-optimum), so that some sort of non-market actions by states or NGOs are indicated – provided that the costs of such actions (costs of success as well as of failure) are not likely to exceed the costs of market failure (and "success") in the absence of such intervention.

Several special credit programmes for the poor, most famously Grameen in Bangladesh, have emerged to address such issues. It should be noted that the features making for success in such programmes echo the features of much older credit interventions. Mutual monitoring by small groups or borrowers, as in Grameen, was the central tenet of cooperative credit before it became politicized. Traditional credit institutions (notably rotating credit and saving associations) are as insistent on saving as most of the New Wave institutions.

Before providing an ordered list of the "rules for success" in credit projects, arising out of the new evidence and consensus, three points should be made.

- There is one special problem about generalization. In West Africa, credit scarcity, even among the poor, appears to be much less than elsewhere in the developing world; either the demand (for consumption smoothing and/or to finance new profit prospects) is smaller than elsewhere, or the sources of relatively unproblematic informal credit supply, especially from kin, are more substantial and diverse [e.g. Udry 1989].

- While it is sensible to ask about policy-proof approaches to credit, some sorts of policy will inevitably warp the impact of credit programmes on the poor [Rugarabamu 1993: 106]. If labour-displacing capital is subsidized at the cost of labour, policies that expand the supply of credit – even if it goes to the poor – will, by reducing its price further, stimulate its use to purchase of such capital, damaging employment, and therefore growth as well as the poor; this happened with some tractor-oriented credit in India in the 1970s [Lipton and Toye 1991]. If, as in Brazil in the 1980s, macro-policy brings about rapid swings in the rate of inflation, lenders and poor borrowers will be bankrupted in turn: lenders as real rates become negative when inflation accelerates unexpectedly; poor borrowers as real rates become huge when inflation is cut back suddenly and unexpectedly by temporary expedients such as a new currency issue.

● There is a subset of credit programmes, such as India's IRDP, where extra resources are linked, in ways intended to avoid fungibility, to the acquisition of specific extra assets by poor borrowers. Such programmes raise special issues (see the "rules" 1, 2 and 8 below).

(iii) Thirteen rules for successful pro-poor credit

The new consensus indicates 13 agreed rules for successful lending to the poor. We list them below, before discussing the evidence for each. (The rules are summarized in Table 4 in the concluding Chapter 7).

1. Respect fungibility. Borrowers usually know the best use of funds.

2. Focus extra lending (or incentives to provide it) upon the poor – but not by targeting it directly on persons, let alone households, labelled "poor" by lenders.

3. Therefore, avoid lending rules that discriminate against the poor.

4. In particular, poor people lack collateral; so protect lenders' capital by other means.

5. Keep down the transactions cost of lending, especially as a share of loan size, and for poor borrowers; appropriate intermediation (participatory or otherwise localized) helps.

6. If local supervision (e.g. peer monitoring) is not to lead to covariate risks, adopt nested organization to keep the lender's portfolio diverse, by location and by sector.

7. Avoid monopoly of lending; formal lender, moneylender and NGO are complements.

8. Before the state acts to increase credit supply, ensure that unmet need (or demand) exists for credit to finance either producer goods or consumption smoothing, and that meeting such demand has a satisfactory financial, private economic, and social return.

9. Subsidize administration and transactions costs of lending agencies readily but temporarily; capital loans very sparingly; and interest rates hardly ever.

10. Don't politicize or otherwise soften repayment – though comprehensive credit insurance (with the expense met by borrowers overall) may be sensible in some cases.

11. Good economic returns to credit (and good repayment) are likelier if there is adequate infrastructure and education.

12. Lending institutions gain by insisting that members save before they borrow.

13. Create incentives for lenders to expand where, and only where, they succeed; some do better by providing credit alone, others by combining it with other inputs.

1. Respect fungibility of credit

The standard 1970s model was for "supervised credit". The normal model was that a state-designated agency, lending with interest-rate subsidy to (supposedly) poor borrowers, sought to ensure that they used the loan for a purpose approved as productive by the agency. But such supervision cannot ensure that the extra funds, made available through the loans, support the extra activity, because the borrower might have undertaken it even without the loan. Anyway, even if it is possible to identify genuinely additional purchases due to the loan, a lender – especially an outside, formal lender – is unlikely to be able to do so, particularly for numerous small loans by poor borrowers. Nor will a formal lender often know, better than the borrower, the activity that will use the extra money with the best rate of return; the borrower might best achieve this by repaying an informal moneylender, or buying food.

The lender is rightly concerned about the impact of "uses of loan" upon repayment capacity. However, his best way to improve such capacity – especially if he is a large formal lender, remote from the borrower's problems and alternatives – is not to ignore fungibility, or to second-guess the borrower about the extra purchases made with the borrowed funds. Where lenders try too hard to do so, borrowers often offload the unwanted asset onto the market, driving down the local price and hence their capacity to repay. In the context of India's IRDP, this may be at least as important, in causing asset dispersal and non-repayment, as the fact that subsidies attracted unsuitable applicants [Gaiha 1994: 103].

2. *Seek poverty focus, but by means other than direct targeting*

To ensure failure in credit projects against poverty, target loans to people defined as "poor" by credit project managers, or those whom they can influence. Such **direct targeting** is not feasible in the context of a project to allocate any subsidized or cost-reducing resource, such as credit. Why?

- People who expect loan subsidies, or other advantages, if they are counted as poor are induced to claim that they are poor. They are also induced to act in ways enabling them to appear so, e.g. by reducing their employment income [Besley and Kanbur 1993].

- Locally delegated managers of parts of a large-scale credit project, such as branch bankers and district-level public officials, are induced to compete in four overestimates. They will overestimate the numbers of poor people in "their" areas who: exist; could benefit from programme loans; would repay them; and have already benefited from them. If there is a targeted index of benefit, even an inappropriate one – such as the number of borrowers who "cross the poverty line" because of a loan[36] – it is this number that local bankers or officials are

---

36. This is inappropriate because it encourages project managers to concentrate scarce loans (and the associated value of expected extra income) on borrowers just below the poverty line, so that many of them can be brought above the line with a tiny loan each. Yet more welfare is created if each such loan (and hence each unit of extra income created by it) goes to very poor people, though they do not thereby reach the poverty line. Also, more welfare and income

induced both to increase and to overestimate. If honest and ambitious, they do so to use extra credit effectively against poverty in "their" ambit; if not, to obtain bribes or to increase their patronage.

● Credit managers lack time and resources to identify the poor with reasonable accuracy. Intensive household surveys to identify poverty, such as the World Bank's Living Standards Measurement Surveys, are difficult, costly and time-consuming; for example, several survey rounds, and expert design, interview and analysis, are essential to separate seasonal from occasional (but year-round) poverty, and both from permanent poverty. Such surveys can be highly accurate because they interview only small samples of persons, use substantial resources per interview, are analysed by trained specialists, and are not greatly clouded by motives to distort responses, among either interviewees or survey staff. None of these things applies to interviews by potential lenders – or other project managers – designed to discover which of their clients is poor. No wonder the instructions to such overworked staff are so simplified that they identify the wrong targets, e.g. in the case of IRDP by measuring poverty in terms of total household income irrespective of household size.

Large-scale credit programmes that have attempted direct targeting have experienced substantial leakage to the non-poor. In six large samples of IRDP loans in 1979-86, the proportion of households "formally ineligible", i.e. not below the stipulated poverty line to which Development Block officials and supporting loan agencies were supposed to adhere, were 27 per cent, 15 per cent, 36 per cent, 16 per cent, 21 per cent and 9 per cent [Copestake 1992: 211-2]; intensive local studies suggest data at or beyond the upper end of this range [Drèze et al. 1992: 20; Drèze 1988]. *Yet it is indeed essential to try and target scarce resources* – whether subsidy or administration, and whether supplied by taxpayers or by NGOs – *(a) on poor people, (b) on those likely to benefit from such resources.*

---

might be created by means of a smaller number of slightly larger loans. Both efficiency and poverty reduction are thus harmed by the target selected.

Four approaches have proved more successful than direct targeting by project or credit managers:

- Selection of potential beneficiaries can be made by appropriate local groups. There is a risk of influence by rich patrons, but this can be avoided by the selection of rules – just as MYRADA succeeded in obtaining the selection of poor women borrowers only when village men were excluded from the selection process [Fernandez 1993: 7-8, 12]. Local popular selection seems to work better than administrative procedures where the process is public and accountable. Several studies show that Indian states where village councils have taken over the local identification of the poor select much smaller proportions of ineligible (non-poor) borrowers for IRDP than do states where formal authorities do the identification [Copestake 1992: 212-3].

- It is also possible to target, not individuals or households designated as poor, but those with particular characteristics, not readily changed or simulated, known to be strongly correlated with poverty (such as location in certain areas, or household size).[3] The apparently successful targeting of the small-farm pilot loans in a pilot project in Thailand in 1984 was probably due much more to the location of the 28 villages in identified "poverty districts", than to the income targeting within these villages [BAAC 1988: 77-81]. In Bangladesh, the Grameen Bank limits its loans to households operating below 0.5 acres of land [Holt and Ribe 1991], and several other large informal lenders use similar criteria [Hye 1993: 76-7]. This *land rule* excludes many *large* poor families, and also families with more land but of *low quality*, and includes some non-poor owners of significant non-land assets; if the data are available, land *owned per person*, measured in "*efficiency units*" rather than in crude area, and modified to allow for main sources of non-farm

---

3 .Household surveys, such as those discussed above, at disaggregated level – e.g. by districts, age groups, etc. – can help to identify the types of characteristics (locations, ages, etc.) strongly associated with poverty. (To avoid the problems of misinformation and incentive discussed above, such characteristics should if possible not be easily simulated or changed in order to obtain a loan or other advantage, once it becomes clear that the previously sampled characteristic, associated with poverty in the "small sample", is to be used as a selection criterion in a "universe"). To the extent that such characteristics are also associated with loan repayment and success in benefiting from loans – or at least not associated with the reverse – these characteristics then provide guidelines for individual selection of loan recipients.

income, would be a better indicator of the likely absence of poverty risk. However, even crude "land-contingent targeting" in acres-per-household, while highly imperfect [Ravallion and Sen 1994], often selects poor borrowers better than would otherwise be feasible in practice for loan managers. Special care is needed when a land rule is combined with group lending; if groups are free to select members, they may anyway choose to exclude the very poorest, and a land rule may further exclude those with significant but very bad land.

- One can "self-target" the poor by selecting and enforcing rules that make loans more attractive to poor borrowers than to others. Such rules can apply either to *loans* or (if the fungibility problem can be overcome) to *activities* that they are to support. uickly available, small consumption *loans*, even at quite high interest rates, can undercut moneylenders and meet the needs of the poor; the rich seldom need such loans, and if they do they have the collateral to obtain them more cheaply from banks. Movable hand-pumps for irrigation, being profitable only if worked labour-intensively and in shifts for long hours, are among *activities* attractive only to landless labourers and marginal farmers [Howes 1982]; loans tied effectively to the purchase of *extra* items of this sort self-target on the poor.

- Finally, loans are likelier to reach the poor if steps are taken to improve loan managers' capacity and incentive to identify the target population. In the Grameen Bank, "the manager of a new branch has to survey the concerned villages for two months without subordinates" [Basu 1981: 360]. But incentives, and training, are probably at least as important as such acclimatization.

void anti-poor rules and actions

The requirement of land as collateral prevents tenants and non-farmers from borrowing. This was a striking weakness of credit programmes in Malawi [Sahn and Arulpragasam 1993], which the Mudzi Fund has sought to address [Hulme 1989]. In the case of KUPEDES in Indonesia, even the requirement of a house or house-lot as owned collateral was associated with the virtual exclusion of the very poorest from borrowing [Getubig 1993]. The large rural credit programmes supported by the World Bank in India during the 1970s frequently excluded not only tenants but also the smallest categories of farmers; in several cases only 30-50 per cent of farmers were eligible [Lipton and Toye 1991]. The notable success of MYRADA, Grameen and BRAC in reaching the poorest stems from the use of alternatives to tangible collateral, together with avoidance of formfilling, remote sources of credit supply, delays, and preference for large loans [Fernandez 1993; Getubig 1993; Hossain 1988].

Public actions on subsidies, taxes, technology policy or infrastructure delivery also create a form of "rules", or conditions, strongly complementary with the success or failure of credit in reducing poverty. A pattern of investment, or of technical progress, that demands a high ratio of labour to capital – and does not demand high capacity to bear risk – can enable poor people to prosper even without credit programmes. However, such investments and techniques are likelier to reach the poor if credit is available for them, and poverty-oriented credit is likelier to reach the poor if appropriate investments or techniques are being spread [Binswanger and von Braun 1993: 179, 185]. In the presence of subsidies for tractors and fuel – and without land-saving, labour-using technical progress in seeds, irrigation, etc. – expanded credit will usually do poor people more harm than good. However, *if much new capital is labour-using* it may be complementary with some labour-saving capital. It would then be self-defeating to deny credit for loans to buy the latter sort of capital, even if there were no fungibility [Lanjouw and Stern 1989: 30]. Also, if poor workers come to *own* new labour-saving equipment as a result of credit, there is little reason to deny it; if the loan is repaid, why should not the poor, especially women, choose to take their extra welfare in the form of time, freed up by a small grain huller?

Often, poor people's requirements for *timing* of credit – and of repayment – are not obvious, and do not meet the standard format for formal lenders. The Bangladesh Swiss Agricultural Project found that, if its customers were to avoid distress sales to lenders, they needed loans immediately after the harvest, not only in the hungry season [McGregor 1988]. MYRADA found that it had to adapt the commercial banks' recovery schedules – both to allow for declines in milk yield in summer, and to smooth repayment by marginal farmers by starting it *before* the harvest, since they were usually also farm labourers who earned wages from sowing, weeding, etc. [Fernandez 1993: 4].

4. Find alternatives to physical collateral

To be viable, lenders need ways to avoid moral hazard and adverse selection, and to enforce the recovery of funds. Yet we know the poor lack collateral. Local lenders can instead – at a cost! – use direct observation, enforcement or substitute "roads to recovery". Can NGOs, formal banks and public-sector lenders copy?

Increasingly, Indian commercial banks are using *local intermediation*. Branch banks play this role, but only in large villages, and only if Head Office operates by devolution and incentives, rather than by politicized targets and centralized instructions. Many NGOs have local units which serve as intermediaries by locally agreed sanctions, mutual lender information, [see Udry 1989 on Nigeria], and the threat of denial of future loans [ibid.; Aleem 1989].

Another approach to this problem lies in *credit insurance*. The record of overall crop insurance, except against easily identifiable hazards such as hail, is not good [Hazell et al. 1986]. McGregor [1988] points out that small NGOs, often with high local concentration and hence covariate risk, will have to impose a high premium if they adopt the insurance approach, because they cannot readily reinsure. Thus the Emergency Fund insurance contribution even in the case of Grameen – no minnow, with over 850,000 loans by 1990-91 [Getubig 1993: 110] and 1.4 million now [World Bank 1994a] – often doubled the interest rate payable by final borrowers. Yet the experience of India's Comprehensive Crop Insurance Scheme – applied for over a decade in several states, and mandatory for formal borrowers planning to plant most crops – is highly instructive [this account rests heavily on Mishra 1994]. To minimize moral hazard, insured borrowers receive standard, crop-specific compensation if, and only if, measured samples of crop yield in their locality fall below set limits. The scheme's huge losses are substantially exceeded by the extra agricultural value-added associated with the more risky, but more profitable, output-mix that borrowers have adopted as a result of the scheme. The losses are thus outweighed economically by GNP gains.

Financially, however, though the scheme protects the formal credit agencies – which have preferential claims on insurance payments – it would be unviable without public-sector support;[38] but this is only because the scheme was applied to very risky areas and crops (especially groundnuts in Gujarat) at premia well below economic rates, and indeed below the rates that farmers appeared willing to pay (on top of normal loan interest). This form of insurance – as a compulsory requirement for borrowers proposing to grow certain crops, or all crops – appears to have raised incomes for small farmers proportionally more than for large ones, despite the per-person (but not per-hectare) bias of credit in favour of larger farms; this is consistent with the existence of somewhat greater risk aversion among poorer farmers [Binswanger 1981]. Furthermore, the extra GNP, and the bias in favour of crops with high risk but also high profit (i.e. high input levels, including labour), should militate in favour of extra employment as a result of the schemes. Comprehensive, compulsory loan-insurance linkage is well worth investigating as a means to improve recovery, and to reduce lenders' risk, in offering credit to poor people with little or no collateral. However, such linkage is likely to be feasible only in areas where capacity to repay (not only for crop-specific loans) depends heavily on agricultural risks, and where adequate and trained rural management, and objective and localized measurement of crop yields (or perhaps rainfall adequacy and periodicity), are available.

Large credit agencies can also try to rely on *local agents as credit filters*. BKK in Indonesia requires a local "big man" to speak for borrowers before a loan is given, and rewards him with a share in recoveries; BKK is explicitly aimed at poor farmers, but this method may prevent it from reaching those with nothing to offer a potential patron, as may be indicated by the substantial average size of BKK loans [Getubig 1993: 110]. The SACP in Bangladesh failed to reach the poor largely because it "handed over large parts of the application and processing stage to locally elected officials" in a context where such brokerage "underpins the existing distribution of economic and political power" [McGregor 1994: 105-7].

---

38. Private insurance would not help in this case, as competitors would cream off the more profitable and/or less variable prospects.

Given the problems with local agency, insurance and intermediation as substitutes for collateral, emphasis has shifted to the role of **group lending**. The central idea is that members of a group are co-signatories, jointly taking responsibility for repayment by each member. If any member defaults, other members suffer even if they meet their own obligations, since they face denial of future group loans, loss of repute, and great difficulty in joining future groups. Hence it may be in the interests of a group to adopt "peer monitoring". This enables lenders to reduce both supervision costs and default risk on small loans, yet to avoid collateral requirements that exclude the poor [Stiglitz 1989].

Group lending and peer monitoring are not new. Traditional lending institutions (burial societies, ROSCAs) rest on them. So does cooperative credit, where it is not deformed by political interference and subsidies. What is new is the combination of group lending and peer monitoring with intermediation, usually by branches of NGOs, and with a primarily developmental role for credit that recognizes the issue of fungibility. Nor is group lending the only route to success in credit for the poor. About a fifth of MYRADA's loans are individual. So are almost all the loans of BKK and KUPEDES in Indonesia. Also, it remains unusual for group lending to go beyond joint responsibility for repayment, and to lead to group management of assets with scale economies – though this happens in Bangladesh, in the case of both Proshika (which finances mainly tubewell purchase by grouped landless labourers, who sell the water) and, increasingly, Grameen [Basu 1981: 362]. Yet success in group lending – which is not cheap – seems likelier if such economies of scale exist not only in loan administration, but also in asset management.

The main reason for advocating group lending is that it permits peer monitoring (which is more poor-friendly than collateral) as a means to reduce the risk of default: five loans of $100, to five individuals, are judged more risky than one loan of $500 to a group of five jointly responsible co-signatories, to each of whom the group then normally on-lends a part of that $500. It pays each member of such a group to monitor whether the borrowing colleagues are acting so as to increase the risk of default on their on-loans, because in that event either the defaulter's debts are made good by the colleagues, or the group is denied future credit and the members' reputation suffers so that they have difficulty in obtaining loans as individuals and in joining future borrowing groups. However, there are costs to each group member, certainly in giving the time to monitor her colleagues' repayment (actual and potential), possibly in accepting her colleagues' monitoring of her own repayment. The latter cost arises because, when her colleagues seek to monitor her own behaviour, their aim is to reduce default risk on her on-loan – and this *may* conflict with what she rationally sees as the optimal mix of her activities, aiming at profit and other aspects of welfare as well as risk reduction.

Sensible rules for group lending will be those that tend to raise the benefits, and reduce the costs, of effective peer monitoring for group members. Such rules, however, need to be designed and overviewed so as to increase the likelihood of membership and borrowing by poor people with high prospects of using the extra credit in ways that have good private and social returns. Failure to avoid this risk led to a reduced poverty focus in rural group lending in Thailand [Siamwalla et al. 1989: 36]. "Group members themselves do not wish to [admit] anyone who will be a bigger risk than they...a village whose mean income is one standard deviation above the mean of all villages has a 21 per cent higher probability of having a BAAC group than a village with [average] mean income" [ibid.: 17]. Even Grameen, in Bangladesh, has experienced some drift of group membership towards those who take larger and more readily monitored loans [McGregor 1994: 112].[39]

What is this "peer monitoring" that successful group lending seeks to encourage? There are eight sorts of peer monitoring. It can take place before the on-loan is made (*pre-emptive*), between the on-loan and the consequent change in the borrower's structure of economic activities or assets (*directional*), or after that change, seeking to affect the production pattern, or more broadly the behaviour, of the loan user (*production* or *behaviour* monitoring). In each category, monitors may seek either to prevent a fellow-member from behaving – even if in her own interests – in ways likely to increase the risk of default on the on-loan (*negative* monitoring); or to

---

39. Obviously the benefit, to a group member A, of monitoring repayment is greater if the loan monitored, and hence the cost to the group in the event of its default, is large; the monitoring cost is probably not much larger, and may even be smaller, than in the case of a tiny loan. Richer members tend to seek larger loans. Hence a group, facing incentives to peer monitoring, will – unless other incentives also apply – seek new members who are rich.

improve her information, choices, or management capacity, in her own interests and that of repayment (*positive* monitoring). Negative production monitoring is probably the least important and the least effective of these eight types of peer monitoring: it often comes too late, makes a minor difference to repayment capacity, relates to an unidentifiable activity, and is costly to, and resented by, the recipient.[40] The analytical and empirical work [e.g. Stiglitz 1989, Besley and Coate 1991, Aghian 1994] concentrates heavily on negative production monitoring; but groups can improve repayment of on-loans mainly by pre-emptive and directional monitoring, and by positive monitoring of overall behaviour and to some extent of loan-specific production. The success of group lending depends largely on whether the group's rules and incentives raise the benefits, relative to the costs, of these types of monitoring.

Credit groups are likeliest to succeed (i.e. to induce acceptance of types of peer monitoring most likely to work – viz. positive, and/or pre-emptive or directional, monitoring) if small, voluntary and homogeneous. Large groups run into the free-rider problem – the attitude that (a) if I don't monitor X "someone else" will, whether I notice it or not, and (b) since others take the same view, probably nobody will monitor me. Grameen in Bangladesh, and Mudzi in Malawi, operate with groups of only five (though this is now being increased to eight for many Grameen groups); BAAC in Thailand operates with 8-12 [Siamwalla et al. 1989: 17]; MYRADA typically with 16-25, much smaller than the village groups originally specified centrally [Fernandez 1993; compare Holt and Ribe 1991; Gaiha 1994: 106].[41]

---

40. It may be too late, because the on-loan and its use (if identifiable) have been committed; production monitoring can seldom retrieve matters if the asset has already been very badly chosen or managed. Repayment capacity may be little affected because the extra resources provided by the loan – and hence the relevance of any extra asset, associated with them, to the borrower's capacity to repay – are often small in comparison with the total resources even of a very poor borrower; may not be embodied in production at all; and, even if large and productive, may affect repayment capacity far less than (for example) drinking behaviour, which MYRADA monitors [Fernandez 1993]. Monitors often cannot identify any specific asset or activity as due to the on-loan, due to fungibility. Negative monitoring is costly to the monitored, but positive monitoring can be seen as a benefit by her; indeed, she may become willing to compensate the monitor out of her own perceived gains.
41. However, among Indian states there is no correlation between the average size of village credit cooperatives and the repayment rate. Kerala, with rather large cooperatives, has an unusually high repayment rate [Reserve Bank of India 1989].

MYRADA, like other successful lenders, also found that initial attempts to impose group membership did not work very well, leading to mutual mistrust, and to low attendance and discharge of obligations by members; and that the principles for group exclusion or inclusion, chosen voluntarily, often rested upon traditional groupings of kin or caste [Fernandez 1993: 12-13, 17-18], corresponding in many African contexts to tribe or clan. Since "successful" credit groups – like "successful" employment schemes – mobilize poor members for a wide range of political actions, there are political risks: such political groupings may divide the poor across communalist or ethnic lines. Homogeneity of the group also creates an economic risk: that covariate risks among members' activities may loom large. That risk can sometimes be met by credit insurance, or by "nesting" the local groups into larger structures so that the central lender is not faced with severe covariance, even if some groups are. High covariance of activities among members of a small group, though it does increase the risk of default (absent credit insurance) with a *given* amount of monitoring, also increases that amount; for it not only raises the concern of each member about joint default, but also reduces the cost of positive production monitoring, and increases the likelihood of benefit, since your advice about my activities is likely to be based on personal experience of similar ones.

5.   Cut poor borrowers' transactions costs

Poor borrowers often transact with moneylenders at high rates of interest, though much lower rates are available on loans labelled "for the poor". This is partly because of inappropriate conditions on such loans, but also because their high transactions costs outweigh their low interest rates. Several trips to the central credit source, perhaps in the district capital some miles away, are often needed, and may involve loss of production or employment. Also, bribes to lending agencies or officials are sometimes required; and there is paperwork that ill-educated people cannot manage, and for which they must buy help. Even repayment may be on a schedule that requires many visits and high transactions costs, further encouraging defaults [Fernandez 1993: 31]. If transactions costs are reduced, many more poor borrowers are able to borrow at interest rates high enough to keep the formal lending agency viable, and much higher than those agencies now charge, although still considerably lower than moneylenders' rates [Gaiha 1994: 104].

The main route to reduced transactions costs for poor borrowers, and also to reduced moral hazard, adverse selection and enforcement costs for lenders, is to install local intermediation. Branch banks and village credit cooperatives show that this is an old idea. However, it is costly to implement, especially in dispersed rural areas; the Mudzi Fund in Malawi was located, rightly, in places of denser population [Hulme 1989]. Lending groups, participation, and the principle of "nesting" all help to decentralize lending sources. This cuts borrowers' transaction costs (and improves lenders' knowledge of borrowers), without incurring the large fixed costs (for often small populations, as well as loaned totals) associated with a new branch bank. Nevertheless, formal branch banking – not just informal intermediation – lowers transaction costs of, and encourages expansion by, small rural non-farm entrepreneurs [Binswanger and Khandker 1992].

There remains the linkage of transaction costs to bribes. This is caused by interest rate subsidies, plus the near-impossibility of direct targeting. There are far better things to do, and indeed to subsidize, if the aim is to focus productive rural credit on the poor.

6. *Reduce covariance of repayment, e.g. by nesting peer-monitoring groups*

Especially if lending is confined to farmers, the lender's risks are highly covariate unless there are many, dispersed borrowers. Yet a lender can maintain overview more easily if borrowers are few and nearby. Even group lending, with peer monitoring, appears to work best with small groups.

Loans to individual borrowers still comprise the majority of lending to the poor. With such loans, risks to local branches are reduced if activities are diverse by economic sector and region. The reluctance of many formal lending agencies to support rural non-farm activities, instead of just agriculture, increases their exposure to covariate risk, such as a bad harvest, a price fall for the main cash crop, or pest attack. It also leads them to concentrate where such risks are lower, although the incidence of poverty is clearly greatest in high-risk, especially semi-arid, areas [Rao et al. 1988]. Even large NGOs that are now successful lenders to the poor tended to have their early experience and background in agricultural credit for farm enterprises; therefore they have had to overcome strong initial biases against non-farm lending, and against part-time farmers whose capacity to repay is to some extent protected from the vagaries of farm income [Fernandez 1993: 4-5; McGregor 1994: 109].

Exposure to covariate risk in agriculture is especially severe for lenders, even big ones, concentrated in a large and homogeneous area without much irrigation and/or with only one or two main crops. In such an area, even diversification of lending towards non-farm activities is an imperfect protection against covariate risk, because these tend to do badly (and therefore to be unable to repay) where, and when, farm activities are in the same position [Hazell and Ramasamy 1991]. Successful large-scale agencies for lending to the poor – Grameen, MYRADA, BKK and so on – even if eventually reaching their clients through individual agents in a village (or as members of small self-monitoring groups), therefore increasingly seek diversi-fication over a large and heterogeneous area, as well as over different sectors. This also has the advantage that, if the central institution also takes in savings deposits, a "run" is much less likely; in a big, dispersed and diverse area, not all savers will want their money at the same season or in the same year.

However, though the central lender is safe, the local agent is not. A village branch bank, cooperative, or informal lending intermediary (such as a Grameen group) still finds that in a bad year there is a rush both to withdraw savings and to postpone loan repayments. It was indicated above that rules for agency, insurance, and peer monitoring can help. However, there is a serious problem – of incentives and "infection" across groups – when a lending group cannot pay as a result of downside, locally covariate risks (perhaps due to a drought or flood). The problem arises from the most important principle for decentralizing, yet impelling, responsible repayment, while diversifying the lender's portfolio to reduce covariate risk. This principle is that of **nesting.**

Nesting of members' and groups' responsibilities works like this. In a group of (say) five members, each has an incentive to maintain some common asset – a courtyard, a fish tank, the access to credit that comes from observing an agreement to repay – and to see that fellow-members do the same. Five such *groups*, and the officers in charge of these groups, feel the same manageable incentive to overview and protect the commons shared by these small groups. And so on up. Nesting, along these lines, is the secret of successful management of many forms of interactive sets of common property rights. For example, a few users of a tiny section of a watershed form a primary group, each of whose members accepts self-imposed and monitored limits (and sanctions) on individual overuse of water in the section; several such groups form a "group of groups" that accepts analogous limits and sanctions against overuse by any primary group (i.e. against diversion of too much water into the group's section); and so on [Ostrom 1990]. That "and so on" is what creates the problem, as we shall see from the following discussion of the nesting of credit monitoring.

In the case of lending that ultimately reaches a few borrowers in each of several thousand villages – but with the credit ultimately coming from a big bank or public-sector agency – nesting works like this. Each person in a primary group of (say) five borrowing neighbours is stimulated to monitor her peers because she is a co-signatory for their loans [Stiglitz 1989] and must either pay if they are unpaid, or face the fact that, if the group defaults, it will not readily borrow again and neither will she. About 20 such village-level groups look to the higher-level "block" lender for future credit; hence each block comprises a "group of groups" with an incentive to peer-monitor each other – since group-level default would mean that the group would be denied future credit by the block-level lender.[42] The nesting goes further: several block agencies, in order to ensure future credit from their district-level lender, are encouraged to peer-monitor each other against default. For example, a block-level coop or bank in India, or the analogue in Grameen in Bangladesh, could not borrow (from district level) if its village groups, and therefore itself, were substantially in default on repayments due on earlier loans. The need for nesting these responsibilities arises from the fact that – while the *agency* needs many, diverse borrowers to reduce covariance among risks – the *group* must have few borrowing members; if a group (whether of primary borrowers or of higher-level agencies) has many

---

42. The higher-level groupings are sometimes developed after pressure or action from below [Fernandez 1993: 45], but are usually structured into the programme initially from above.

members, each member relies on the others to monitor – and each comes to feel that there is little risk of *being* monitored!

In big organizations with many primary members (borrowers), the nesting sometimes goes further still. Not only is the block lender the apex organization for the village groups, and the district lender for the block agencies, but also a state or provincial agency can continue or deny credit to the district lenders, and finally a commercial bank, or NGO headquarters, at national level can (and sometimes does) exclude a whole province from further credit until it has improved its repayment rate, and thus that of its districts, blocks, village groups, and ultimately individual members. Not only does the central lender retain control and incentive for repayment at each stage, however decentralized, of the web – "The spider's touch, how exquisitely fine! Feels at each thread, and lives along the line" [Pope 1733: 217] – but the smallest borrower can, by his or her repayment or default, trigger a series of actions at each level upwards. Each nested level of responsibility – centre, province, district, block, village, household – is at once protected (up to a point) against covariate risks *below* the next level down, yet stimulated to induce repayment *by* that level, so that it can itself repay. Above all, units at each level have incentive, and sufficiently small numbers, to monitor each other's repayment prospects and performance: five group members monitor one another, but so do the 10-25 groups in a block, the 15-35 block lending agencies in a district, etc.

Where, then, is the problem? Unfortunately, like many complex structures claimed to produce optimal results, the nesting system does not perform perfectly. Many borrowers reason: "If I default, so may the village cooperative branch bank or *other* peer-monitoring group. Then it (and I) will get no formal credit next year. But will that be different if I and my fellow-villagers repay? Even if our village repays the block lender, many villages in our block will default, so that the block, too, will have to default on repayments to the district lender. Then, the block will not get credit from the district next year, and we in this village will have repaid without benefit. Even if more villages repay than I expect, so that our block does not default, several nearby blocks will; then the district, including all these blocks as well as that containing my village, must default, and will have no access to credit from the higher-level lender next year, so that even if my own area does not default it will get no loans. All in all, I had best default!"

If there is no collateral, therefore, drought (or lax repayment discipline), *near* a group – whether as a small set of individual borrowers, or in a true peer-monitoring arrangement as in Grameen or MYRADA – undermines its members' incentives to repay, and to monitor fellow-members' repayment. This was observed in regard to comparative credit in Sri Lanka in the 1960s [ILO 1971]. The **paradox of nesting**, in its application to credit, is this. The system is designed to stimulate decentralized responsibility, centralized reduction of covariance among prospects, yet peer monitoring of repayment at each level. But the levels interact, discouraging repayment (and peer monitoring) within each unit. That is because units do not look just at members of their own group, but also ask: "Will I and my fellow-members look foolish if we repay, because we shall still be denied subsequent credit when other groups, at the same level as my group *or at higher levels*, default?" That might stimulate each member to press his group to peer-monitor other groups, but this further time-consuming process will be "preferred" to the erosion of repayment discipline only if there is good hope of success, and particularly if there is confidence that the higher levels of lending will not themselves be denied credit. *Breakdown of nested peer monitoring, once past a certain point, thus grows of its own volition.*

Yet several lending agencies have maintained high repayment rates, and other indicators of success, through nested peer monitoring. To the Asian examples analysed by Getubig [1993] should be added MYRADA in India, and the several clones of Grameen, such as that in Malawi [Hulme 1989]. All these agencies, however, can maintain widespread activities – including the enforcement of repayment – only because the apex agency (1) subsidizes, at each level, the administrative, supervision and training costs of peer monitoring (but does not subsidize the interest rate of on-lending), and (2) receives major outside support, permitting it to maintain such subsidies. Grameen, for example, could certainly continue without subsidized help from the government and aid donors, but only on a smaller scale, and probably with much less coverage of areas that are especially difficult for recovery of loans, owing to climatic fluctuations or to severe past erosion of repayment discipline. Yet these are the poorest areas. *To reduce poverty sustainably via group lending, therefore, one may need local agency and/or credit insurance* to supplement nested peer monitoring.

7.   Avoid lending monopolies

The initial aim of the massive expansion of state-supported rural credit in India was to eliminate, or at least greatly weaken, the moneylenders. Their rates were seen as extortionate, and it was felt that cooperative, and later on state-backed commercial bank, credit could replace them. Indeed, the share of lending from informal providers has been greatly reduced in India, though less so than official estimates suggest [Bell 1989]. But the lesson from India, and many other countries, is that borrowers still need informal credit to meet many sudden, or small-scale, needs; and that informal lenders require high interest rates to meet high costs and risks. Competition from formal sources – even if they do not reach many of the poor – keeps down the cost of informal credit by preventing local monopoly. But laws that enable one particular formal source to monopolize credit, even locally, lead to the neglect of credit requirements that the monopoly finds it unprofitable to supply, and to price increases and supply restriction by the monopoly (often through bribes rather than published interest rate schedules).

This does not mean that competitive lending is always practicable, or solves all problems, or always reaches the poor. Commercial banks in India have seldom found that it paid them to set up a competing rural branch bank in a village, or next to a village with a branch of another bank. Work in Thailand and Pakistan, and supporting theory, shows that competition can increase the costs of rural credit, and that apparently "competing" credit suppliers find that it pays them to share information about potential clients, and implicitly to divide up the market [Aleem 1989; Siamwalla et al. 1989]. Also, more credit supply, e.g. from competing lenders, need not bring lower interest rates for poor borrowers if suppliers believe that such rates would encourage borrowers to take on riskier prospects [Stiglitz and Weiss 1981]. Nor does the case against monopoly credit mean that the public sector has no useful role to play in the sector. However, that case is very strong. Except in the very unusual case where the poor themselves both control the credit system (or its political masters) and have strong incentives against the over-expansion of credit supply, any laws or other public actions tending towards local, or other, credit monopoly are likely to damage the poorest by reducing credit supply, promoting its rationing (to the better-off) through bribes and other economic rents, and raising its price.

8. Ensure that extra credit can be productive before raising its supply

State action to expand the supply of credit to the poor normally involves real cost. This can be exceeded by benefit to the poor only if (1) they can undertake a welfare-increasing set of activities that has been constrained by lack of credit supply; (2) the expansion of state credit reaches poor people who will use it to undertake such activities, and (3) is not offset by contraction of these people's private credit (or own-resource savings); and (4) poor people gain more from the release of this credit constraint than from the use of state resources in the activities from which the credit expansion has diverted them. Where the public sector acts to expand credit, too little attention is usually paid to establishing that these conditions, especially the first, are met.

Where there has been a technical or marketing breakthrough that greatly increases the returns to using resources (especially land and labour) owned by poor people, the demand for such resources will rise and the poor will benefit, even without expansion of public credit supply or incentives. When the "green revolution" struck the Indian Punjab, little was heard about credit constraints, either on growth or on the expansion of employment income for the poor (indeed, credit subsidies eased the path to mechanization that *reduced* growth in employment for the poor). On the other hand, if the profits or risks of extra production in an area are unattractive, or are attractive only if the production is highly capital-intensive, no amount of credit will be likely to increase productive inputs or investments in a way that helps the poor. *It is in the intermediate cases – where there are opportunities for productive expansion by, or using the labour of, the poor, but these are not quite profitable or safe enough to be taken up – that state action to increase the supply or competitiveness of credit for production are likeliest to help the poor.* Their welfare can also be helped, in a wide range of cases, by credit that eases "consumption smoothing" [Besley 1995], or that enables the poor to spend more on education or health care; but, where this cannot be transformed into extra productive capacity, the issue of where the resources are coming from is acute. Distributional benefits may accrue even without extra output, but probably not if poor people's extra credit comes at the cost of other pro-poor activities, as is likely in any given balance of political power.

Even if extra publicly-induced credit does reach poor people, and is associated with activities that durably raise their income levels, "success" is likely only if further questions are asked *early*. Does the credit increase, or decrease (perhaps by a large part of its own value), the credit available to these poor people from other sources – private, family, or community? Where credit is genuinely additional and is embodied in productive inputs or investments, are these labour-using or labour-displacing; risk-reducing or risk-increasing; suitable for small family enterprises or for large formal concerns? And – a question insufficiently considered by some credit programmes integrated with the purchase of particular "developmental" items, such as milch cattle under IRDP – can the new, poor owners of assets, bought with the new credit, ensure the purchase price is fair, manage the assets technically, and market their product?

9. Subsidize transactions costs and administration, not interest

It is not true that subsidized credit is always biased against the poor, or that it is never justified. Suppose that expanded productive activities in a particular area, or for a particular targetable group, offer a good return eventually but have an initial risky period, or a period of learning. Then subsidized credit, as a means to encourage experiment (especially by the poor, less-literate and risk-averse), may be preferable to subsidies for specific production inputs. That is because, cash being fungible, each recipient of subsidized credit can select the preferred use of the extra resources, whereas an agency subsidizing inputs can seldom judge which inputs merit which subsidies (and this differs across areas anyway). However, it cannot be efficient to divert credit to places where its return is less than could be attained elsewhere, and interest-rate subsidies, especially if "directed" (however inefficiently) towards particular aims or groups of recipients, tend to do that. Such subsidies also tend to undercut, and thus to repress, alternative sources of credit, even when those sources do things that the subsidized lender cannot, or will not, do efficiently.

Prolonged interest-rate subsidies on some forms of credit distort the whole credit market, even for non-subsidized credit. They also set up expectations for public-sector credit subsidies that tend to increase, leading to the nightmare of negative real interest rates over long periods, bankrupting credit agencies or else requiring ever more inflationary injections of public funds. Large interest-rate subsidies almost always go disproportionately to wealthy borrowers. In a study in Tamil Nadu, such subsidies also tended to discourage saving [Wiggins and Rogaly 1989]. It is unlikely, too, that heavily subsidized interest rates will reach many of the poor.

However, this does not mean – as was believed by many critics in the 1980s – that the state does best for the poor, or for productive efficiency, if it withdraws entirely from credit, apart from the provision of a legal and regulatory framework. Partly because interest-rate rationing does not pay many local private lenders, whereas commercial and public-sector lenders are deterred from supplying poor people or remote areas by high transactions and enforcement costs, it is likely that poor people are substantially "under-borrowed" in many developing countries. In other words, the social rate of return to expanding credit for the poor exceeds the private rate. But it is self-defeating to use this as a pretext for financial indiscipline (whether through lax repayment or through substantial interest-rate subsidies) by branches of the agency, let alone by final borrowers.

Yet *almost all the success stories of credit for the poor* – whether through banks, NGOs, groups of the poor themselves, or public-sector agencies directly – do *rest upon substantial subsidies* from the state, or from international concessional lenders relying on the state as guarantor of "sovereign risk". However, these subsidies are *to the agency, in order to reduce the administrative or transactions costs* of lending in ways that are convenient to poor borrowers – costs that they would otherwise have to recover from those borrowers. In other words, the Grameens, MYRADAs, and so on could lend to the poor without artificial support, but only on a much smaller scale. The subsidies are *not direct to borrowers, especially not as reduced interest rates for on-lending*. Indeed, even where the subsidies are expressed in the form of low-interest loans *to the agency* – as with Grameen or MYRADA – the final lender usually insists that the agency should not pass on any substantial interest-rate subsidy *to the final borrower*, but should use the support to defray his or her (or its) transactions costs, and to support administration, training, and loan recovery. Evidence from Bangladesh, Indonesia and elsewhere indicates that very poor borrowers are prepared to pay market interest rates to "new wave" semi-formal lenders if the transactions costs of borrowing are brought down [Gaiha 1994: 104]. The cost to the final lender that stands behind the agency, and to the integrity of the financial system, are usually far less – as is the diversion of on-lending away from the poor – if a given sum, used to support an agency, is used to subsidize administration and transactions costs, rather than interest rates to, or lax repayments by, final borrowers.

There is a necessary link between the two arguments (1) that withdrawal of interest-rate subsidies need not harm the poor, since their interest-elasticity of demand for "new wave" credit is very low, and (2) that loans should not be tied to particular purposes as long as they are repaid. For a poor person, who spends 60-80 per cent of outlay on food and most of the rest on other necessities (and who usually saves little), higher payments for an item like credit because of a price rise (i.e. price-inelastic demand) implies reduced consumption of basic essentials – unless the item itself is, or can be used to acquire, such essentials. To say "Charge the market price for primary education, because the poor are prepared to pay – their demand is price-inelastic" is to say "Let them eat less". This does not apply to injunctions to charge the market price for credit, since that can be used to buy, or to free up cash to buy, food and other essentials (as well as to support higher production, for income to buy such essentials later on). But if the borrower is so effectively supervised that fungibility is not possible, then indeed raising interest rates on a *given supply* of credit to the poor harms their access to non-credit essentials. This, of course, must be offset against the fact that *subsidized credit may lower the supply* of credit to the poor, because it undermines the viability both of lenders that provide it, and of those who try to compete against it – and because it is seldom the poor who can politick or bribe their way to items, such as credit, that are both scarce and rationed by administrative discretion. Yet, to ensure that credit at market rates benefits the poor, lenders should avoid tying and directional monitoring, unless desired by borrowers (positive monitoring).

10. *Avoid politicizing or softening repayment but anticipate emergencies*

The "electoral credit cycle" is only too familiar in some Indian States, as in Sri Lanka in the 1960s and 1970s [ILO 1971]. For most of a government's term of office, its agencies struggle to recover formal credit, in order to increase the viability of the lending agencies and the financial system as a whole. Local branches and agents of banks and coops are cut off for weak repayment performance, and credit shortages develop, especially for poor borrowers without collateral. As election time approaches, the parties compete, first to renew credit despite past incomplete repayment, then to promise partial or total write-offs of overdues. At the next comparable (pre-election) stage in the electoral credit cycle, the previous experience of write-off induces borrowers to postpone repayment until elections approach, or even to postpone lending so that there is a better chance of deferring repayments until they are eased or cancelled. The whole climate of repayment, even when elections are far away, is harmed.

It is a misperception that lax repayment discipline helps the poor. Like Heine, the poor know that "it is wise to pay your loans back; there's a lot of life to come, and you'll often have to borrow, as you have so often done". A rich borrower faces less such pressure, and more choice of lenders even if his or her repute is less than perfect. It is the better-off who can work the system to avoid repayment; it is the rich who default because they can, not the poor because they must. Default risks usually increase with loan size and with borrower's wealth [Lipton 1976]. Women borrowers – almost always relatively under-supplied with credit, because inheritance practices deny most of them land collateral – repay significantly larger proportions of their dues than do men [Hulme 1989; Holt and Ribe 1991]. *Strict repayment discipline is associated with larger, not smaller, proportions of credit reaching the poor (and women), and in the medium term with larger, not smaller, total amounts of credit for the agency to lend.* In Bangladesh the politicized, non-recovered loans to the rich by the public-sector NCBS contrasts sharply with successful loan recovery by the "new wave" BRAC, Grameen and Proshika [McGregor 1988]. The successful "new wave" semi-formal credit institutions reviewed by Getubig [1993] have repayment rates of 90-99 per cent, as do MYRADA [Fernandez 1993] and, until recently, Mudzi in Malawi

[Hulme 1989]. Most "old" formal lenders and coops, which have been far less successful in reaching the poor, also have much worse repayment rates, often in the range of 50-75 per cent. Often, as with MYRADA, new-wave lenders have to overcome an initial hurdle created by past politicization of debt repayment: the perception that the banks or other apex agencies, whose resources the local MYRADA branches were intermediating, were making gifts rather than loans [Fernandez 1993: 6].

Repayment of capital, in the case of collateral-free and hence poor-friendly loans, must be enforced strictly in normal circumstances. However, there are two special cases. The first is a bad year. With locally covariate risks, group members, etc. can rarely help each other out. If there is no credit insurance, and poor borrowers depend mainly on income from farming or farm labour, loans may have to be rescheduled in years of drought, flood, very badly timed water supply, severe pest attacks, or price collapse for the main cash crop.

The second case for caution, in enforcing repayment, arises if a poor borrower faces an unpredicted and (for him or her) uninsurable life-cycle event, such as the death of the main earner. Even a much smaller income shock can impede, for a short period, hitherto regular repayments, even of a small loan. If the borrower is part of a co-signatory group, other members may help out for a short period, or it may be feasible briefly to call on the "group fund", built up by compulsory contributions in most such groups. With individual lending, formal rescheduling is required. One reason why the poor turn to moneylenders, rather than to formal credit, is that moneylenders (apart from being readier to schedule repayment on a regular basis) often permit skipping of a week or two in the event of a sudden shock to repayment capacity; successful semi-formal lenders (including group intermediaries) need to follow that practice, judiciously, if they are to compete with moneylenders.

However, in both these special cases rescheduling has to be just that, not part of a political process leading to debt forgiveness by formal or "new wave" agencies. The rich are usually the main gainers from such debt forgiveness; many of the poor cannot or will not borrow at all, and many others depend on moneylenders and traders who hardly ever forgive debt. Also, it is the poorest – with the fewest credit options, and the most pressing needs – who stand to lose most in future, if lax repayment leaves the formal and "new wave" lenders (and some of their undercut informal rivals) unviable and thus unable to offer credit later.

The facts that even the best-run agency will experience some *defaults*, and that small loans to the poor have genuinely high ratios of *enforcement and overview costs* to loan size, mean that a viable lending branch must have fairly high *interest rates*. The three trade off: in the experience of a leading international NGO, Women's World Banking, local (NGO or group) intermediation reduces administrative costs – and therefore break-even interest rates for on-loans – by 1-2 per cent of loan values; and "good" administration can make another 3 per cent difference, between default rates of, say, 5 per cent and 8 per cent of loan value, in a "new wave" lender.

11. Infrastructure and education may complement credit

There is no clear verdict on whether credit agencies do best by providing credit alone or "credit plus". BRAC started with a programme of "conscientization", in which all borrowers had to receive education and training – including basic literacy and numeracy – as a condition of borrowing. However, it is not clear whether this reaped good returns in terms of better loan repayment or use, though literacy and numeracy are desirable anyway [Chowdhury and Mahmood 1991]. In Latin America, there is nothing to choose between the performance of credit programmes and "credit plus" programmes [Holt and Ribe 1991].

However, all this means, not that credit alone is sufficient, but that it is not clear whether credit and other programmes are best combined in a single agency, or provided separately. I know of no research into whether there are gains from providing both of them jointly, rather than separately, to a particular group or area irrespective of the agency of provision – research, that is, into the impact of infrastructure or education on the rate of return to credit, or on its outreach to the poor. The statement that the impact is important and positive rests on analogy and on common sense. The analogy is to the favourable effect of education on health, child mortality and total fertility rates. Even when income is held constant, that effect is substantial. The commonsense case is that borrowers trained to read the small print, to count the likely costs and returns of new credit and input decisions, are likely – given their initial income, and their attitudes to risk – to be better at selecting good uses for their extra resources after receiving credit. As for infrastructure, transport and telephones are ways of reducing transactions costs, both of obtaining credit and of choosing things to buy with it; such possibilities are especially important for the poor, because they tend to make small loans, so that transactions costs (and therefore a given proportionate reduction in them) loom large relative to the amount borrowed.

12. *Savings requirements improve borrowers' performance*

It is the almost unanimous experience of successful lending groups that borrowers are most likely to repay, and to select successful uses of credit that ease repayment, if and only if they have previously been small savers [Holt and Ribe 1991; Rubaragama 1993: 107; Getubig 1993: 76; Fernandez 1993: 10, 32]. Even a tiny, but regular, commitment to savings demonstrates a person's financial discipline, and thus is likely to indicate somewhat greater probability of repayment. More specifically, members of a group whose savings build up a "group fund" have extra rewards from ensuring that their fellow-members use that fund responsibly. Of course, this is not different from the old cooperative principle that members must buy shares in the local branch of the coop commensurate with their loan obligations.

13. *Create incentives to lenders and borrowers for repayment*

In Indonesia, KUPEDES "imposes a penalty of 0.5 per cent of the amount borrowed per month for late payments, which is collected from all borrowers but subsequently reimbursed to those who repay on time" [Gaiha 1994: 105]. The advantage of such incentives to borrowers for repayment is clear. However, even with group lending, incentives from the higher level assist repayment and its peer-monitoring. In the case of Grameen, the primary group (of five borrowers) is encouraged to levy individual penalties for repayment "indiscipline"; and access both to personal savings, and to the proceeds of the "tax" on individual loans in order to build up group funds, is restricted unless the group's repayment record is good [Matin 1994: 2]. In MYRADA the Group Fund similarly creates incentives to individual repayment [Fernandez 1993: 33-4].

Lenders also need to impose on employees and agents the sense that their incomes, careers, and ultimately jobs depend on their success in inducing good repayment performance. The key issue is to remove the natural feeling that lax repayments discipline is good for the poor *or* for bank officials; it helps the rich, imperils bank jobs (whatever the short-run gain for the dishonest few), and, on balance, hurts the poor. The discussions of the various "new wave" lenders also contain many instances of incentives to permanent officials to recover loans. These officials have to be brought to realize that the survival of the agency, and therefore of their own jobs, depends on good repayment discipline. Positively, part of their pay can be linked to repayment performance. The mental block, often needing to be overcome by planners and donors, is the false notion that slack repayment is good for the poor.

The economics of poverty reduction has passed through its ideological adolescence. We have much experience of what works and what does not. After the first wave of faith that state-mediated and subsidized credit expansion could massively reduce poverty, and the second wave of belief that simple state withdrawal would suffice, there is growing experience of successful "new wave" lending focused on the poor.

5. Public works to create employment for the poor

(i) Introduction

Manual labour on public works, especially if the wage rate is rather low, attracts only people who have few other opportunities to earn money, and who need income much more than they need leisure. Public works programmes, in other words, tend to be self-targeting upon the poor. This largely avoids the often corrupt and arbitrary outcomes of direct targeting by project managers upon those labelled as "poor". Self-targeting also avoids, to some extent, the imperfections of indirect or indicator targeting upon groups or areas believed to have high incidence or severity of poverty. This avoidance is not complete: there is corruption and arbitrariness even about selection for public works gangs, especially when an intermediate labour contractor has a local monopoly; and many of the poorest are able neither to do hard manual work, nor to depend for incomes on those who can. Nevertheless, the self-targeting feature of low-wage, manual public works programmes renders them attractive to policymakers serious about poverty reduction, but starved of cash.

Third World experience with public works to reduce poverty via employment income is quite hopeful. However, care is needed. First, while the great advantage of public works, as compared with credit schemes (and indeed schemes to transfer land or human capital) for the poor, is self-targeting on, and relative cheapness in *currently* benefiting, the poor, there is an offsetting disadvantage. Public works employment, as compared with credit and other schemes for the poor, normally provides them only with *current* benefit. Thus, unlike the alternatives, public works programmes must be financed as long as there remains poverty judged in need of remedy. Unlike credit, land, or skills for the poor, public works do not enable permanent escape from poverty – unless accompanied by special measures such that the works programme itself builds up assets (savings, physical capital, skills, health, or infrastructure) owned by, or providing future employment income to, the poor.

Two historical analogies underpin the need for caution. Workhouse in-relief, to which the able-bodied poor were restricted after England's 1834 Poor Law Amendment Act [Himmelfarb 1984], explicitly "self-targeted" on the poor by aiming to provide pay and conditions "less eligible" than the meanest available alternative. The able-bodied poor received less, and more demeaning, relief than under the previous system of parish-based out-relief. They may also often have been deterred by stigma and indignity, with damage to family members, especially small children, who had no choice in the matter. In short, extreme self-targeting can redistribute income (i) away from the poor as a whole, as compared with somewhat less rigorous self-targeting, and (ii) *if there is an adequate budget* even from the poorest, as compared with alternative means of provision.

The second historical analogy is the counter-cyclical public works programmes adopted by several Western countries during the slump of 1931-36, and again during milder recessions around 1950-75. The partial success of these was related to two features not replicated in many developing countries using such schemes. First, residual *poverty* in the West in the 1930s and 1960s *was not due mainly to the absence of skills or other assets in the workforce.* Second, such *poverty was*, perhaps, *due substantially to cyclical constraints on the demand for labour*; correspondingly, aggregate supply of goods and services could be substantially expanded during the recession by the application of extra unskilled labour, and thus was highly price-elastic during the recession (i.e. during the early life of the counter-cyclical works). This helped to justify a policy of balancing the budget only over the business cycle, i.e. with substantial deficits to finance public works employment (but also thereby to push out the frontier of production possibilities) in recessions, and substantial offsetting surpluses to contain inflation (as aggregate demand pressed against that frontier) in booms. This "Keynesian-neoclassical synthesis" of the 1960s has been severely challenged by subsequent experience and theory; but it made some sense in the West, and probably still does, as a partial justification of some counter-cyclical public works employment. Yet in most of South Asia and Africa today the two features required for that justification obviously do not apply. Many of the poor lack the skills to obtain long-term work, even if aggregate demand recovers; and aggregate supply of the main consumable, viz. food staples, is price inelastic in the short run.

Enough caveats. This book is about principles of success in anti-poverty policy. There is plenty of evidence that, done the right way in the right place at the right time, public works employment can succeed in significantly alleviating (not perhaps in durably reducing) poverty in developing countries. Strikingly, (1) the thirteen rules for successful operation, listed in Chapter 4 (iii) for anti-poverty credit policies, appear to apply *mutatis mutandis* to public works employment policies also; (2) the largely rural location of success against poverty, noted above for credit policy, appears also to apply to public works policy. Before reviewing these guidelines to success, we need to examine briefly the *scale*, the *income impact*, and the *poverty targeting* of some major programmes.

(ii) Scale

The scale of several public works programmes has been substantial. Three per cent of the workforce, or about 30,000 persons, were employed in mid-1987 under Bolivia's Social Insurance Fund. In Chile, comparable projects engaged 6 per cent of the workforce in 1976, and 13 per cent in 1983 (the latter at a scheme cost of only 1.4 per cent of GNP, indicating very low wages but also successful self-targeting). In Honduras in 1990-93, some 5 per cent of the workforce was engaged on similar public works projects, implying a 20 per cent cut in open unemployment through direct effects alone. In Cape Verde in 1983, almost 30 per cent of the workforce was engaged in labour-intensive public works, and their income appears to have prevented rising mortality despite prolonged and severe drought. That also applied in Botswana, where in 1985-6 some 74,000 workers (3 million person-days), in a total workforce of perhaps 300-350,000, were involved in the rural Labour-based Relief Programme. Such figures [Glaessner et al. 1994; Drèze and Sen 1989: 137, 156; Gaiha 1994: 117; Ahmad 1993] cover direct effects only.

To estimate total impact one needs to *add*, to these direct effects, employment and labour income due to (1) **multiplier effects** of spending out of incomes created by the public works programmes and (2) **capital effects**, as workers earn net extra income from employment in using and maintaining new assets or skills created by those programmes; and to *deduct* (3) **opportunity-jobcosts**: employment and income (and their multiplier effects) foregone by public works employees, i.e. the part of employment and income, obtained on public works, that the employees could have derived from other sources in the absence of those works. Estimates for (1) and (2) are not available, but estimates from Asia for (3) range around 20-30 per cent of the direct effects of the works.

Though data for these effects (1) to (3) are seldom available, the largest programmes – in number of workers employed, and in duration – are clearly Bangladesh's Food for Work Programme and the successors of Food-for-work in India (now largely based on cash payment): the National Rural Employment Programme (NREP, now incorporated into JRY) and Maharashtra State's Employment Guarantee Scheme (EGS).[43] The EGS appears to reduce rural unemployment by 10-35 per cent; in a range of survey villages almost half the *participants'* wage employment is supplied by the scheme. EGS at its peak in 1986 provided 190 million workdays. That amount has since halved, partly due to reduced demand by workers, and the real wage rate about doubled – leaving the scheme costing some 10-14 per cent of the state budget [Dev 1994; Datar 1990].

For India apart from Maharashtra, between 1980 and 1989 the NREP – which unlike EGS does not offer a *guarantee* of employment – provided some 320-370 million person-days per year [Bandyopadhyay 1985; OASS 1985; Hirway 1991: 67]. The JRY, including an expanded NREP together with some other national employment programmes, provided about 830 million person-days of work each year from 1989-90 to 1992-3. In 1993-4, with the help of an "intensified JRY" launched in 123 backward districts (and the new demand for jobs created by unemployment in the wake of economic stabilization), the total rose to just over a billion workdays. Adding an estimate for workdays from EGS in Maharashtra, we reach a current figure – still expanding – of about 2.2 million full-time-equivalent working years from major employment schemes in India, the vast majority of them rural. That still comprises well below 2 per cent of India's rural workforce, and not all of this is additional employment: low wage rates on JRY encourage departmental officials to use it for

---

43. A word of warning. EGS is probably the most studied, and the best analysed, poverty reduction scheme in the world. However, the evidence relies far too much on statements, purporting to be about EGS as a whole, which in fact arise from an excellent panel survey in just two, probably untypical, villages of the several tens of thousands in the State! In discussing EGS we make this clear when we refer to this two-village data set.

construction that would have taken place even in its absence [OASS 1985]; and there is some negative "opportunity-jobcost". However, India's public works schemes since the early 1980s must have created enough *net* workplaces, including multiplier and subsequent effects, to represent a significant success in poverty reduction. This is to say nothing of partly successful earlier pioneers, such as Karnataka's Land Army [Donovan 1973] and Kerala's Pilot Rural Employment Scheme [Gopinath et al. 1978], which did well for a time but appear to have fallen foul of the huge extra outlay required to sustain such programmes over a large population, especially in a bad year, and as they become better known to the poor.

On scale, we conclude that several works schemes, in a wide range of developing countries, have created very many workdays since about 1980. There has been great improvement on the dismal earlier record [World Bank 1976]. That is mainly because schemes are much better pre-planned, reducing real cost (especially non-wage cost) per job and per unit of real assets created. However, as we shall see, the impact in reducing poverty durably – as opposed to relieving current need – is much less. This means that, if employment programmes are not to gobble up increasing resources for ever, they must be supplemented as anti-poverty weapons by other sorts of programme, or by whatever general poverty-reducing impact can be achieved from growth and/or macro-policy.

(iii) Apparent impact on the poor

Few and non-comparable data are available for this. There are two components: the proportion of poor people who participate in these schemes, and the proportionate increase in their incomes (net of negative effects) from the schemes. Ideally, we should wish to allow for the three secondary effects (multiplier, capital, and opportunity-jobcost) as well.

The average participant in Bolivia's FSE projects increased wage earnings by about 45 per cent in 1987 [Glaessner 1994]. In Maharashtra's EGS, a series of large samples produced estimates of 20-35 per cent for the share of participants' total income[44] derived

---

44. Barely a fifth of these earnings (i.e. 5-7 per cent of total income) needs to be deducted for "opportunity-jobcosts" of participating in EGS [Ravallion 1991].

from the scheme (and this is a scheme in which probably well over 80 per cent of participants, as against 40-45 per cent of rural people in Maharashtra, were poor) [Dev 1994: Table 2]. More evidence is reviewed when we discuss the rules for pro-poor targeting of these schemes below.

A related issue is whether the assets, created by the schemes, have significant impact on the poor. This can be done in several ways. India's Million Wells Scheme and its successors, recently linked both to JRY and to EGS, seek to create *durable assets on small and marginal farms*, enabling poor farmers to generate subsequent self-employment income. Some forms of *village infrastructure*, such as the drought management works favoured by EGS in the early 1980s and again recently, may well help the poor most (although there was a strong drift of EGS resources towards roadbuilding around 1984-90, which did most for the wealthier rural population) [Dev 1994]. *Human capital creation* – employment schemes to build primary schoolrooms, for example, as in Kenya's Harambee in the 1960s – can also focus on the poor; Bolivia's FSE in 1993 increasingly concentrated on "small basic health and education projects", creating social services likely to benefit mainly the poor, on the assumption that others already tended to obtain basic educational and health care; in Honduras, health-care and primary-school attendance both appear to have risen by about a quarter as a result of new facilities created by the FHIS employment projects [Glaessner 1994]. However, as Dev [1994] and others have emphasized, there are conflicts: if only the poor benefit from the assets created, there will be few powerful people to support these costly employment schemes; and some schemes that create pro-poor assets, such as building primary health centres, have low ratios of wage-costs to capital and raw-materials costs. Ravallion [1991] argues that employment schemes are designed mainly to alleviate current poverty, not to create assets; that is a useful by-product, but there are better ways to do it.

(iv) Targeting on the poor

As Ravallion emphasizes, too often targeting of *employment schemes* on the poor is *post-evaluated* through imperfect indicators of poverty. It probably makes sense for a hard-pressed and honest administrator of a *credit* scheme to *allocate* scarce resources to the obviously landless, rather than to those who can convince or bribe his officials to allow them as eligible because "poor"; but in post-evaluation it is whether a scheme has reached (and benefited) those who started poor that matters, and the poor overlap very imperfectly with the landless. Moreover, with a largely self-targeting programme such as a low-wage employment scheme, failure to reach the poor is much likelier to be due to design faults or leakage to officials than to seizure of ditch-digging jobs by the rich.

We discuss the rules for targeting and self-targeting on the poor below. At once, we should add two notes of caution. First, one must resist naïve assumptions that either high or low wage rates on these schemes are in general pro-poor; that is very context-dependent. Second, one cannot always argue, from the fact that a public works scheme is good at apparent immediate self-targeting, and also cost-effective in creating income for the poor in isolation, that it is cost-effective as a way of benefiting the poor in general equilibrium; this depends inter alia on the cost of participation, in the alternative schemes, for the poor. Ravallion [1991], however, has recently shown that a major component of this cost in the case of public works schemes – alternative employment and self-employment income foregone to work on them – is lower than had been thought, at least in the (big) example of EGS: barely 20 per cent of earnings from the scheme. Furthermore, a general-equilibrium model for India [Parikh and Srinivasan 1993] appears to show that a given level of public outlay on employment programmes as a whole is, on several alternative assumptions, somewhat more effective in reducing poverty than is similar outlay on plausible steps to accelerate labour-intensive agricultural growth, and much more effective than spending the money on food distribution programmes.[45]

Here we stress only that apparent immediate self-targeting on the poor by these programmes has usually been very good (though the ill, the weak, and those with major child-care obligations may be unable to participate; in two villages in Maharashtra, EGS participation, while generally focused on the poor [Deolalikar and Gaiha 1992], was negatively correlated with two attributes of many of the very poor, viz. shortness and a large number of children in the

---

45. The model, however, is in need of development, especially insertion of a labour market [Dev 1994] and a capital market.

...old). In Bangladesh's Food for Work Programme, the quartile of rural households with least income-per-person provided 60 per cent of participants, and obtained 70 per cent of workplaces [Ravallion 1990: 25, 45]. On EGS, most estimates suggest that 90 per cent of *employment* goes to the poor, who constitute "only" 40-45 per cent of Maharashtra's rural workforce; but the share of scheme *benefits* – as opposed to wage benefits – must have been eroded as the wage component has fallen, from over 80 per cent of EGS costs in 1976-84 to 55 per cent in 1988-92 [Dev 1994: Table 2]. There may well, however, be a trade-off between the short-run gains to the poor from a very high wage component and the construction of assets of long-run use, especially to the poor.

Especially where these schemes use piecework, targeting on women is also good. EGS is typical of the bigger schemes in that the share of women in participant-days rose steadily from 41 per cent in 1979 – already well above the share of women in the rural workforce – to 53 per cent in 1987 [Dev 1994: 3]. That is important in alleviating the worst effects of poverty, in the long run and in the short. In the short run, extra income for women appears to make considerably more difference to children's health, nutrition and survival prospects than extra income for men [Kennedy and Peters 1992]. In the long run, expected future earnings for women, relative to men, appear (at least in India) to be a major explanator of inter-district differences in the ratio of female to male infant and child death rates; where EGS or anything else raises women's relative prospects of employment income, little girls are less likely to be underfed or denied health care [Rosenzweig and Schultz 1982].

(v) Public works: Rules for success against poverty

The above discussion already suggests a substantial overlap between the rules for success in reducing poverty through credit and through employment. This is surprising, because credit tends, especially if subsidized or supported by public action, to gravitate to the non-poor, whereas manual work for low wages tends to self-target the poor. Yet, without artificiality, we can list thirteen rules for success against poverty, closely analogous to those for credit (see Chapter 4, (iii)), for schemes of public works employment.

1. Time in employment is often transferable between schemes and other uses. Design the scheme so that poor people gain from participating when their opportunity-cost is low.

2. Use self-targeting, plus location, etc. – not direct targeting.

3. Arrange works and rules (quick payment, piece-rates, nearness, crèches, timing) so as to discriminate in favour of the poor.

4. Try to allow for poor workers' frequent weakness, undernutrition and smallness.

5. Minimize transactions costs of participation by the poor (transport, registration, bribes).

6. Reduce financial strains on the scheme by compensatory devices in structure or timing.

7. Maintain competition between the scheme, private employers, and food retailers.

8. Estimate whether labour demand or labour supply constrains local income of the working poor, and adapt the scheme locally to allow for this.

9. Use subsidy (i) to build up sustainability, coverage, and (via maintenance and poverty-focus of scheme assets) workers' prospects to "graduate" out of it – not (ii) to raise wage rates unless a positive anti-poverty impact is proved, and financing of job targets is sustainable.

10. Encourage participants to form pressure groups, e.g. to improve the scheme's village-level integration and political sustainability, to spotlight faults, and to reduce leakages.

11. To raise returns to schemes, and reach those they leave out, encourage complementary infrastructure and social capital.

12. Before schemes begin, build up *their* capacity to expand (and fluctuate), by creating a shelf of schemes – and *participants'* capacity, by improving information, transport, health care, etc.

13. Create performance incentives and career structures that lead successful components of schemes to expand, and others to shrink.

1. *Designing employment for low opportunity cost*

This implies ensuring that the scheme is available in the slack season (which is why agricultural labour seldom features in such schemes). However, it is not obvious that the poor are best served by making public works employment offers *strictly* seasonal, as in Botswana, where Labour Relief "jobs were temporary, stopping during the cropping season for two or three months" [Harvey and Lewis 1990: 302]. That certainly maximizes "stabilization benefits" to the poor, but may reduce their "transfer benefits"; for public works, if continued in the peak season, could tighten the market for private labour and thus bid up the wage rate. That effect is much less likely in the slack season, when labour is plentiful, and demand for it therefore wage-elastic [Ravallion 1990; Gaiha 1994: 114]. In the Kosi area of Bihar State in India, public works in the slack season only may have reduced the equilibrium private-sector wage rate in the peak season [Rodgers 1973] (though the reverse result is also possible if people substitute leisure for income as the latter rises [Robbins 1930]). Use of public works to raise peak demand for labour implies a political choice: to increase the bargaining power of the workers [Dev 1994: 8], at the possible cost of alienating big-farm employers from the scheme. Whether this renders the scheme more sustainable politically, or less so, is a context-specific political judgement; the point to note is that the choice needs to be explicit, when timing the provision of works (or guarantees of employment) in a scheme. Of course, if the works or the guarantees of employment become rationed (rule 2), this decision is constrained, tainted, or made altogether infeasible.

In most schemes, limited resources and high wage and other costs impose a need to ration, at least, the times and places where work will be made available. Usually, social safety nets are not plentiful enough to permit the designers of employment schemes the luxury of going for "transfer benefits" rather than "stabilization benefits" and, if the labour-market conditions so indicate, crowding much of the scheme work into the busy agricultural season. There is urgent need to provide employment income to those without reserves in a drought, or a slack season following a below-average harvest; providing maximum job chances to the poor at such times, when there are few job opportunities elsewhere, takes priority over transfer benefits. Only the physical feasibility of works – such as roadbuilding or irrigation maintenance in soggy land – constrains capacity to time employment into slack periods.

As indicated, substantial numbers of scheme employees are women, and it is desirable that this should be so. It is therefore important to ask whether the opportunity cost of women's participation is affected by the timing or other details of a scheme. Evidence from Kerala [Kumar 1977] indicates that, in some seasons but not others, reductions in child care when women do extra work can outweigh the benefits, for small children, of improved income and nutrition. The compulsory provision of crèches in EGS is certainly one reason why high female participation has not been associated with any such opportunity cost there. Moreover, while over half the EGS participants are women, NREP – where there are no crèches and no employment guarantee – attracts only 15 per cent [World Bank 1991].

Small and decentralized works, which can be located near each of many villages, reduce transport time and hence opportunity cost. This is especially important for the poor, who are likeliest to be compelled to use slow and time-consuming transport, and for women. The de facto rationing that took place after 1988 in EGS, when it was compelled to double its wage rates (see below), mostly took the form of much more distant job offers. That excluded not only those less desperate for the work, but those less mobile and further away.

2. Seek alternatives to direct targeting – but wage effects are complex

We have pointed out the natural advantage of self-targeting enjoyed by public works employment. In Botswana, targeting greatly improved when drought relief shifted from provision of food to provision of employment income – the rich eat more than the poor, so that all-round food distribution had meant anti-targeting [Drèze and Sen 1989: 153-4]. Experience with EGS, however, suggests that narrow targeting is an important route (alongside pressure from poor participants themselves: see rule 10 below) to reducing leakages of scheme benefits to participants [Lieberman 1990]. This is especially important in a scheme that provides but does not guarantee work, or that (like EGS in recent years) is forced to ration its "guarantees" because the wage bill is otherwise too high relative to funds

[Ravallion et al. 1993]. Narrowing the self-targeting via extra, non-fudgeable indicator targeting, e.g. by location or household size, is welcome – provided the indicators are not readily distorted by, or discretionary for, managers or politicians.

The main problem of leakage in schemes using unskilled labour at low wages is not that rich workers take the jobs, but that poor workers must share benefits with scheme officials or politicians (e.g. via bribes for scheme access). Therefore, the main challenge for direct targeting among workers – apart from reducing such leakages – is to design public works schemes that will, in fact, provide the sort of unskilled jobs that will target the poor. This raises a number of problems: the need to avoid stigmatizing the work, so that poor but proud people go hungry rather than doing it (one of the problems with the English Poor Law workhouses after 1834); the desirability that the work should impart some skills; the frequent reality that useful capital works need a significant input of skilled labour.

The most widely suggested means to improve self-targeting, therefore, is to keep wage rates low (though obviously not "too low"). Very low wage rates will attract the most severely poor people, who can do no better outside the scheme; slightly higher rates will attract workers near the poverty line, whom the scheme might push above it, thereby reducing the numbers of poor people. Hence the wage policy, required for optimal self-targeting, depends partly on whether the public works programme seeks mainly to reduce *severity* or *incidence* of poverty [Ravallion 1990, 1991].

Ravallion is clearly right that the validity of "targeting by low wage rates" depends on a scheme's financial resources, and on the feasibility and efficiency of putting large parts of them into wages. If both are severely constrained, adequate coverage of the poor will mean low wage rates. Quite apart from their targeting benefits on the side of labourers' demand for scheme jobs, they are the only way to avoid rationing out potentially poor people for want of scheme resources. For example, the doubling of EGS wage rates in 1988 led administrators to concentrate job offers on occupations with lower piece-rates, as well as to reduce (and hence make harder to reach) the number of workplaces [Ravallion et al. 1993] – plainly damaging the extent and "year-roundness" of access for the poor. However, if scheme resources are substantial, wage rates slightly above contemporary market levels can be set. EGS pulled up private wage rates by about 10 per cent [ibid.], a good secondary outcome for the very poor – provided it does not, in turn, lead to substantial displacement of unskilled workers by tractors, weedicides or bulldozers.

While above-market wage rates, such as the legal (but privately unenforced) minimum wages that EGS must pay, can reduce both self-targeting and the scheme's capacity to offer large-scale employment, it is obviously not sensible to lower the wage without limit. At the extreme, few or no workers will be forthcoming. At very low rates, there is a possibility of attracting only the weakest and least competent workers, and of providing scant motivation – and little extra food to spare for their hungry families.

Despite some elements of oligopoly in labour markets, there is little doubt that imposing (or raising) a minimum wage rate somewhat reduces the equilibrium level of employment. However, the gains to people who stay in work can exceed the losses to those who lose work; to establish the net poverty impact, we need to compare the gains multiplied by the poverty indicator among the gainers (numbers and/or severity) with losses multiplied by the poverty indicator among losers. Net damage to the poor is certain if, say, a public works scheme with a tight budget sets a minimum wage at double the market rate, especially if there is a big spin-off to lower-level private-sector wage rates; but if a scheme raises its minimum wage to 10 per cent above the market rate, but reduces its jobs by 5 per cent so as to stay within budget, it is not obvious that the overall poverty indicators will deteriorate.

There is a more subtle point, which has become clearer during the debates about minimum-wage legislation in the United Kingdom in the 1990s. Suppose that, when scheme wage rates rise, unemployment rises somewhat, due both to scheme budget constraints and to the transmission of the wage rise to the private sector. Who becomes, or remains, unemployed? United Kingdom evidence suggests that these marginally unemployed tend to be secondary workers in households where at least one other person already has a job, which normally provides enough income to escape household poverty; whereas the low-income employees who keep their jobs and get the wage rise tend to be primary workers, drawn from initially very poor households. In such cases, imposing a minimum wage might reduce poverty, although increasing unemployment. There is no evidence about whether this applies in developing countries, but the issue underlines the importance of examining the effects of both a wage rise and any consequent extra unemployment upon household income per person (among the actually and potentially poor), not just on the incomes of the persons directly affected.

3. Use scheme rules and conditions to discriminate for the poor

Apart from crèches, we have already reviewed *wage rates* and *slack-season* timing as means of increasing the gains to the poor. Wage *payment systems*, and the precise *phasing of works*, are less discussed, but are also important components of success.

Piece-rates are especially favourable to participation by women [Dev 1994: 11], small persons, and others who may prefer longer to more intense work, and who are often excluded (or feel compelled to exclude themselves) under time-rate systems. Dandekar [1983] showed that, in a statistical reality almost reflecting the definition of a piece-rate, this has its dark side: women's daily earnings are significantly below men's. In the context of minimum-wage laws, there is some pressure in EGS to apply a mix of piece and time payments; but any time-rate component, together with costly or imperfect supervision, would lead to "peer pressure" by workers against relatively unproductive colleagues. While desirable to save public money, that might stop smaller and weaker people – often the poorest – from taking part in a scheme. Already, although only in two villages, and offsetting the general pro-poor biases of EGS there, EGS employment was significantly likelier for taller persons [Deolalikar and Gaiha 1992]. Piece-rates also have the advantage that several members of a large, poor and perhaps weak household can share the work.

We have mentioned the stabilization benefits to the poor (and the possible trade-off with transfer benefits) from monthly and yearly adjustments in the scale of EGS. Landless workers in two EGS villages – where EGS work was negatively correlated, time-wise, with – had about 50 per cent lower coefficients of variation of income than similar workers in an agroclimatically comparable village without EGS [Bhende et al. 1992; Walker and Ryan 1990; Dev 1994: 9]. It is notable that this stabilization is apparent both before and after 1988, the date from which wage legislation plus budget limitations compelled EGS to impose informal work rationing (longer distances, concentration on work with lower wage rates, etc.). Since poor people's participation rates (age- and gender-specific), employment prospects, and wage rates tend to fluctuate adversely together, more than for the non-poor and affecting a greater proportion of their income [Lipton 1983], stabilization benefits home in on the poor, improving the targeting and the cost-effectiveness of these schemes.

However – as we saw in the case of credit – poor people's timing requirements are more complex than is usually recognized in outsiders' perceptions of a bad season or year [Chambers, Longhurst and Pacey 1981; Sahn 1989]. For example, Drèze [in Drèze and Sen 1990] stresses the importance of getting employment income to at-risk areas *before* the worst shortage threatens, so as to provide effective demand that will pull food staples into those areas. Responsiveness to local variations in average patterns of requirements, and flexibility in face of fluctuations about that average, may substantially determine success in programmes of public works employment, as in programmes of credit. Food for Work in Bangladesh was poorly timed to match the localized, seasonal patterns of need, both for food and for work [Clay and Harriss 1988]. And, even if there is no great seasonal need for jobs in a particular village, that is no consolation to a landless worker, just recovered from illness, and denied the "public work" needed to catch up to a tolerable income level.

Unfortunately, the typical circumstances of departmental budgets – a rush to use up funds at the end of the year, tightness in mid-year – does not match average state-wide, let alone drought-affected local (or disease-affected personal), timings of need. *For local adaptiveness and temporal flexibility, there are advantages in (a) an employment guarantee with wide coverage and provision (even at a low wage rate if need be) and funds to support this; (b) a substantial "shelf" of useful works or other employment-intensive activities, ready for use when circumstances require; (c) local organization of the poor, perhaps around the public works themselves (rule 10).*

4. *Allow for poor workers' frequent physical difficulties*

This has been a recurring theme. Labourers, and the poor in general, are often removed from work by illness or injury, and are more prone to such loss of time and income than the non-poor [Lipton 1983]. We have emphasized that the old, the chronically sick, etc., especially if not supported by relatives or community provision, need anti-poverty help other than employment guarantee schemes. But there are large numbers of people who are able to work, but impaired by weakness from working well. What can public works schemes do for them?

First, such people find a meal before work, nearby schemes, and prompt payment especially important. If payment is delayed for some weeks, as happened in the early years of EGS [PEO 1980] and as is frequent in some African countries, the weak and hungry cannot participate.

Second, it may be possible to provide lines of work less demanding of physical energy, and to steer the less able-bodied towards such activities, at little or no cost to the programme. Unfortunately many of the small and weak are also illiterate, making it harder to place them in clerical work. This underlines the complementarity of cost-effective anti-poverty programmes with primary health and education – a fact recognized in the case of credit, e.g. by the policies of BRAC in Bangladesh, but less often in public works.

Third, where a large proportion of the poor are impaired from participating in public works by ill-health, it may help to steer those public works towards health improvements. Primary health care centres, control of insect vectors, and even improved local roads (cutting the calorie cost of movements to and from work and clinics) may all be relevant.

Finally, the pattern of illness, and especially of injury, is usually highly seasonal [Chambers et al. 1981; Lipton 1983]. It may be possible to extend or shift local public works slightly in order to avoid the illness peak. More frequently, it may be possible to fine-tune the local pattern of public health provision, water management, or insect vector control. The local specificity, and occasional sharp variability, of such needs strengthens the case for their local management (as is beginning in EGS via village-level integration and decentralization) and even more for representative, local and politically active groups of beneficiaries (rule 10 below).

5. Minimize poor participants' transactions costs

As Dev [1994] reminds us, the serious leakages from public works programmes are to or through officials, not to rich participants in the workforce. The main "transactions cost" (as opposed to opportunity cost, or cost of access via transport) for potential workers in public works programmes is the cost of obtaining access. Part of the wage may be forfeited to a contractor, official or politician in return for access, or not paid at all because it is misappropriated to begin with. Where access is guaranteed, as in EGS (assuming no rationing), this is less of a problem, though even in that case the more attractive forms of work may be rationed. On EGS "corruption is mostly in wage manipulation and falsification of expenditure ... by officials who may overstate the wages paid out ... or exaggerate the costs of materials. [However,] compared with other anti-poverty programmes in India ... relative corruption is lower in the EGS" [Dev 1994: 12].

NREP is a public works programme with much less by way of participants' pressure groups than EGS – probably because NREP, unlike EGS, has no statutory right of access to embolden participants, and to present a legitimate claim around which they can agitate. In NREP, workers are often mobilized and put in touch with local works managers and planners by a contractor; in Haryana in the mid-1980s this *mate* system created substantial corruption and leakages [OASS 1985] because it was the only way for poor, unorganized would-be employees to obtain access *without* huge transactions costs.

The standard labour-linked transactions costs are labour management costs, viz. labour search, screening and supervision. The immediate *incidence* of these costs (except for some search costs) is on the employer, i.e. the public works programme. However, the true *impact* is largely on the worker's wage rate and/or employment prospects in most cases, viz. when and where unskilled labour is in wage-elastic supply and wage-inelastic demand. Also, if programme funds are fixed, their diversion to such transactions costs leaves less to pay the workers. If the impact of transactions costs falls on the worker, or on the potential worker who is not employed because of these costs, it is especially important to consider payment or management systems that reduce such costs.

Piece-rates, if properly supervised and enforced, are one approach. They do, however, tend to move production towards activities where output can be readily standardized into a given quality and quantity per "piece". Such activities – construction rather than maintenance, roads rather than irrigation – may well not be the most productive or, when completed, poverty-reducing. The usual network of terminal bonuses, penalty clauses, etc. might also apply, but there is no reason to expect it to be more satisfactory in these schemes than in other production.

In view of the problems with these efforts to reduce the transactions costs of shirking, is there an alternative, more in keeping with the aims of these schemes to be participant rather than top-down, and (albeit as a subsidiary aim to employment for current poverty reduction) to create durable assets for the poor? One possible approach to reducing the transactions costs of labour management is partial or total joint ownership of, or other perceived benefit for workers from, the completed asset. If workers form a closely knit group (e.g. from the same village), this could lead to a form of peer monitoring that will reduce or remove the incentive to shirk.

6.   Reduce covariate stresses on public works resources

This recipe for success – or at least for avoiding disaster – is not nearly as well understood as is its analogue in anti-poverty credit programmes, viz. the need to diversify the lender's portfolio, with regard both to the known timing of stresses and to risks. In any one place, stabilization will usually be required at much the same time. If national, state or local authorities need to prepare cash-flow to meet that demand in many places with the same season of stress, then fiscal and monetary (and perhaps cross-border borrowing and repayment) policy must be adapted accordingly.

Often, however, it will be possible to include, in the portfolio of a state's public works activities, regions with different, or at least not perfectly coincident, peaks of need for public works employment. As in the case of credit, so with public works employment: if the provider is heavily or solely orientated to rural activities, and particularly to support of farmers and farmworkers, the "portfolio" is especially vulnerable to concentration of peaks, both in normal years and (especially) in bad years. Even more than in the case of credit programmes, this imposes not only a direct financial strain, but also a severely fluctuating demand on the agency's equipment and, above all, staff. That means higher costs, per unit of wages paid or works completed, than if a smoother flow of work could be achieved by appropriate risk management, i.e., for the most part, by obtaining a less covariant mix of activities, regions, or client incomes.

7. Use retailer, employer, and public works competition "for the poor"

When extra income is generated by public works, it is spent; if received by the poor, it is spent mainly on food, especially staples. There has been much controversy about the circumstances under which this is best handled by providing wages in kind, especially food-for-work. This book will not review that controversy, but one thing is clear. Reliance on *monopolistic* food delivery imposes heavy delays and other transactions costs, and possibly price gouging, upon the poor. In Botswana, drought relief worked moderately well in the 1970s because food was supplied through a variety of retailers, always potentially and often actually competitive. However, the programme was substantially more cost-effective in benefiting poor drought victims in the 1980s after the switch from direct food distribution to labour-based relief, because the whole competitive retail system (not just food suppliers) responded to the extra wage demand, with no attempt to "force" food [Drèze and Sen 1989: 156].

Even more important than retailer competition for food is employer competition for labour: a market relationship, understood in advance by the programme authorities, between them and private employers. Indeed, while public works employment always implies public (or community or NGO) financial *provision,* the *production,* for example of roads or irrigation maintenance, can sometimes be carried out by private employers, selected after competitive tenders to the public sector. Public works schemes normally include paths towards efficiency (e.g. stipulated tasks, rates, and supervision systems) and towards effective poverty reduction (e.g. rules on labour intensity, wage share, etc.). However, given public *provision* of a set amount of resources for public works, there is no iron law that public *production and management* will meet the efficiency conditions or the anti-poverty conditions better than private employers facing them as (subsequently monitored) rules for competitive tenders. Both sets of controls are imperfect (and corruptible); which is better, for which works and in which circumstances, is an empirical question.

Lacking provision for tendering to private constructors or work organizers, public works managers certainly face laborious requirements to orientate activities towards efficiency and the reduction of poverty. This is partly because financial and physical controls inevitably involve conflicts between finance departments and executing (line) departments. In private firms the board of directors, or the individual boss, resolves such problems. In publicly managed works programmes, they are in principle resolved at political level, e.g., for Maharashtra's EGS, the district zilla parishad or the lower-level block development office. Yet the conflict between line departments and the revenue department remains, as do high enforcement costs.

Elaborate arrangements are made to deliver the EGS benefits to the recipients. The revenue department must be prepared to provide work on demand but it is the irrigation, forestry and other departments which draw up advance plans for work in groups of villages and then, on instruction, execute individual projects using the EGS labour. Official instruction, informal guidelines, extensive monitoring, unscheduled field visits, vigilance tours by officials at various levels, and the advisory and supervisory role of non-official statutory committees help in delivering the EGS benefits [Dev 1994: 14].

EGS is a successful scheme, though perhaps decreasingly so. Yet, even there, the above inevitably costly and exposed process of public production and management is not obviously better than competitive tendering for private execution (also a risky process). The options should be fully and publicly reviewed, when the scheme is planned and at intervals thereafter, separately for various types of works and local circumstances. It is easier to keep this review process, and public works as a whole, accountable where the potential beneficiaries of employment schemes can organize and speak out (rule 10), and, in general, where there is a functioning, free and noisy "civil society". This is enjoyed by Maharashtra, and by many other places with public works programmes against poverty, such as India as a whole, Botswana and Chile. However, in less open polities that attempt employment-oriented public works, an accessible review process is needed even more; and the *prima facie* case against public monopoly of works execution and management is stronger.

Apart from the execution of the public works themselves, the nature of the nearby labour market is important to the secondary effects. The effect on the poor of decisions about public works wage rates, timing, location, and much else, depends in large part on the variability, price elasticity and competitive structure of supply and demand. This applies especially to the categories of labour demanded by the public works, but also to types of labour, skill, and (perhaps most important) capital equipment that might displace or complement this labour. Specific implications of these issues are discussed elsewhere in these sections. Here, we make five general points.

- The responses in private labour markets, to changes in the seasonal availability of labour due to public works, can hugely affect – double or destroy – the poverty impact of public works.

- Therefore, *the impact on employment, poverty and output of such responses must be estimated (roughly, but with analysis of sensitivity to error) before starting work on major public works.*

- Scheme planners should assume that private firms and households, in search of income and security, will respond intelligently to new wage, employment, and other options and incentives created by public policy.

- In economic terms, such responses will involve changes in output, as well as in labour supplies and demands, that reflect changing scarcities (and therefore prices) and risks, overall and seasonally.

- There may well be a political response; for example, big farm employers may well find it worthwhile to lobby for works that improve their irrigation, will oppose works that increase peak-season labour scarcity and wage rates, and may not feel strongly about works that improve small farmers' irrigation.[46]

8. Before starting, check that low demand for labour causes poverty

As with credit, so with employment: anti-poverty provision makes no sense if a shortage of supply is not causing poverty. If all labour supplied is fully employed (i.e. gets as much work as it wants) at an equilibrium wage rate sufficient to prevent poverty for almost all households, there is no case for a scheme of public works employment to reduce poverty. Such a case can arise in four ways.

- First, there may be involuntary unemployment: of *all* workers, e.g. because in the slack season employers do not find it worth while to employ anybody at a wage rate sufficient to attract labour; or of *some* workers, e.g. because employers prefer to hire stronger workers who need less time (and hence less supervision) to complete a task, so that small and weak (and usually poor) workers, though willing, are screened out of work.

- Second, although all the categories of labour get all the work they seek (each category at its own equilibrium wage rate), the demand – and hence the equilibrium wage rate – for some types of workers, usually the unskilled and poor, may be so low that it does not pay them (e.g. in terms of energy foregone) to supply sufficient labour to avoid poverty; a special case arises if demand for labour is price elastic for a given size of workforce around a poverty wage rate (or less), so that more labour supply means less total labour income for the workforce.[47]

- Third, particular groups of workers may be kept poor by being prevented from entering into the labour market, fully or at all, by gender, group (e.g. caste or tribe), or personal circumstances (e.g. illness).

---

46. Unless such works divert public funds from work on irrigation, etc., for larger farms – or, in the medium term, by creating new opportunities for deficit farmers on their own farms, lead to labour shortages on big farms.

47. Under these circumstances, greater labour supply and absorption will increase poverty *incidence* among the initial workforce; may lower it among the new workers; but is likely to reduce the *severity* of poverty, if the new workers had been extremely poor previously.

- Fourth, some people may be kept poor because, for a variety of reasons, equilibrium is not reached in a part of the labour market, e.g. because some groups of workers are prevented from undercutting, even slightly, a very high wage rate established for a few privileged workers.

The first case is the classic origin of public works to create extra employment for poverty reduction, notably in the case of Keynesian involuntary unemployment; but not all involuntary unemployment is susceptible to public works remedies. In the second case, they will work to the extent that public works offer a higher-than-equilibrium wage *and this does not "knock on" to the private sector and price out many poor employees there*. In the third case, public works employment is relevant to the extent that it pioneers the employment of outgroups (e.g. the sick or disabled) by accepting some losses for a perceived social benefit, or demonstrates a gender-blind or caste-blind employment policy – or even "affirmative action" (reverse discrimination) as in much public employment in India.

In the fourth case, which characterizes urban and public-sector employment and is usually found mainly in open democratic societies, the role of public works policies is complex. It depends on their capacity to reduce costs of employment by avoiding various rules and restrictions on recruitment, dismissal, and wage rates that apply to the formal sector as a whole, and are normally enforced with special rigour in the public sector. Glaessner [1994] attributes the success of anti-poverty public works employment in Latin America in substantial part to the relaxation or removal of such rules for the works agencies concerned, in the context of their partial independence of the general government machine. Yet one needs to be careful that the "removed rules" do not offend against genuine requirements of safety or of natural justice; the public sector, even in order to employ the poor cost-effectively, should not give a lead that encourages, say, lax safety rules on construction sites, or *arbitrary* dismissal. Also, some cost-raising provisions on public works have proved essential in enabling particular poor groups to benefit (see discussion of rule 1 for the impact of crèches on women's participation in EGS as compared with NREP).

The lesson is to ask: (1) Is unemployment, a low real wage rate, or something else the main cause of poverty? (2) How cost-effectively will proposed public works employment remedy the cause, allowing for secondary and knock-on effects in the private sector? If poverty arises mainly because illness or discrimination cuts labour *supply*, a programme to reduce poverty via public works labour *demand* may not help.

9.   Subsidize coverage, sustainability, graduation – but seldom above market wages

Successful public employment schemes for the poor often involve paying somewhat more for the end-product than could be achieved outside such schemes. This is a hidden subsidy. However, just as successful credit for the poor usually focuses any subsidy on things other than the interest rate, so successful public works employment usually focuses them on things other than the wage rate.

For a programme with a given budget, or given limits on its growth rate, there is a definitional trade-off between high coverage, high non-wage component, and high wage rate: more of any of these normally means less of at least one of the other two. Minimizing the non-wage component is assumed to be good, but where this assumption is made (as in EGS) the constructions with low shares of non-wage costs tend to be done first, and for this reason (and others) the non-wage element rises over time [Dev 1994: Table 2]. Nor is the assumption always right: squeezing project skills, capital and overview to the limit soon damages cost-effectiveness in production, and ultimately even in poverty reduction. Moreover, capital intensity in a small part of a district's capital assets may be needed to increase labour intensity in other parts [Lanjouw and Stern 1989]. General incentives to keep the non-wage component down are nevertheless usually right; but when that process reaches its limits the choice between spending on coverage and spending on higher wage rates has to be faced. Basu [1981] argues that the wage on food for work programmes in the late 1970s was above the "optimum" level, viz. the wage rate that exhausted scheme resources while employing all who wished to work at that wage.

We have explored the limits on propositions such as "the higher the wage rate, the worse the targeting", or "the lower the wage rate, the worse the poverty impact", or "minimum-wage or other employee-protecting rules harm the poor as a whole". There is a strong presumption in favour of using scheme resources to support wider coverage rather than above-market wage rates, but only if (1) the cost of eliminating poverty is high, (2) those who graduate out of poverty (e.g. via the public works scheme) are unlikely much to increase the resources for financing that cost, (3) the scheme authorities aim to reduce some index of the severity of poverty rather than "merely" to push the just-poor over the poverty line, (4) the complementary requirements for a cost-effective rural public works programme are met. These conditions are often met, but it is (4) that is likeliest to be violated. It is not sensible to keep scheme wages well below some statutory minimum if the *only* reason is to free up resources for extending the scheme into some region where the poverty reduction is not constrained mainly by inadequate demand for labour, or where the infrastructural requirements for poor people to work in such a scheme (e.g. transport, health and nutrition conditions) are not met. Also, some schemes such as PIREP in Kerala underspent because the administratively feasible rate of expansion, and/or the demand for jobs at the offered wage rate, had been overestimated [Desai 1975; Gopinath et al. 1978]; in such cases it would be folly to reduce already low wage rates only in order to increase coverage.

Nevertheless, *it is a good general rule* – subject to empirical investigation in the particular case – *that scheme support and subsidy should be geared towards higher coverage, not above-market wage rates*. This is fairer *among* the poor than concentrating coverage *and* above-market wage rates on a favoured few regions or groups. Fairness among the poor matters, because these schemes need all the political friends they can get; as has been shown, they are expensive and may well not please some of the powerful rich. Also, there is bound to be some perceived "unfairness" in the early years, when it is not feasible to go for complete coverage (if it ever is); to compound this with the sense that some are being denied coverage so that others may get higher wages than "necessary" is probably bad politics, as well as cost-ineffective poverty reduction. Of course, to be cost-effective, increases in coverage involve costs beyond those of exact replication; locally specific surveys, exploratory pilots (usually involving matching grants to NGOs or grassroots organizations), and training for officials and potential participants are required. Experience, however, suggests that "going to scale" in employment programmes is usually less expensive and problematic than in credit programmes.

If subsidies to **coverage** are to be kept manageable or phased out in any anti-poverty scheme, two relevant considerations are to improve **sustainability** – of the projects financed, of the scheme's own operation, or of the escape from poverty of its initial beneficiaries – and to improve the rate of **graduation** of beneficiaries, out of the groups so poor that they will require (or be willing to do) the self-targeting, low-wage, largely manual work that the scheme has to offer. Obviously, that principle applies to all anti-poverty schemes: in credit programmes as in public works programmes, more *sustainable* embodied projects, scheme management systems, and "exits" from the scheme's ranks of clients all mean that the scheme can *cover* a larger proportion of the remaining poor at a given level of support costs, as does a higher rate at which existing employees or borrowers *graduate* from poverty and thus "exit" from scheme support.[48] But the formulae for improving sustainability or graduation vary greatly as between, say, credit and employment programmes. For example, many activities supported by credit schemes lead to end-products owned by beneficiaries (most of them, it is hoped, thereby graduated out of poverty), while much construction supported by employment programmes is in the public sector and/or provides undirected, or even rich-farmer-oriented, benefits; in the latter case post-project maintenance, and sustainability of favourable poverty impact as well as of productivity of the end-product, poses different (and usually harder) problems.

Will public works assets sustainably benefit the potentially or actually poor? The problems are different for the main sorts of asset: privately owned physical capital, economic infrastructure, or social infrastructure.

---

48. Much poverty is transient or temporary, especially in drought-prone scheme areas such as Botswana or Maharashtra. In such cases, graduation and exit should be measured between comparable climatic points. Even during successful scheme operation leading to rapid poverty reduction, short-term rises in scheme demand are normal during drought.

It is unusual for privately owned physical capital produced by public works to be owned by the poor. A frequent criticism of EGS is that it provides water or land development on the cheap for big farmers. This may increase employment prospects and thus sustain poverty reduction later on, but not as much as if the assets were on the land of marginal and poor farmers (who tend to use them more labour-intensively). In a sense, public works employment (like credit) is a way of attacking poverty without grasping the nettle of land reform or other radical redistribution; and unless the nettle is grasped it is not easy for poor people, especially the rural or urban landless, to benefit from the sort of assets readily created by public works.

However, there are successful examples of this. India's Million Wells Scheme created durable assets owned by small and marginal farmers, many of them around the poverty line. As for the landless and near-landless, Bangladesh's Proshika is a credit programme, but illustrates a principle applicable to public works as well. In Proshika, groups of very poor people receive training and credit to purchase tubewells that subsequently provide them with capital and labour income, as they deliver water to farmers [Wood 1984]. In adapting this principle from credit to public works employment, the big problem is finance; the more the employees are asked to put aside their (usually quite low) wages to save up for ultimate ownership of the assets they are working to create, the more they sacrifice their modest living standards now in order to sustain them at a higher level in the future. Some credit element would be needed alongside, possibly matching, such savings.

Even then, it is not clear that the most sustainably poverty-reducing use (after the works employment is complete) of any accumulated savings and credit is (1) to allocate it to those among the poor who have already received the public works employment, and (2) to "tie" it to the particular assets they have been employed to construct. The latter does have the great advantage of motivating higher-quality work, and of reducing the need to supervise shirking (thanks again to peer-group monitoring, in this case of workers rather than of borrowers). But the experience of urban site-and-service and slum-upgrading projects – a form of urban public works scheme that was itself rather successful in many cases – suggests caution. In their early years, such schemes were damaged by efforts to tie the work done to subsequent ownership of the house or improvement by the worker. Both poverty impact and efficiency are often greater if the employed person and the subsequent owner of the particular asset created – while, one hopes, both helped out of poverty – are distinct. Employees may do better to use their incomes to accumulate other assets than those they are working on, or to buy health or food rather than to accumulate at all. Poor people able and willing to manage such assets may be more cost-effectively served through a credit programme, leaving employment programmes for others.

However, the concentration of public works benefits in rural areas on large farmers can be extreme. In Botswana the "emphasis on creating projects useful to farmers *such as dams and firebreaks*, and to encourage increased food output on *commercial* farms" [Harvey and Lewis 1990: 304; my italics] implied that public works involved durable benefits (as opposed to short-term employment incomes) largely for people who were wealthy, sometimes extremely wealthy, and especially prone to use labour-displacing methods of farming. This is a much more extreme case than the large-farm bias of benefits from public works to construct percolation tanks in Maharashtra's EGS [Gaiha 1994: 121] and in Bangladesh's Food for Work scheme; "large farmers" in such cases, though rarely poor, are seldom wealthy, or very much more capital-intensive than smaller farmers. In both sorts of case, but especially in cases like that of Botswana, it remains worth asking whether direct ownership of public works scheme assets by the poor is feasible. Where the poor have a little land, this can sometimes be achieved by restructuring the planned works to serve it, e.g. by reducing the distance between irrigation outlets. Even the landless poor – if engaged on public works, with a savings component out of wages – many attain joint ownership of a new asset, the output of which (e.g. tubewell water) they later sell, Proshika-style. Such involvement of the workers in constructing their own asset makes them keener to work well as a group, and thus harnesses peer monitoring by workers on the scheme, reducing labour supervision costs. Moreover, if poor workers build assets for their own subsequent benefit, scheme administrators may save costs by planning for employment and asset-based anti-poverty components together – provided the economies of scope outweigh the costs of steering into untested waters. There are financing problems, and strong training requirements – both for administrators and for employees who are to become owners – but it is worth trying.

Much more common is the use of schemes to produce social infrastructure favourable to the subsequent employment income of the very poor. Under EGS, water conservation in Sholapur District was planned with subsequent horticultural production in mind [Dev 1994: 8]; this is both suitable for very small farms and intensive in the use of hired, as well as family, labour. In general, the sort of assets created under EGS have a good deal to do with the decline in demand for the scheme, as a growing proportion of the poor – not necessarily the former scheme employees – found their labour could be used more rewardingly elsewhere [Hirway 1991: 68]. Conversely, NREP social infrastructure was not usually well suited to subsequent employment of, let alone ownership by, the poor [ibid.].

There are four problems with building on such success to enable assets, created by public works employment programmes, to provide durable incomes for the poor afterwards and thus to assist the graduation process.

- Maintenance of scheme assets is usually delegated to line ministries or local authorities, and is often inferior to maintenance of public-sector assets with which they have more direct experience and identification [Dev 1994: 17; PEO 1980].

- The poor (and their communities) are often best served by using public works resources to construct social infrastructure such as schools or primary health centres; these do not yield much subsequent demand for unskilled labour.

- If both the works and the employment are oriented almost entirely towards the poor, there may be little reason for the rich and powerful to support or finance the programme [Dev 1994]; then the sustainability of poverty reduction through scheme works may be offset by reduced political sustainability for the scheme itself.

- Most public works schemes – especially later, unplanned components – contain little or no facility for the poor to learn skills, on the job or otherwise, that will later assist with employment on (let alone ownership or management of) scheme works [Gianchandani 1991].

The history of these schemes, however, shows that resources can successfully be applied to overcoming these problems, so that the public works create durable assets that are labour-intensive in subsequent use. Roads, a common component of these schemes, often show good social returns. However, they are labour-intensive neither in use nor (as a rule) in construction, and, when complete, usually raise rich people's incomes proportionately more than poor people's. Public works schemes such as India's NREP tend to emphasize roads, but the emphasis can be reversed, as was the drift towards roads in Maharashtra's EGS [ibid.: Table 2; Bandyopadhyay 1985].

Support and subsidies for public works employment schemes – i.e. the element of scheme cost in excess of (1) the value of the assets created or (2) their lowest attainable production cost, whichever is the smaller – have several possible uses. Great caution is indicated in using subsidies to support wage rates above market levels; it is usually, but not always, better to use the resources to extend scheme coverage, and to permit the poor previously covered to graduate from the schemes by making the assets themselves labour-intensive, or suitable to generate income streams for the poor (via employment, skill generation, or ownership) after the works end. Financial viability of the schemes is likely to depend on steady graduation of this sort.

10. Encourage grassroots pressure groups to improve the scheme

"[T]he enfranchisement of the rural poor is a notoriously arduous task ... the reliable availability of public employment seems to provide the poor with a unique opportunity to organize around common interests, besides improving their bargaining position within rural society" [Drèze 1988, cited in Gaiha 1994: 111]. It is the legal guarantee of employment, rather than discretionary provision, that encourages the poor to be so bold [Echeverri-Gent 1988]. Dev [1994: 8; cf. also Hirway 1991: 69] cites numerous locations where EGS employee groups have been formed, and ways in which they have applied pressure helpful to the scheme's performance and sustainability. Confronting the problem that contractors cream off some of the benefits intended for the poor on many a public works project in an Indian district that he studied, Galab [1993] argues that labour cooperatives might replace contractors. Such control of leakages to officials, as well as the development of integration with village-level development requirements, and the organization of political support for the programme (without undue reliance upon, and hence drift of benefits to, the powerful non-poor), are examples of the uses to which participant beneficiaries can put their political organization.

While many writers stress the importance of these local political organizations of beneficiaries, I have found no discussion of what scheme managers can do – or how they can be encouraged – to help such organizations into existence, or to protect or encourage them (without co-opting them). The shortness of this sub-chapter does not indicate its relative importance: *political and hence financial unsustainability is the main single problem of anti-poverty programmes, and organization of beneficiaries – potential, if possible, as well as actual – is perhaps the main remedy.* Three observations are presented here as hypotheses, with scanty evidence.

First, a major problem in sustaining common-benefit organizations (or any other commons) is free-riding. Everyone would like to leave the costs, risks and pains of political organization and negotiation to others, and free-ride on the benefits: what Olson [1982] characterizes as the contributors' dilemma, so damaging to large organizations (such as trade unions) seeking members' subscriptions, let alone direct involvement. It may be feasible, without co-option or corruption, for a small grant to be made out of scheme resources to provide some clearly designated, non-discretionary incentive for the organizer of an employee's representative group linked to a particular set of works.

Second, a big cause of free-riding is the sense that one's share in the benefits of the common project is small relative to one's share in the political costs or risks of organizing it. Rules on each works that provide roughly comparable net benefits to the participants may help here. Such rules, however, should not override the need for convenient access to bigger or smaller "pieces" of scheme work according to the needs and capacities of the different employees.

Third, groups of employees on public works schemes, which are largely self-targeting on the poor, do better to advance the interests of the poor as a whole in such schemes than "village development committees" or other bodies. Even if these are democratic and representative, they are likely to reflect substantial power among the rich. Thus in Botswana, which is an open multi-party democracy, labour-based relief projects were in large part "chosen through Village Development Committees" [Harvey and Lewis 1990: 302], but this did not prevent the constructed works from being severely biased towards very large farmers (see above, rule 9). Dev [1994] provides examples of political pressure by scheme beneficiaries that helped to oppose the tendency (and was by no means focused mainly on bidding up wage rates to the possible disadvantage of *potential* beneficiaries, who after all probably include the actual beneficiaries' families and friends).

11. In performance and outreach, employment schemes complement others

This is true in two senses. First, the net economic and social benefits to most public works are increased, and/or the costs of production reduced, if other appropriate activities are being, or have been, pursued at the same time in the same region. Second, in the sense of complementarity of outreach, groups of poor people in an area who are not reached by a public works programme are liable to be reached by appropriate anti-poverty programmes of different types.

The net economic benefits to a public works project, as measured by its economic rate of return, are likely to be higher where other forms of poverty-oriented activity are being *effectively* provided (not necessarily produced) by state action. The cost of works will tend to be lower, given the wage rate, if even unskilled workers are literate and numerate, healthy, and readily able to get to work (e.g. by public transport on adequate urban metro services or rural roads). Furthermore, the completed works will normally produce more net output in such circumstances, and also if users and owners, even if poor, can readily obtain credit at market rates.

All this applies to the *economic* rate of return, without income-distribution weights. However, net benefits can, and in the case of poverty-oriented schemes should, be measured through the *social* rate of return, so as to give a higher weighting to benefits (and costs) that accrue to the poor than market prices would suggest, and a correspondingly lower weighting to benefits and costs accruing to the non-poor. If the social rate is used to measure net benefit from public works, the impact of complementary anti-poverty programmes upon that benefit will be proportionately higher than if the economic rate is used (on the plausible assumptions that the complementary programmes are better than random in their targeting upon the poor, and do something to improve productivity). Not only will the extension of primary education, or access to credit, or public transport, in general make public works cost less and yield more net product (assuming that wage rates are not pulled up too much, given the wage elasticity of demand for labour); such extensions will also cause a larger part of benefits from the works, and a smaller part of the costs, to accrue to people at the lower end of the income scale.

The second sense of "complementarity" refers to outreach. Many of the poor are unlikely to benefit from public works schemes, but can benefit from other anti-poverty programmes. That obviously includes people who cannot work more than they now do, e.g. because they are old or sick, and who do not receive extra income from household members whose wage receipts rise as a result of those schemes; such people can be helped by food distribution or other forms of social security, but not by public works (or by sound credit programmes, as a rule).

Some groups, not reached by public works but accessible to other anti-poverty programmes, are less obvious. Some societies impose strong sanctions against work *outside the homestead* by widows, even if healthy and willing to work; credit for poor widows might help. In some countries, many of the poor still get most of their income from farming rather than from employment, and have little opportunity to take up public works jobs even in the slack season; pro-poor technical change in agriculture advances the interests of such people, who may be left out by public works schemes. Such progress may also reduce the price of food, or its seasonal fluctuations, in towns or food-deficit (e.g. cash-crop) rural areas with high transport costs of food from ports or domestic food-growing areas. Such local food price effects increase the real income of the local poor as a whole, whether in or out of public works schemes, thus complementing them in both rate-of-return and outreach senses.

In another (but regionally overlapping) case, complementary health/nutrition programmes may be indicated. In northern India, Pakistan and Bangladesh, there is strong evidence of intra-household discrimination against little girls in the provision of food and health care [Harriss 1989]; since such discrimination may be worse in households around or slightly above the poverty line, we cannot assume that in such households girls will benefit from public works, even if it raises their parents' earnings. This is especially the case if the cost to children in terms of reduced child care, when women take up employment, exceeds the gains from extra income. This happened in a case in Kerala studied by Kumar [1977], though only in some seasons, and though it did not happen in the two EGS villages analysed by Deolalikar and Gaiha [1992]. In general the gains to child nutrition are *more* if extra income accrues to women than if it accrues to men [Kennedy and Peters 1992] and discrimination against little girls declines as female earning opportunities catch up with adult males [Rosenzweig and Schultz 1982]. Normally, therefore, high female participation, as in a public works scheme like EGS, is better for girls' health than low participation, as in NREP. However, net harm to girls *and* boys when mothers seek work (because worse child care outweighs greater household income) is a real risk in some households, as Kumar [1977] indicates. This fact, plus the presence of small children in some households from which no member can take up public works employment, makes a case for complementary health/nutrition schemes where public works are introduced, especially into the poorest communities or those with nutritional gender discrimination. It also strengthens the case for providing crèches at public works sites.

What is the policy implication of the fact that public works schemes against poverty are in general complementary with other *cost-effective* schemes for the same area or group – complementary in the sense that the other schemes increase both the social returns and the outreach of the public works scheme? The word "cost-effective" is crucial. There is a fixed cost in starting each particular type of scheme and learning about it, nationally and also in any particular region. No country can carry out, at the same time, many different anti-poverty programmes in many different regions without sharply declining effectiveness for some schemes and some regions; the schemes remain complementary within each region, but the benefits, both to social returns and to outreach, are eventually much outweighed by the losses due to declining marginal cost-effectiveness of particular schemes in particular regions. That is especially true for the newest *type* of anti-poverty scheme, or the more marginal regions to which a given scheme has been extended – in each case, almost certainly with inadequate survey work, training of staff and potential beneficiaries, piloting experience, and infrastructure. Older-established but already marginal or faltering schemes and regions also suffer, as staff are thinned out to operate the new programmes or areas.

Hence complementarity (of returns and outreach) cannot possibly mean that every village and suburb should have access to every type of anti-poverty programme, even if some individuals in each place would benefit from each scheme located there. The scarcer and less efficiently or honestly organized are administrative resources, the more concentration is needed. But what sort of concentration? Here, complementarity of returns has very different implications from complementarity of outreach. Complementarity of (local) *returns* indicates that, for cost-effectiveness, a small number of areas should each enjoy several different anti-poverty programmes, rather than assigning Programme A to region r, Programme B to region s, and so on. The "lucky" regions to get several programmes would be selected on a basis that, in practice, combined several criteria: need, economic returns (perhaps weighted together via the social rate of return), political persuasiveness. Complementarity of *outreach* need have no such implication; there is no obvious reason why, because poverty group 1 is being helped by an anti-poverty scheme of type A in region r, therefore poverty group 2, which is best addressed by schemes of type B, should get access to such schemes in region r rather than, say, in region t or region u. A sense of "fairness" among regions indicates the opposite; and though economists will retort that it is fairness among people that matters, and that fairness among regions is valueless, try telling that to voters or politicians! Complementarity of returns may, however, go hand in hand with complementarity of outreach, in that multiplier benefits and favourable externalities are greatest if several poverty groups in a region are being developed and disimpoverished at once. That is the idea behind area development, integrated programmes, and the old concept of "balanced growth".

For reasons that have been indicated, public works employment programmes are especially likely to be affected by the need for complementary inputs if they are to have high social rates of return. This creates a dilemma: the sense of fairness requires dispersal of programmes, but cost-effectiveness, even in poverty reduction, requires their concentration. The dilemma can be softened, though not solved, by concentrating public works employment on regions, urban or rural, that will really benefit (in terms of poverty reduction) from the employment programme, given the level of administrative efficiency and integrity that can reasonably be expected, the impact of expansion upon programme-wide returns, and "returns complementarity" among programmes in the same region.

12. Build up capacity of schemes and workers before works begin

The absence of a "shelf" of properly pre-evaluated works is one of the reasons why rapid, widespread expansion into new regions of public works schemes (and of credit schemes tied to new productive works, such as the Comilla project in Bangladesh) so seldom works well. Such a "shelf" is a crucial, yet often neglected, requirement for good social returns, and good outreach to the poor, in public works programmes.

In Botswana, the transition from food distribution to labour-intensive rural works was prepared by recognizing and planning for future drought problems well in advance, while rains were good; in the 1980s, when small-scale works were needed in large numbers to provide employment income during severe and prolonged drought, such works had been well prepared, in large part with a view to reducing vulnerability to drought later on [Drèze and Sen 1989: 154]. Years before Maharashtra's EGS began, it had been the subject of political debate and administrative preparation, so that a large "shelf" of micro-projects had been prepared, ready for construction where and when the demand for jobs expanded; the high (but declining) quality of EGS works is attributable to the large (but dwindling) project shelf, as well as to the normal effects of diminishing returns. In contrast, the employment programmes of drought relief during Kenya's anti-famine programme in 1984 did not include properly prepared micro-works. Hence this part of the relief largely failed. Yet this was in the context of an otherwise very successful programme [Drèze and Sen 1989: 140].

A review of food-for-work projects supported by USAID worldwide concludes that *a shelf of pre-planned projects, ready to be drawn down in emergencies, is the most important condition for success.* The reviewers add that the variation and improvement by donors of FFW conditions, so as to ease local purchases and national-currency transactions, had helped improve matters in this regard [Bryson et al. 1991]. It is important that the shelf be filled with projects that are pro-poor and sound in engineering and economic terms, but also that scheme rules do not impede rapid implementation of relevant items from the shelf.

People, as well as local works, should be prepared, if the scheme is to have good results. Administrators and supervisors of works have to be trained. Potential scheme participants have to be informed, and sometimes taught specific skills. Links to local health and nutrition may need to be prepared. Importantly, the bases of community participation and political pressure by poor beneficiaries, actual and potential, may need to be laid early, if the mix of projects in the scheme is not to be skewed towards the well-to-do (rule 10). Conversely, the political basis to support durable financing of the scheme needs to be secured. The long-lasting success of Maharashtra's EGS owes much to the existence of a large city, Bombay, to pay most of the costs [Herring and Edwards 1983], but a city already the beneficiary of substantial urban bias on other accounts, and concerned to reduce migration from the villages. Nevertheless, prolonged preparation of the better-off for a scheme that was to cost up to 15 per cent of state revenues was essential, and has paid off.

13. Use performance incentives for officials and participants

As with credit, direct incentives should be used, where possible, rather than rules (especially discretionary rules), to improve scheme performance. We have discussed piece-rates, and peer monitoring secured by group ownership of assets. The problem of incentives to officials is somewhat less fraught than in the case of credit programmes, because the *self*-targeting of low-wage unskilled labour upon the poor removes the acute need to provide incentives to officials for the achievement of possibly counter-productive *external* targets: a problem pervading credit-based anti-poverty programmes. The question of control of works, however, remains; and the differences among and within public works programmes in this regard does suggest that performance incentives for officials may be important.

Lieberman [1984, 1985] reviews possible incentives for field officers in the context of the need to reduce corruption, and improve supervision of works, in Maharashtra's EGS. Employment guarantees reduce officials' capacity to apply normal work disciplines, especially since they promote (otherwise highly desirable) political organization among beneficiaries. The tension between, on the one hand, local supervision through the District Collector and the Revenue Department, and on the other hand responsibility for design and implementation with the line departments responsible for physical completion of works, can create cross-cutting pressures, and odd results, that create undesirable incentive structures.

6. Land, farming, social services, food, towns: Testing rules of anti-poverty success; implications for governments, NGOs

(i) Introduction

In Chapters 4 and 5 we found that the "rules of anti-poverty success" applied to the two types of policies widely used to reduce poverty: credit and public works. Given limits on time, space, and coherence, we deliberately refrain from attempting anything like similar detail on other categories of anti-poverty policy. Yet some of these categories are at least as important in poverty reduction, and have at least as many instances of success and failure, as the topics we have reviewed. These categories include policy for: land reform; agricultural growth and technology; social services – both for human capital via health and education and for safety nets; and in some circumstances food supplementation or subsidization.

This chapter very briefly examines the above categories of anti-poverty policy in turn. In each case, the reader is left to decide – with a few suggestions, one hopes not too biased, from the author – which of the 13 rules apply. Our expectation is that the rules will do well in categories such as food-distribution policy, where poverty-focus poses many targeting and regional problems similar to those in credit and public works – but that the rules will need much alteration where political contentiousness is sharper and/or macro-policy more dominant, such as land reform and the acceleration (or labour-intensification) of technical progress in agriculture.

We close with a question: Why have anti-poverty policies had so much more specific and production-oriented success in rural than in urban areas of developing countries, notwithstanding the urban bias of public policy, the generally slower growth of farm than of non-farm output and prices, and hence the continuing and probably widening gap between rural and urban poverty and well-being?

(ii) Land reform

With this classical but recently undervalued form of anti-poverty policy, we move into a different world from that of credit reform or employment schemes. Many otherwise well-informed people believe that, since the post-war reforms in Japan, the Republic of Korea and Taiwan (China), there are few if any success stories of land reform. They believe that it has been legislated with so many loopholes that very little has happened; or that it has been evaded, or has failed to get land to the poor, or has been reversed; that it runs against modern farming, with (alleged) economies of scale and complex techniques of production and marketing; that, even where desirable, it is politically infeasible; in short, that the golden age of land reform, if it existed at all, was over by the mid-1960s. *All these statements are false, and are generally agreed to be so by subject specialists, whatever their analytical or political preference.* There is almost no area of anti-poverty policy where popular, even professional, opinion is so far removed from expert analysis and evidence as land reform.

To introduce the question of "rules for success", we therefore set out a series of propositions. Evidence and reasoning appear, inter alia, in [Binswanger et al. 1995; Gaiha 1994, ch. 5; Lipton 1993; el-Ghonemy 1990; Hayami et al. 1990; Thiesenhusen 1989; Berry and Cline 1979].

- The only land reform that normally reduces poverty, and enhances efficiency and growth, is **privately redistributive land reform (PRLR)**: redistribution of land from large to small farms, which usually does both. Other things often miscalled "land reform" – enforced registration of individual title, collectivization, state farming, prohibition of tenancy – almost always do net harm, to the poor and to farm efficiency. So does tenancy restriction, except alongside PRLR.

- There has been massive PRLR since 1945. It has taken place in China, most of Latin America (though not Brazil or Argentina), much of South Asia and parts of Africa.

- Though PRLR slowed after the mid-1970s, it never stopped. Attempted reversals (as in Chile) reduced collective areas, but actually increased the proportion of land in small family holdings. The pace of PRLR is again picking up in much of Latin America [Carter and Mesbah 1991], much of Eastern Europe starting with decollectivization in Romania, north-eastern Brazil intermediated by local authorities and NGOs [Tendler 1993], and South Africa.

• PRLR has often happened only after an enforced detour via collectivization [Bell 1990], but this has usually been undone – often after great and needless suffering – by peasant action and/or by the sheer weight of its own perverse incentive structure. Farmland then becomes distributed to households, much less unequally than prior to collectivization.

• Greater equality of owned or operated farmland, as between pairs of agricultural censuses or surveys in the past 30 years, has hardly ever happened without PRLR [el-Ghonemy 1990]. Even half-hearted PRLR creates incentives for big farmers to dispose of holdings, reducing inequality of farmland [Vyas 1976; Lipton 1993].

• Rural poverty incidence is strongly correlated with inequality of farmland [Tyler et al. 1993].

• Smaller holdings, such as those created by PRLR, are usually observed to be more socially efficient, i.e. to produce at lower average opportunity cost, especially where land is (increasingly) scarce relative to rural labour. *This is not to say that large farmers are privately inefficient!* The observation is due mainly to the *inverse relationship* (IR) between farm size and (i) gross annual output per hectare (due mainly, not to higher crop-specific yield on small farms, but to their higher cropping intensity and more labour-intensive and hence valuable choice of crops); (ii) to a lesser extent but still clearly, total factor productivity; (iii) tendency to choose methods and crops requiring a lot of land and purchased capital, relative to labour, in circumstances where the opportunity cost of labour is less than the wage rate.

• This IR is not much weakened by the "green revolution"; applies to many so-called plantation crops; and is not much weakened by mechanization (itself often a socially inefficient response, made privately profitable for big farmers only by their success in lobbying for subsidies on fuel, credit and tractors to displace labour).

- Some of the IR is due to better quality of land on smaller farms, but not as much as is often thought; anyway this better quality is in considerable part due to the greater efforts made, per hectare, by small farmers to improve their lands [Binswanger et al. 1995; Berry and Cline 1979; Hayami et al. 1990; Lipton 1993].

- The IR is due mainly to the fact that small farmers with several family workers per hectare have lower transactions costs in seeking, screening and supervising labour – their own or that of employees – than do large commercial farmers. The latter therefore maximize profits by choosing more extensive farm inputs, outputs and methods than do family farmers.

- As land is redistributed from big to small farms, therefore, not only family labour per hectare, but (although to a lesser extent) hired labour per hectare, increases quite sharply [Boyce 1987: 204-13; Thiesenhusen and Melmed-Sanjak 1990: 397-404]. Furthermore, land reform beneficiaries divert family labour from the job market to their own farms (and perhaps to leisure). For both reasons, the employment position of those who remain landless even after PRLR improves.

- An area with smallish, fairly equal farms is likely to devote expenditure (both average and marginal) much more to labour-intensive, locally-made purchases – thereby providing secondary income for employees – than an otherwise similar area with very unequal farms.

- If land ownership starts very unequal, the economic advantages of small and equal farming are unlikely to be realized to a great extent by land sales or tenancies alone. This is partly because land markets are thin, imperfect and often localized or restricted to transactions among members of a particular group; partly because farmland is held, in part, for speculative or precautionary reasons, so that its sale price (or rental) overstates the present value of its future (expected) net value-products; and partly because big owners fear that tenancy laws will damage them if they rent out their land in small units. Markets can be improved, or stimulated, to reduce these obstacles; but usually PRLR is also needed to achieve substantial progress towards poverty reduction, and the increased social efficiency of farming, associated with smaller and more equal landholdings.

- There are two main reasons why PRLR does not always happen. First, there are genuine economies of scale in providing many farm inputs, and in collecting, processing, marketing, and bulking-up some farm outputs; these economies of scale have been conflated institutionally with the farming process, often leaving big farmers (e.g. of tea) also to provide processing. Complex institutional innovations, often not perfectly supplied by the market unaided, are needed to unbundle processing from farming – so that processing proceeds in big units with scale economies, leaving farm populations in smaller, more equal and on balance usually more productive units.

- PRLR laws and implementation are also impeded by political obstacles. These are usually blamed on political opposition from big farmers. But these could be compensated, both by profits from supplying the "unbundled" farm-input services, and directly by the state and by land-reform beneficiaries together. That would still leave the beneficiaries to enjoy a net GNP gain, due to the IR. The real political barriers to IR may come largely from urban groups unwilling to pay towards the transitional costs of the reforms, and fearful of losing things now provided by big farmers: farm surpluses, savings, and perhaps alliances for social control.

- Prospective gains from PRLR are most, and the balance of power is usually least, able to prevent it, if land inequality is extremely large; if there are labour-intensive crop-mixes and technical choices open to smallholders (i.e. if the agroclimate does not dictate a monoculture, and if choices of crop and method are considerable); if the rural person/land ratio is relatively high; and if complementary services (research, extension, credit, transport) are either available (privately or publicly) to the new or enhanced smallholders, or are not required by them.

- As a majority of the poor comes to depend on labour rather than land for livelihood, the employment gains from PRLR come increasingly to determine its effects on poverty and the proportion of poor people likely to receive significant farmland directly declines. Many pessimistic assessments of the prospective gains from land reform refer to places such as Bangladesh. There, in contrast (say) to Brazil, land is much less unequal; the correlation between access to land and absence of poverty, while still considerable, is weaker; and the proportion of rural poor without land (and unlikely to get it even in a quite radical PRLR) is higher. So *evaluations of the impact of land reform choices on poverty need to assess effects on employment income, at least as much as effects on the distribution and amount of net income from land.*

- The above discussion – solely to simplify the argument – has proceeded as if farms contained land of the same quality, as if each household comprised the same number of persons, and as if all households were dependent on farming for the same proportion of income. Equity and poverty-reduction require, in principle, that quality of land owned, size of family, and non-farm sources of income should be taken into account when undertaking PRLR. In practice, a search for completely accurate targeting in these matters would involve much cost, delay and evasion.

- The possible injustices associated with the resulting imperfect targeting of PRLR strengthen the moral and political case for undertaking it in decentralized, market-friendly fashion and with some degree of consent. Yet the classical model for PRLR has involved the take-over by a central land authority, often with a large confiscatory element, of land owned above the ceiling, and eventual redistribution of the surplus to the landless or near-landless. That model, while it has scored considerable success, has increasingly proved prone to corruption, bad targeting, evasion and delay. Recent "new wave" reforms [Tendler 1993, Lipton 1993] involve more decentralized, less confiscatory approaches. However, some element of threat or fear, at least among the largest owners, either of land invasions [Binswanger et al. 1995] or of possible enforcement of the classical model, is usually required, if owners are to release much land consensually without price rises that either exclude the poor from benefit or impose crippling fiscal burdens.

While very summary, the above observations may give some "feel" for the issues involved in designing and implementing successful PRLR. *PRLR is undoubtedly one of the most important weapons against poverty. It has achieved many successes,* but in the past 15 years has been unduly denigrated. As experience has taught potential losers the art of evasion and avoidance, there may be a case for more consensual approaches. However, *the combination of great land inequality with the IR makes a powerful case for PRLR in many places, often on "new wave" lines.* The extreme rural inequality of (say) South Africa and Brazil, and the need for a multi-pronged attack on poverty in some less unequal but still very poor places like Bangladesh and Kenya, make it certain that we shall hear much more of PRLR. Claimed rules of success – appropriate provision of post-reform services, speed of execution, etc. – are familiar from the literature, but hark back to a time when reforms were assumed to be central and confiscatory, and when many people assumed that the whole panoply of rural services was needed by reform beneficiaries and was best provided by the state.

Hence one would, rather, turn at this stage to our "rules of success". They may prove more generally applicable – with the caveats mentioned there – to classical as well as "new wave" land reforms. For example, Singh and Hazell [1993], in a study of panel data from five agro-climatic zones (two villages each) in India, illustrate the importance of three of the "rules of success": recognition of *complementarity* between anti-poverty policies, review of indirect market effects (here via *employment*), and careful *targeting*.

Hazell and Singh simulate the effects on poverty of various policies, including PRLR that – by obtaining land from households with more than 10 ha. – brings every household originally landless, or operating less than 0.2 ha. of farmland, up to 1 ha. This on its own – while it reduces poverty incidence by almost 30 per cent in the wealthiest zone, which has the highest rainfall and the greatest initial income inequality – does much less well elsewhere. It reduces poverty incidence in the ten villages as a whole by only 3 per cent. However, if the land reform is *complemented* by transfer of a pair of bullocks to each beneficiary, poverty incidence falls by 74 per cent! (Bullock transfer alone brings only a 34 per cent fall.) The poverty impact is increased because the smaller, post-reform farms *employ* more hired (as well as family) labour per hectare, especially with the above complementary bullock transfer. The PRLR would be *better targeted*, and thus more poverty-reducing even on its own, if households to lose or to gain land were specified, not by land per household as here, but by quality-adjusted land per person; then fewer of those losing land would be initially near-poor (and at risk of becoming poor through the reform), while more of those gaining land would be among the initially poor.

A closing word is needed about property rights. Many people oppose land reform because they see secure property rights as essential if enterprises are to be induced to plan, invest, and take risks in order to benefit from growth later on. Success in land reform does indeed depend on creating the assurance that post-reform rights – especially the right to rent – will not be unreasonably abridged. However, prior to reform (or in the aftermath of imperfectly implemented reform), the great mass of *de facto* property rights to big farms in many developing countries, especially where distribution is very unequal, result from inheritance, not from earning, skill, enterprise or saving – and often originated in force or fraud, not seldom with racial or colonial associations. What is more, many – probably most – very large farms in developing countries are held in contravention of ceilings legislation enacted by legitimate and accountable government, or else are due to the unauthorized enclosure of public land [Tendler 1993]; these are not genuine property rights, but wrongful violations of the property rights of others. Much land reform, even of the consensual new-wave type, takes the form not of violating genuine legal property rights, but of implementing them, thereby asserting the law as against "property wrongs" hitherto enforced by the abuse of economic and political power. De Soto [1989] rightly stresses the importance to the poor of such law enforcement for *urban* house sites and informal-sector enterprise. The same applies to much rural land reform.

(iii) Agricultural growth and technology

The "causes of success", in attacking poverty through policies affecting agricultural growth and technology, have been extensively reviewed [Lipton with Longhurst 1989; Binswanger and von Braun 1993; David and Otsuka 1994]. There are two main issues. First, under what circumstances and to what extent does agricultural growth tend to reduce poverty? Second, what structures of institutions and incentives can improve this impact?

Despite some controversy, there is general agreement that faster agricultural growth is *associated with* somewhat faster poverty reduction. The wrong sort of technical progress, or a bad year, can destroy or even reverse this association. Moreover – as a study of ten villages in central Gujarat, India, shows – century-old differences in the history of land tenure (here *ryotwari* as against other modes) can drastically affect the extent to which current growth, associated with a given technical change, reaches the poor [Singh 1985]. So it is unsurprising that one can often find a village, even a district, here and there in which, despite rapid agricultural growth, the remaining villagers have become poorer – though often such findings, even when based on panel data, omit the villagers who, having escaped poverty, have migrated.

To evaluate the general linkage between farm growth and reduced poverty, one needs to look at slightly broader issues and data sets. As for the issues, surely nobody would deny that the *negative* growth in real farm output per person in much of Africa has *harmed* the poor, both by reducing their claims on income (including self-consumed food production) from farming and farm employment, and by depleting food stocks so that local prices rise and the dangers from drought become sharper. Conversely, it would be unpersuasive to deny that the huge growth in the rural farm and non-farm economies, in the wake of very rapid agricultural progress, was a main cause of the dramatic fall in PCP (to the lowest level of any Indian state) in the Punjab and Haryana, the "green revolution" heartlands.

However, unless the cross-sectional or time-series differences in growth rates are dramatic, the poverty impact may not be very large – and may more readily be offset, even sometimes outweighed, by changes in technology or crop-mix, due to "wrong" incentives or institutions, that harm the poor. Panel data for six semi-arid villages in India show sluggish, though positive, poverty impact from similarly sluggish real growth [Gaiha 1994a]. This has been shown across Indian states; for time-series data in several developing countries; and [Tyler et al. 1993] across a set of developing countries.

The poverty benefits of all but the most inappropriate forms of agricultural growth should not be confused with trickle-down [Gaiha 1994: ch. 3]. Faster agricultural growth (unless confined to cash crops, or in a small country or region trading freely, at very low transport costs, with foodgrain surplus areas) normally restrains the local price of food staples, and/or permits stockbuilding which stabilizes that price. This helps those below the poverty line, since food staples form 40-60 per cent of their consumption. Moreover, agriculture is usually more labour intensive than other sectors of the economy, and farmworkers tend to be poorer than other workers. So agricultural growth bids up the employment, and sometimes the wage rate, of persons likeliest to start poor. Agricultural growth is also linked to increasing local non-farm incomes for poor people [Hazell and Ramasamy 1991].

The experience of Kerala since 1975 shows that poverty can be significantly reduced in spite of a very weak performance in terms of overall and agricultural growth [Kannan 1993], and of underlying technical progress in agriculture. However, the financial and economic sustainability of such a process is limited. That will be the case especially in places that, unlike Kerala, do not have (i) democratic government, (ii) ruling parties dependent mainly on the active support of the poor, (iii) fertility, and hence population growth, that has proved more than usually responsive to better health and education, and (iv) substantial and often taxable remittance income from abroad. Similarly, a modest acceleration of agricultural growth in Bangladesh may have been offset, between 1975 and 1986, by a worsening of distribution, so that poverty declined little if at all [Khan 1990].

The impact of agricultural growth on poverty, however, needs to be assessed by a more complete range of comparisons than can be provided by "success stories", or failure stories, on their own. Ravallion and Datt [1994] analyse the results of 20 household surveys in India, spanning the period 1958-90, and find that "the poor gained from higher farm yields, though the effect was distribution-neutral in the long run. The long-run elasticity of [PCP] to farm yield was over two, and 40 per cent was through wages. Growth also reduced the depth and severity of [PCP], both initially and in the short run."

These are only tendencies, correlations. Some sorts of agricultural growth have no, or even negative, effects on the poor. If the growth is associated with labour displacement, and takes place on the farms of the rich, GNP may rise only because the increase in total farm profits (and rents) outweighs a negative effect on labour income. Even the "green revolution", almost an ideal structure of technical progress in being labour intensive and raising food supplies and stocks of food staples, has had a disappointing (though positive) total impact on the poor: partly because problems of access, or of perceived risk, delayed the adoption, by poorer farmers, of the new technology, and when they did so the prices of its product (food staples) were already being pushed down; and partly because farm employers reduced the effect of rising demand for labour on workers' income by using (and obtaining subsidies for) alternatives to labour, such as weedicides and reaper-binders [see Lipton and Longhurst 1989 and sources therein].

Does this suggest any formula for policy success in managing growth to reduce poverty? First, to bias growth against agriculture normally harms the poor. That is because agriculture is normally more labour intensive than other sectors, and more likely to improve or stabilize the supply, or reduce the price, of *local* food staples, even given the prospects for trade. Second, even if conditions for transforming farm growth into poverty reduction seem favourable, incentives and institutions should not be so structured as to encourage or subsidize labour displacement, or the concentration of output on larger (and normally less labour-intensive) farms, during the growth process. Third, in more difficult circumstances, where farms are already very unequal and labour-displacing equipment and practices are in place, stronger corrective action will be required to get the gains of growth substantially to the rural poor. Fourth, if pro-poor institutional changes (such as land reforms) are sought, they are cheaper and easier to impose *before* rapid land-enhancing technical progress – whether based on new irrigation, green revolutions or biotechnology – has alerted big farmers or landlords to the full potential value of their assets. That was the sequence in the Philippines [Hayami et al. 1990], where the gains to the reform beneficiaries – but also the unanticipated opportunity cost of the reforms – were much increased by the subsequent spread of higher-yielding rice varieties.[49]

The path of technical progress – which plays a big role in determining both the pace of agricultural growth, and its impact on various categories of poor people – is greatly influenced by policy in a few developing countries that together contain a large majority of the world's poor: countries with economies and agricultures large enough to have powerful and substantially autochthonous agricultural research establishments (Brazil, China, India, Mexico and a few others), or committed enough to devote large parts of small resources to those ends (South Africa, the Philippines and a few others). Clearly a lot of cost-effective agricultural research, if pushed by incentives, career patterns and habits, and institutions to develop results favouring small farms and labour-intensive choices, can help the poor. Yet that is not what the political or financial market ordains, even if the economics of factor scarcities suggest it. *The crisis in financing of national and international agricultural research, especially pro-poor research, is the main threat, though a hidden one, to success in poverty-reducing policies. It may well undermine the basis on which such success must depend while rural workforces are still increasing: cheaper food staples, more expensive unskilled labour.*

The three main categories of technical progress are land and water development; biochemical innovation (manure, fertilizers, seed selection, pest control); and mechanical innovation (notably the sequence from hoes via ploughs to tractors). The three main classes of innovation normally take place in that sequence, as established by Ishikawa [1968] for South and East Asia:

● After agricultural settlement, there is a period when new land-water resources can be harnessed without much rise in average cost of farm production. Initially this happens through breaking in new land; later, by exploiting "easier" paths to irrigation, for double-cropping or intensification.

---

49. It is in this context irrelevant that the reform beneficiaries, as sitting tenants rather than farmworkers, were seldom the poorest – and that the latter may have lost, as farm size was increased because landlords resumed personal cultivation to escape the tenancy reform. The point is that reform - whether wise PRLR or unwise tenancy reform – is easier and cheaper before land-enhancing technical progress than afterwards.

● Next, responding to higher populations and diminishing marginal productivity of new lands, farm communities labour-intensify via natural manures and/or fertilizers. These are made much more profitable when linked to new plants and improved seeds. This set of innovations is as old as farming, but accelerated sharply with new biological inputs in tenth-century China, in the sixteenth century following the Columbian Exchange, and most recently in the "green revolution".

● As rural labour becomes scarcer relative to land, the third phase – mechanization and other forms of labour displacement – becomes appropriate.

Which policies make each set of innovations more cost-effective, timely and pro-poor?

There are few parts of the developing world where environmentally sustainable agricultural growth can still be achieved economically by breaking in new lands. Where feasible, such activity creates work and food for the poor, on the "new" lands not much less than on the old. There is, however, some scope to simulate this by policies to slow down land loss – and the resulting destruction of employment for the unskilled poor (and of productive and relatively stable food-producing lands) – due to ill-planned urban expansion, and to some extent due to soil and water depletion.[50]

As for irrigation, this can be of special help to the poor (who have the greatest difficulty with consumption smoothing) because it increases not only the amounts of food supply and labour demand, but also their stability – across seasons by double-cropping, across years by compensating for bad rainfall. Rao et al. [1988] have demonstrated the huge impact of irrigation in reducing chronic and transient poverty as between Indian states (my work in progress confirms this even more strongly at disaggregated, viz. district, level). Yet the case for irrigation in much of Asia has apparently been weakened – and the pace slowed – by diminishing returns to new works, falling efficiency of old ones, and falling world prices of most farm products relative to manufactured goods prices. In Asia, much of the remaining irrigation

---

50. The latter is, in turn, largely due to the incentives to use resources for current income (rather than to keep them for future income) created by the unprecedented duration (1979-96?) of very high real and shadow rates of interest.

activity has shifted from construction to rehabilitation and maintenance. In most of Africa, despite the sluggishness of rainfed farm output (and research), the conventional wisdom remains that irrigation works, per hectare served, "must" cost three times as much as we are used to in apparently similar agroclimatic and economic circumstances in Asia, and yield half the value-added – so that new irrigation should be largely confined to farmer-managed micro-schemes. There are indeed several horror stories of large-scale irrigation in Africa. Moreover, the micro-evidence from Asia is that dug wells are likelier to be used on the land of the poor than are more large-scale irrigation systems [Narain and Roy 1980]. Yet *it remains implausible that Africa's widespread, severe food-employment constraints on poverty reduction can be much relaxed without radical rethinking of the conventional mantras against large-scale irrigation.*

The biochemical type of innovation – fertilizers and new seeds or plant types – is responsive on some models to the high supply of rural labour and the growing shortage of land. Such innovation is in any case likely to increase the demand for labour. However, there is widespread evidence of declining (though still clearly positive) elasticity of farm employment to increases in farm output, even if they are caused by improved seed-fertilizer technology.

This is in part because – for reasons connected with financial markets and political lobbying, and not in most cases with the economics at undistorted prices of inputs and outputs – the "green revolution" has often been connected with a thrust towards mechanization well before labour became scarce (at wage rates when its employment was still profitable). Reaper-binders and combines simply displace labour; if there is no labour constraint they cannot increase output, though they can shift income from wages to profits. Tractorization decreases employment per hectare in cultivation, and in the care of draught animals; only if the tractors permit a *more than offsetting* increase in employment by bringing new land under cultivation (allowing for the fact that new land is likely to be less suitable for intensive farming than old) can wage income increase. This is not an argument against tractors – any more than the fact that the poor spend half their income on food staples is an argument against cash crops. However, successful policy, whether for growth or against poverty, is harmed by subsidies, institutions, research choices, credit arrangements, or (unequal) farm-size structures that artificially push agriculture away from labour intensity, or into forms of cash-crop production, that would not be attractive otherwise.

What does this imply for success in anti-poverty policy? Apart from avoiding price incentives that militate against labour intensity or food staples production – and thus against research to assist them – governments in poor countries need to ensure that career structures, institutional changes, and perhaps above all politically mediated demand from small farmers and landless labourers, are brought to bear upon agricultural research institutions. It can be done; Sri Lanka, through all its travails, has been persistently a model of intelligent and politically sophisticated research response to the needs of poor people dependent on rice production, consumption and employment [Lipton et al. 1996]. But research cannot do the trick alone (and its financial base in countries with small agricultural populations and many crops or agroclimatic zones will anyway be small). The main policy thrust needs to come from political pressures – from above and below – to set priorities for and within farming through appropriate incentives and institutions, and to provide adequate finance, staff, and research conditions. That can permit, but not ensure, good results – in particular, research end-products (methods, seeds, etc.) making it attractive for small farmers to increase the output of food and, by a somewhat smaller proportion, the use of labour to grow it. Nobody (except Mother Nature) can guarantee, in a specific agroclimatic zone, a good *supply response* – to incentives or political demand – of such pro-poor end-products. However, relevant *demand pressures* can be developed, and policy can help.

If the potentially poor – who in Asia and Africa remain overwhelmingly rural – have access to land and jobs, they can effectively mobilize demands, political and· economic, for technologies to reduce their poverty; if not, they cannot. *Policies that correct institutional, public-expenditure, political and price biases against farm and rural output, growth and employment, especially on small farms, will almost always improve the prospects for success of other anti-poverty policies, including those in the field of research and technology.*

(iv) Health, education and poverty reduction

This much-analysed area interacts strongly with the last. Jamison and Lau [1982] have shown that farmers, and even farmworkers, improve their prospects of escaping poverty through agriculture if they have some education. At village level, the close and mutual causal connections at individual and household level between better health, better education, higher earning power, and poverty reduction are manifest; the total impact of education plus land, or education plus bullock power, in reducing poverty impact considerably exceeds the sum of the individual impacts, in data for ten Indian *villages* over eight years [Singh and Hazell 1993]. Also, there are strong links between a *region's or a nation's* health and education (especially if obtainable together, and if primary education reaches women and is completed) and its subsequent growth and poverty reduction. The cross-section evidence, from household surveys to international data sets, has often been summarized [Gaiha 1994: ch. 9; World Bank 1990; Schultz 1988; Behrman and Deolalikar 1988; Psacharopoulos 1981] and will not be repeated here.

Striking, however, are the huge differences among (and within) countries at similar income levels, and often with comparable power structures, in the educational and health levels of the poor. It is surprising, because each experience should inform the laggards that improvements in mass health and education would normally and cost-effectively raise efficiency *and* reduce poverty. That is also true of land reform, but unlike land reform more widespread primary health and education for the poor would not appear to threaten, and in some ways would benefit, the powerful and wealthy. Two more components of the jigsaw puzzle: those countries that have devoted substantial public resources to providing and subsidizing health and education have often concentrated on the tertiary sectors – universities, kidney machines – despite strong evidence that both need and social return are much more for basic and primary provision; and those countries that have moved towards universal provision, notably of primary education in parts of Africa, are pervaded by the belief – right or wrong – that this has been at a catastrophic cost in quality, vitiating the benefits expected in terms of growth and poverty reduction alike. The most persuasive explanations of "why governments misbehave" in social-sector spending, preferring activities that do little for efficiency or equity, run in terms of rent-seeking [Birdsall and James 1993].

There is convincing evidence of good returns and cost-effective poverty reduction when we compare individuals or regions in the same country receiving education with those not receiving education. Some of the data sets also suggest diminishing marginal returns, i.e. when we regress poverty reduction or income growth upon the level of a person's or group's education and upon the square of that level, then the coefficient on the former is positive and on the latter negative – though primary education is something of an exception, since incomes (and poverty risk, health status, and family size norms) appear to be little if at all improved by primary education that lasts only two or three years and is not resumed or completed. Within a country, therefore, *success in anti-poverty policy is usually advanced by increasing the proportion of health and educational resources going to basic and primary care and/or to the poorest groups or regions*. This has to be modified: (1) because of complementarities between different levels of education (and to a lesser extent of health provision); (2) because capacity to benefit from education depends partly on nearby economic prospects to use the acquired capacities; and (3) because very rapid expansion in a particular area is likely to involve lower marginal benefits than more planned, piloted change. However, the general rule seems valid.

A final issue is the role of social services in providing safety nets. These are desirable because the poor are both statistically likeliest to be exposed to unstable employment income [Lipton 1983] and to periodic ill-health or lack of support in old age, and also because these risks compel many of the poor to adopt safety-first and therefore unenterprising strategies in production and in life as a whole: the fear of acute poverty keeps many people in chronic poverty. But is social security the way to go?

Health provision (and food policy) inevitably has a dual role, as safety net and as creator of human capital for the poor. It is widely claimed that poor countries cannot afford social security provision. This, however, is belied by the experience of Sri Lanka, and in India of the State of Kerala, where old-age and widows' pensions are the rule. Usually, however, especially in Latin America, so-called "social security" has ignored the really poor, and has become heavily subsidized (and often fiscally burdensome and unstable) out-relief for the not-so-poor in the organized formal sector, especially public-sector employees. The "lesson for success", given the immense political difficulty (even in the United States and Europe) of reducing subsidized middle-class entitlements once they are in place, is to look to the experience of Kerala and Sri Lanka and examine the prospects of providing accurately targeted programmes for the poor; actuarially fair and self-balancing programmes for the remainder are a second priority, to be attempted only when the state has sufficient administrative resources. A good review of the safety-net role of social security is Ahmad [1993].

It needs, however, to be stressed that safety-net provisions are of three sorts: those provided by stable sources of real income, such as properly water-controlled agriculture; those provided by family and community; and those provided by the state. Before expanding the latter, one must ascertain that it is cost-effective in reducing vulnerability among the poor after allowing for net effects, possibly negative, on the first two sorts of safety nets.

(v) Food distribution and subsidization[51]

Low-wage and unskilled manual employment, or guarantees of employment, on public works "self-target" on the poor. Credit, unless carefully planned, can well self-target on the rich (even if labelled "for the poor"). Food looks more like employment than like credit in this regard; after all, the poor devote a larger proportion of their consumption to food than the non-poor, and probably a larger proportion of their income to consumption as well; and the poor are worse affected than the rich by unstable food availability or prices. This appearance, however, is misleading. Spending per person on food as a whole, and even on many staples (including rice and wheat), is usually higher *in absolute terms* among the non-poor than among the poor. Therefore, overall food subsidies, and even, though to a lesser extent, subsidies on many food staples, provide more consumption support per person to the rich than to the poor – not good targeting.

---

51. This discussion is brief and cursory. The excellent work of IFPRI over many years has greatly improved our understanding of the "rules for success" – and the pervasiveness of failure – in this area. An excellent summary, much fuller than is possible here, appears in Gaiha [1994: ch. 8].

The cost of bad targeting – one side of which is the extension of free or subsidized food to the non-poor – is high. At its peak in the 1970s, the universal, subsidized rice ration absorbed over 10 per cent of Sri Lanka's GNP, and such burdens are not unusual. In Andhra Pradesh, India, the state government was almost bankrupted in the 1980s by efforts to make good on populist promises of heavily subsidized rice, and eventually had to abandon them.

The other side of the cost of bad targeting is not fiscal but operational: the apparently universal support for food consumption often fails to reach the neediest, for at least three reasons. First, the food or subsidy tends to be perversely distributed regionally, especially where governments rely on their own channels of distribution rather than on competitive retailing. For example, both India's fair price shops and the consumption gains from Egypt's food subsidies are concentrated in urban areas, where the incidence and severity of poverty are less than in the countryside. Second, the search for channels of food distribution often becomes a search for politically attractive options that in reality serve the hungry very imperfectly. For example, school meals often miss the poorest [Beaton and Ghassemi 1982]; their central role in the "Chief Minister's Noon Meals Scheme" in Tamil Nadu State, India, has proved unhelpful to pre-schoolers, and to children whose parents did not send them to school (often because poverty compelled them to rely on child labour). Third, the untargeted nature of these schemes precludes steering them in ways that minimize the ill-effects of food maldistribution *within* poor households, as might be done if food support were concentrated upon small girls, children exhibiting growth faltering, big families, or areas with a high incidence of one or more of these groups.

These limits, serious enough, are confined to the areas of fiscal cost and consumption targeting. A further problem arises with production impacts. Sometimes the food schemes are supported through extra imports; to the extent that these would not have happened commercially and do not correspond to extra cash-backed demand for food, the effect is to raise domestic food availability ahead of demand and thus to reduce producer prices, adversely affecting subsequent food production and employment (though much of the loss is made good as the land and labour are switched to other uses). Often the government – as in India in the 1960s – is tempted to reduce the fiscal burden of these schemes by compulsory or monopoly procurement from farmers at below-market prices, and/or by closing interregional borders to food via zoning rules in order to simplify such taxation and procurement. This, too, has disincentive effects on food production, locational efficiency, and employment. And all this is to obtain benefits for the poor that are likely to be much watered down if general-equilibrium, multi-market effects are considered; for instance, if food subsidies raise the real wage of unskilled labour, and its supply elasticity is high, employers will be able to reduce their money wage and capture many of the benefits of the food subsidy.

This certainly does not mean that food subsidies and food distribution have no part to play in a successful set of anti-poverty policies. It means only that the lessons of experience in this sphere have led to a rather clear selection of specific policies for specific situations, and to rather sharp applications of some of the "13 principles", notably indirect targeting, complementarity, and advance multimarket anticipation of responses and results.

First of all, in dire emergencies the need to get the food to the famine-stricken is unquestioned. However, that should be done early, for two reasons. It is price rises, and anticipation of these, that often denies food to those at risk of famine, not lack of food availability [Sen 1981]. And waiting until the desperate have congregated in camps, or otherwise involved themselves in migrant or refugee situations, is to be avoided if at all possible. Such conditions can breed almost as much disease, even death, as the food prevents. The lessons – the need to obtain "early warning" of emergency, and to look for signs on the side of deficient demand and entitlements as well as (and usually rather than) on the side of food availability – has been well learned, perhaps overlearned; in parts of West Africa there are apparently competing and overlapping "early warning" systems in place. Today at least, there is abundant evidence that the reasons for failure to act in time lie much more in absence of early, integrated and planned *response* than in absence of "early warning". Drèze and Sen [1989] give several striking examples, especially in Africa, of successful policy choices and management by government in these crisis situations. Even severe drought seldom causes heavy excess mortality without war or societal and political breakdown; and that can cause massive famine deaths even without drought.

Even when famine threatens, and more so in less extreme cases, provision of access to cash – as income or as entitlements – is normally, probably usually, preferable to food distribution. The needy can then reveal their preferences among (say) food, fuel and health care, and the market can provide the desired mix. This may be a dangerous approach, however, if short-run supply elasticity of the food staple has been forced down by absence of nearby stocks or breakdown of transport systems. Also, the relieving agency – government, NGO or UN-linked – may have access only to a food staple, not readily sold except to the target population (though even then the option of injecting it into the retail system and providing cash to the people at risk should always be considered). If direct food distribution is the only way forward, it is obviously important to avoid "relief dependence" and durable decline in production among the people relieved; as their health and strength, and perhaps the local water conditions, improve, so the relief agency should begin to redirect resources from specific food provision to cash-for-work. This may well sensibly be supplemented by – or correspond to construction activity for – resumed production (especially replenishment of seeds and youngstock); droughtproofing via improved water management; and – via loans for transport, information or other infrastructures – food retailing in areas that are drought-prone, and remote or sparsely populated.

Food support or subsidy also has an important role in poverty reduction in general, but targeting is needed. This can be by area, by food product, or by type of recipient. Urban slums and remote or ill-watered rural areas contain very disproportionate proportions of the poorest almost everywhere; regional targeting has improved poverty-focus of food support in north-eastern Brazil [Gaiha 1994: 142-3].

As for types of food product, agencies can do a lot better than the nonsense of subsidizing chickens and beef. Coarse grains and roots are self-targeting on the hungry and poor, being "inferior goods" (in the sense of demand theory, not at all of health); in Bangladesh, when ration shops offered the choice of wheat flour or a larger quota of sorghum flour, the poor preferred the latter [Alderman 1991]. However, there are problems. The poor are often over-represented among employees, and even farmers, engaged in the production of coarse grains and roots (as well as among the consumers of these products), and may suffer if food subsidies depress the demand for market purchases of such products. Moreover, cheap and bulky foods impose high ratios of storage and transport costs, per ton distributed, on the agency.

Targeting of foods on the needy, in conjunction with targeting of health care, was a striking feature of the very successful Tamil Nadu Integrated Nutrition Programme (TINP). The TINP involved giving a package of food and health support primarily to under-fives revealing growth faltering. Of course the TINP required a comprehensive monitoring programme; otherwise the neediest – especially the homeless, or migrants – would have been missed. Even allowing for such costs, however, the TINP proved many times more cost-effective, in terms of prevented child deaths per rupee spent, than the untargeted "Noon Meals Scheme" in the same state [Berg 1987].

All these are important improvements, increasing the options of the poor, while reducing the wastes and delays involved in providing food, or food subsidies, rather than access to cash or other more general entitlements. (Food stamps, by reducing administrative costs of food distribution as in Sri Lanka from 1978, are another useful step in the same direction.) However, many will be reminded of the remark that Rover is a good dog: almost as good as no dog at all. There are ways of targeting food support better, but why not, as a general rule, enable the poor to earn (or if old or sick to receive) the cash they need to buy what they judge most important to them? An exception to this rule is certainly provided by programmes such as the Narangwal pilot [Taylor et al. 1978] or the TINP, which aim to provide a "package" of strongly complementary merit goods, some private like extra food, but others (such as health improvements) unlikely to be provided to the vulnerable poor except publicly. The case is even stronger when the package is effectively targeted on small children, or other persons unable to choose how family income is used.

(vi) Whatever happened to the towns?

Despite the urban bias of most development expenditures, policies and incentives, most of the examples and analyses of anti-poverty policy, including the efforts to isolate and explain "success", are rural. This may be partly because past history, including the bias, has kept poverty mainly rural. The reader may object that the proportion of poor people who live in urban areas is increasing. That is true, especially in Latin America, North Africa and West Asia (although both the rate of net rural-to-urban migration, and the extent to which the poorest can benefit from it, are habitually overstated as a result of inaccurate readings of the data). The facts remain [Lipton and Ravallion 1995] that the rural incidence of private consumption poverty (PCP), in developing countries with reliable survey data, is between 1.3 and 5.1 times the urban incidence; that this disparity is increased because the PCP poverty gap is wider in rural areas; and that the impact of greater rural PCP is sharpened by generally much worse rural health and education services (in India, one of the less urban-biased of developing countries with rural PCP incidence only 1.3 times urban, the infant mortality rate in rural areas is almost double the urban rate). It is also arguable, though controversial, that urban poverty – while certainly a big problem in its own right – exists largely because of rural poverty, so that the most cost-effective way to reduce urban poverty incidence may be to provide better life chances for the rural poor.

We shall return to this argument later. In any case, however fast or slowly the urban poor are increasing or likely to increase, the "poverty research industry" owes its clients some explanation for the lack of urban content in its rather substantial results for the developing countries. (It is interesting that in the developed world the analysis of poverty and its remedies is almost wholly either location-free or urban – which is not clearly true of the location, let alone the causation, of poverty itself.)

Perhaps the answer can be approached through the exception, not the rule. In one area of urban anti-poverty policy, there has been massive empirical and theoretical work, much learning from experience, and considerable success in benefiting the poor. This area is the improvement of housing conditions, including services such as clean drinking water, waste management, and electric power.

Policy here has gone through several phases. First came the efforts around 1950-75 to "solve" the problem by slum clearance, zoning, restrictions on migration (as in Jakarta, Addis Ababa, and – for a much longer period – the main cities of China), and "low-cost" housing. This expelled some of the poor from their handhold on urban prospects, exposed others to arbitrary harassment by settled townspeople and "their" police and civil servants, subsidized the dwellings of these same persons, yet allowed policymakers to feel some aesthetic and (unjustified) moral satisfaction. It is quite surprising that it proved possible for mere facts to terminate such élite-friendly policies, but to some degree the trick was managed. Perhaps it was because the urban poor proved inconveniently difficult to manage or expel, especially as the non-poor required their services and their rents.

The second phase was to recognize the poor as a lasting urban presence and to enlist their help in developing their housing areas – first through site-and-service, and subsequently, in the early and mid-1980s, through slum upgrading, which reached down to much poorer people, though seldom the poorest quintile. Part of the learning process was that paternalist and apparently pro-poor restrictions were abandoned as counter-productive, when they ran too much against fungibility combined with maximizing responses. For example, in the early site-and-service and slum upgrading schemes, beneficiaries of materials or loans were "forbidden" (not usually very effectively) from hiring in labour, or hiring out their improved dwellings; support, work and residence had to stay in the same family or group. That sounds nice – who wants to "subsidize slum landlords" or to "pay idle employers"? – but when we get past such rhetoric the only effect of such restrictions was to prevent renters-in of, or workers on, the cheapest housing from sharing the benefits of the upgrading schemes with the dwellers. Since the dwellers were usually less poor than the excluded tenants or workers, this was hardly a good move from the standpoint of poverty reduction. Learning that lesson certainly contributed to the success of many of these schemes, and echoed the learning process in several of the rural anti-poverty activities we have discussed.

The third phase has been to improve, mainly through better financial management and cost recovery, the provision of services to these upgraded urban areas – and to a lesser extent to the much poorer unregistered slums. An associated movement, deriving in part from the major contribution of de Soto [1989], has been to secure and clarify the property rights of the urban poor. There is no doubt that much of the urban housing-based policy, through this three-phase learning process, has been cost-effective in the sense of generating substantial welfare benefits per unit of cost for poor urban people, though perhaps not the very poorest.

There are, however, three linked, radical problems with this entire approach. They illustrate the *central difficulties of urban anti-poverty policies* in developing countries:

- Extra urban prospects pull in immigrants at rising marginal congestion cost, often eventually reducing even the *total* social returns to the works;

- The urban approaches *lack a substantial income-earning component*,[52] comparable to the focus on agriculture of the great mass of rural anti-poverty programmes from land reform through small-farm technology to rural public works. This is partly because employing the poor has a much higher cost-per-job in cities than in villages – even in the informal sector, once the marginal urban cost of a worker in terms of social and infrastructural capital is taken into account;

- There is no obvious case for locating some of these extra services, such as better sanitation or drinking water, in urban areas, given that initial levels of provision and of outcomes (e.g. infant mortality) are so much worse in rural areas.

The new phase of urban anti-poverty policy is beginning to benefit from applying some of the "13 rules". In particular, complementarity is tending to be embodied much less in single-provider, central plans for the provision of numerous services, and much more in the planned recognition of likely responses by firms and households to the new options provided by municipal authorities, followed by steps to select the options where those authorities have comparative advantage, and where benefits are targeted indirectly or self-targeted on the poor. But many of the urban poor, being either engaged in doubtfully legal activities or places of residence, or persons of no fixed address or residing in unregistered slums, are

---

52. There are a few exceptions, such as the incorporation of informal worksites into the third phase of Manila's Tondo slum upgrading programme in the late 1970s and early 1980s; the construction of municipal sites for renting to small informal-sector traders in several places; and the pruning of regulations and restrictions, often implemented in the past so as to restrict or zone informal enterprises in the interests of the large formal firms.

harder to identify and therefore to target (even through indicators) than are most of the rural poor. Also, the above three problems are rather fundamental: they mean that policy against poverty may "do worse by doing better" if it raises the share of anti-poverty resources devoted, even cost-effectively, to the towns. That is because such an increase might well have little direct or durable productive impact; could divert social and infrastructural investment away from more urgent (though less articulated) rural needs; and could self-destruct – at least as regards improving urban life and conditions – by pulling in more rural immigrants at rising marginal congestion costs which, because mainly not borne by the individual immigrant but externalized, would not deter future immigrants for some considerable time.

Blunting one of these three objections might sharpen others. If urban anti-poverty policy becomes more focused on the affordable creation of durable work prospects (informal or formal), that strengthens the pull of persons from village to city (with rising marginal, and largely external, congestion costs) and perhaps diverts resources more decisively from places of greatest need. The example of urban agriculture – much neglected, but typically employing 10-15 per cent of the urban workforce and a much larger proportion of the urban poor – typifies the problem. Urban agriculture is surely a long overdue "suitable case for treatment" in any attempt to develop successful urban anti-poverty policies based on durable production. Yet success would divert resources and demand from rural agriculture, and increase conflicts of use and production-to-consumption externalities (such as nitrates in drinking water) for the cities.

The above discussion, like much of the literature, uses the terms "rural" and "urban" without further analysis. In regard to the borderline, this reflects international variations in practice; censuses set the border at 5,000 in much of Asia, at 2,000 in much of Latin America, and with the use of varying and arbitrary mixes of political and geographical characteristics in many countries and regions. More important, for the design of successful "urban" anti-poverty policies, is the aggregation of all conurbations, irrespective of size, as "urban". Most household surveys – our only reliable source for data on the scale and characteristics of the poor – do not separate even the main size-classes of urban area: the policymakers' information on the incidence of poverty in Calcutta is aggregated with their information for scores of small towns in West Bengal, if not in India as a whole. Yet the public perception of anti-poverty policy relates mainly to the big metropolis. Poverty may well be more serious, or growing faster, in intermediate or even small conurbations in the range 5,000-100,000; certainly the composition of the poor by age, gender, employment status, duration and severity of poverty, literacy, and so forth will be different. Disaggregated policies against urban poverty, and probably more focus on smaller towns, will be required for greater policy success – and will, in turn, require larger household surveys, so that they can be disaggregated by size (and type) of conurbations without losing statistical significance in the findings.

7. Conclusion: The "Rules of success against poverty" reviewed

This book began by isolating three overarching principles that seemed to apply to poverty policies.

- The principle of joint requirements tells us that several conditions had to be met together if many people were to escape poverty, and that this usually (though not always) creates complementarity among different anti-poverty measures in the same area.

- The principle of total effect indicates that anti-poverty policies, especially big ones, need to be evaluated for impact beyond their particular area and overt set of policy goals.

- The principle of joint planning indicates that, before implementing a poverty programme, one should have clear and reasonable expectations, jointly, about targeting of its services on the poor, sustainability, quality of yield, and acquisition of yield by the poor.

Next, we examined the macro-evidence, confining ourselves to the 40 or so developing economies (including three transitional economies) for which reasonably reliable data on poverty were available for household surveys. We found that differences among nations in average real private consumption (measured in US dollars of constant purchasing power) were associated with about 35-50 per cent of international variance in the incidence of "private consumption poverty", or PCP. We conclude that there is ample policy scope to reduce PCP at a given level of average private consumption; the remaining half to two-thirds of international variance in PCP incidence is associated with policy, or other variables, affecting distribution between poor and non-poor persons.

We then turned to indicators of "illfare". Such indicators are normally concentrated among the poor, and indicate how much a given incidence of PCP is liable to harm them. International differences in per-person GNP (again at standardized and constant purchasing power) were associated with just under half the international variances in infant mortality and illiteracy – but these variances were not associated with differences among nations in private consumption poverty (once a nation's real GNP per person was allowed for). We conclude that, while more GNP per person makes it easier to reduce the "illfare" connected with poverty, there is ample policy scope to do so at a given level of real GNP per person – and that this scope is almost unaffected by the incidence of PCP.

In Chapters 4 and 5 we derived "rules of anti-poverty success" by exploring two types of policies widely used to reduce poverty (given the level and growth of average real GNP or private consumption): credit and public works. Within each of these two policy types – despite much failure, leakage and waste – we found strong learning effects, and, to our surprise, we found that "rules of anti-poverty success" emerging from the study of anti-poverty credit policies applied astonishingly well, *mutatis mutandis*, to the analysis of public works employment policies.

In Chapter 6 we reviewed policies for: land reform; agricultural growth and technology; social services – both for human capital via health and education and for safety nets; and in some circumstances food supplementation or subsidization. We refrained from applying in detail the rules to these categories of anti-poverty policy, but could give some indication of their relevance. The rules do well in categories such as food-distribution policy – with targeting and regional problems similar to those in credit and public works. But the rules will have to be altered when political contentiousness is sharper and/or macro-policy more dominant, such as land reform and the acceleration (or labour intensification) of technical progress in agriculture.

The accounts of the credit and public works employment policies suggested that the rules performed tolerably well. We now attempt, therefore, to present a general form of the rules, to see whether they can be applied to different categories of project that are intended to reduce PCP or its ill-effects. The rules, applied to both categories of policies, are presented in Table 4.

Table 4. Rules for anti-poverty projects

Principle	Application: Credit programmes	Application: Public works
1. People are rational.	Credit is fungible among uses.	Scheme labour should have low opportunity cost.
2. Response to targets is rational.	Target indirectly via: (i) local group selection; (ii) self-targeting; (iii) characteristic targeting; (iv) managerial monitoring.	Use self-targeting, but explore total market impacts before setting wage rates.
3. Rules can have unintended screening effects.	Avoid rules denying credit to poor.	Discriminate in favour of poor via: (i) quick or prior pay; (ii) piece-rate; (iii) nearness.
4. Review physical constraints on poor.	Seek alternatives to physical collateral (group lending, peer monitoring).	Allow for workers' frequent physical difficulties.
5. Reduce transaction costs.	Explore local intermediation.	Low: (i) transport costs; (ii) local discretion to hire.
6. Reduce covariance of risks.	(i) Not just farm lending; (ii) "nested" hierarchies of independent lenders (but note problems).	Diversify: (i) borrower and lender activities; (ii) regions.
7. Avoid monopoly supply.	Compete fairly with local lenders.	Contract to, or compete with, local employers and food retailers.
8. Pre-test demand for programme.	Is their unmet demand by poor for credit at price permitting viable lending?	Is poverty worsened by lack of effective demand for labour to perform worthwhile tasks?
9. Subsidize only if this is the best way to ensure the poor gain from external effects.	Subsidize administration costs (temporarily), not interest rates.	Don't subsidize above-market wage rates; subsidize for sustainability, coverage, poor "graduating".
10. Plan for likely political pressure.	Pre-publish rules for extended repayment in emergency; resist or deflect pressures to forgive debt or interest.	Encourage scheme workers' local pressure groups.
11. Plan for complementarities.	Infrastructure and education may complement credit.	Social capital can complement physical works.
12. Strengthen beneficiaries.	Seek (small) saving before admitting borrowers.	Shelf of projects, and training, before scheme begins.
13. Build performance incentives.	Reward lenders and borrowers for project performance and steady repayment, not for meeting outreach or spending targets.	Provide performance bonuses for scheme participants and officials.

1. The first rule is that, in designing and implementing any anti-poverty programme, governments and NGOs should respect and welcome, not seek to impede, the rational use of fungibility by the clients of such a programme. Fungibility and rationality, taken together, mean that people can, and usually will, transfer resources – however much a planner may label them or seek to tie them to particular uses – to the activities in which the users, not the planner, believe those resources will do them most good. That applies to most of the goodies made available by anti-poverty policies or programmes: credit; working time, intended to be attracted to (say) a public works programme; cash (or inputs, especially saleable ones such as land or fertilizers) labelled as being for specific uses such as farming, e.g. after a land reform or a campaign to extend a new technology; or chances to acquire, or to use in alternative ways, new health and education options.

2. Second, experience suggests that direct targeting, on people labelling themselves as poor in the context of "pro-poor" programmes, leads to information and incentive problems [Besley and Kanbur 1993]. This is likely to apply not only to anti-poverty programmes of credit and public works, but also of land, choice of techniques, food distribution or subsidy, schooling and much else. Effective targeting is essential in view of resource constraints – universal benefits may sometimes be sensible in rich countries but very seldom in poor ones – but should concentrate on self-targeting and/or on steering the benefits towards persons or areas with clear indicators of poverty, indicators that are hard to dissemble and unlikely to change rapidly as a result of the programme itself. Coarse food staples, basic primary health and education, and land requiring labour-intensive methods are self-targeting on poor users, just as are manual public works employment at market wage rates and tiny loans at market rates of interest. And fairly constant indicators of poverty are specific to people, households or groups, not to categories of anti-poverty policy.

3. The search for rules discriminating in favour of the poor is also likely to make sense in any category of anti-poverty programme, though specific applications will vary greatly.

Rules helpful to poor women – and to large families, which are heavily over-represented among the poor – require special attention, not least in the case of land reform.

4.   We identified particular constraints that were especially common among the poor, to which programmes needed to give attention – lack of collateral in the case of credit, shortage of strength (based on health and nutritional problems) in the case of public works. A similar "most often binding constraint" may or may not exist for other categories of programme. Food distribution programmes, apart from ensuring that the food-deprived can and do benefit, need to be aware that it is shortage of dietary energy relative to requirements – not protein or micronutrient shortages – that comprises the main explicit link between poverty and nutritional deprivation [Lipton 1983a]. A pervasive constraint on primary school attendance among the poor may well be the parents' overriding felt need for children's time in household activities, or in earning income as child workers. Constraints impeding the poor from taking up, or benefiting from, land-reform options are likely to be more varied: access to water in some cases, to technology or inputs elsewhere, to seasonally available working time in yet other (probably rather few) cases.

5.   The need to minimize transactions costs of participation by the poor – frequent visits to remote bankers for small loans, time or bribes used up on contractors in public works programmes – is also likely to apply to other pro-poor programmes, and indeed to structure what sort of programmes are pro-poor. Registration of title is likely to be an anti-poor type of land reform if the poor have to face especially high transactions costs (per unit of gain) because of their illiteracy, lack of access to the legal system, or informality of initial claims – though it can be a pro-poor reform if carefully planned to anticipate and avoid such constraints; some of the ways to do this are discussed, largely in an urban setting, in de Soto [1989].

6.   Protecting the anti-poverty agency against sharp, sudden stresses, without imposing intolerable financial strains on the public purse, is vital. The means for implementing this rule are highly specific to the category of programme concerned:

diversification of a credit agency's portfolio, flexible seasonal or inter-year financing for public works programmes, etc. However, it is probably a crucial principle of anti-poverty work in all categories. That is because risk cannot normally be passed on from the programme agency to the poor beneficiaries. Indeed, it is the fact that these have succumbed to, or are unable to bear, risks that can lead to the collapse of rural lenders, or the overloading of public works programmes, when misfortunes strike.

7. The need for competitive use of available markets, rather than creation of programme monopolies (with strains on administration and dangers of rent-seeking), is again likely to be of special importance for all categories of programme with poor or politically weak, dispersed, or inarticulate clients. In credit programmes, that implied not seeking to crush rival private lenders (but perhaps learning from them, or even using some of them as agents). In public works programmes, the competitive principle implied the careful review of the impact of the schemes on poverty (and production) via private labour markets. In food distribution programmes, great administrative strains have been imposed, and access by poor people in remote rural areas impeded, by the limitation of distribution to single channels – whether privately, or via state-controlled "fair price shops" – as against the use of functioning retail systems as in Botswana [Drèze and Sen 1989]. In land reform, the poor benefit, and output tends to rise, when land is redistributed from large to labour-intensive small farms that can operate as they choose – but the poor lose from being forced into collective or state farms, or into restrictive tenancy regulations [Binswanger et al. 1995; Lipton 1993]. Even clearly desirable land redistribution may be more feasible politically, and may benefit the poor more swiftly and reliably if achieved, in the context of the "new wave" from Romania through Brazil to South Africa, which follows rule (7) by using a range of decentralized implementing authorities and/or market-friendly, partly compensatory reform, rather than the old model of a single (and confiscatory) land authority [ibid.; Tendler 1993; Lipton and Lipton 1993].

8.   The rule of ensuring effective demand by the poor before providing, say, programme credit or public works employment, and establishing that meeting this demand will reduce poverty, seems fairly obvious. Plainly, land reform where land is almost free (few such places are left) makes little sense. In one area of anti-poverty policy, however, this concept of effective demand, and perhaps therefore rule (8), is moot. Steps to benefit the health, schooling or nutrition of some household members, usually children but sometimes women, may be impeded by self-interested or short-sighted actions by others, usually the male household head.

9.   For both credit and public works, anti-poverty impact is usually improved, and leakage and rent-seeking are reduced, by using subsidy and support to improve administration and outreach, and to reduce transactions costs – not, as a rule, to tilt prices (interest rates, wage rates) in favour of scheme beneficiaries. *This rule requires modification for some other categories of anti-poverty programme.* In the case of *land reform*, the poor would seldom need it if they could afford to buy, or even to service a loan for, land at full market prices. Yet focusing reform land on persons willing and able to repay fairly priced credit, supplied for the land purchase, does filter out those who do not plan to farm the land but seek it only because it is cheap, and helps to target reform land towards people with the keenness and capacity to make a profit from farming it. Probably the solution – assuming that the poor can be effectively targeted as potential land recipients – is a transparent, up-front subsidy to the capital cost of acquisition; the alternative, an interest-rate subsidy, not only distorts capital markets, but also promotes rent-seeking and the almost undetectable disguising of other transactions as loans to obtain reform lands, in order to attract the subsidy (fungibility strikes again). In the case of *primary education and basic health care*, the recent claims that even the very poor have low price elasticity of demand for such services do not, as some people allege, mean that the welfare consequences of charging for such services are acceptable. Poor people typically devote 60-80 per cent of consumption resources to food and the rest largely to other necessities. If they (or the male head of household) can

and do pay for health and schooling out of a given income, this simply means less money for these basic needs (perhaps for pre-schoolers, especially girls). Since the returns to basic health (and primary education) often fall sharply if there is inadequate early food intake, charging the very poor for the former at the expense of the latter is probably inefficient as well as inhumane.

10. Rules for something as situational as pressure politics are bound to be context- and programme-specific. On public works, we illustrated the advantages of localized pressure groups of poor beneficiaries; on credit, we warned against the political softening of repayment, usually by rich people and in their interests. *Land reform* usually grows out of popular demand; the central, neglected political issue, as we shall explain, is whether the urban rich are at least to share, with the rural rich and not-very-rich, the costs of a venture widely agreed to be "good" for efficiency as well as the reduction of poverty. The impact of *food distribution and subsidy* schemes depends substantially on focusing the gains on the hungry, and the costs on the non-poor; that means skilfully resisting the political pressures to subsidize the diets of non-poor but politically articulate townspeople, and to place the cost burden on dispersed farmers by procuring their food on the cheap.

11. Planning for complementarity – as we showed in Chapter 1, a likely but not certain result of the Principle of Joint Requirements – is a key rule, or precondition, for success in most types of anti-poverty programme. It does not imply "integrated area development" or even offices of coordination; Tendler [1993] shows that in north-eastern Brazil such offices worked only to the extent that their senior officials stopped "coordinating" others, became enthused by specific necessary actions, and risked cutting their fingers by breaking bottlenecks. But success in land reform is clearly complementary to incentives, or institutional measures, to increase the flow and attractiveness of labour-intensive and lower-risk farm methods and outputs. Pro-poor health, education (especially female), family planning efforts, and child care are each more cost-effective when the others are present than when they are not. Extra primary schooling attracts the poor in proportion as it

offers a good expectation of returns – i.e. when they have or will get the land, jobs, techniques, etc. to raise the returns to new-found literacy and numeracy.

12.   Building up the capacity of both anti-poverty programmes and their beneficiaries before major expansions of activity is a sound general guideline, but it needs modification in certain political circumstances. If a land reform is very conflictual or confiscatory, it is either done swiftly or not at all. (Given the costs of mistakes, that is one argument for reducing the levels of conflict and confiscation somewhat.)

13.   The final "rule for success" – to provide well-considered incentives for both anti-poverty agencies and potential beneficiaries, and to anticipate the market effects of their responses in using or avoiding the schemes, were explored for anti-poverty credit and public works programmes. The rule is almost always sensible. Incentives, however, must be to right action, though – not to the achievement of mechanistic targets, or even of sensible but uncheckable or simulable ones. The effects of incentives on other parties, too, need review. In a land reform, what happens when big farmers partly evade or avoid land ceilings? (The effect, surprisingly, usually itself redistributes land.) What happens when landlords evade tenancy rules by rapidly moving tenants around, or avoid the rules by resuming direct cultivation? (Both are generally highly unfavourable to the poor.) In general equilibrium, major land reform may also have big effects on persons who neither lose nor gain land: on farmworkers, middle farmers, rural artisans, townspeople. When poor people's health or education is greatly improved, the supply of many categories of labour will shift; what, once again, are the effects on quantities and prices of work and outputs, and hence on efficiency and poverty?

The above would be a somewhat technical, research-oriented note on which to close a report on principles, and rules, for success in anti-poverty policy. As announced, we deliberately refrain from stating whether the 13 rules, developed for credit and public works policy, are guides to success in other fields. We have presented some evidence of what works and what fails in those fields, and many examples of the extent to which they follow or diverge from the

"13 rules". Certainly, too, there is more work to be done in developing underlying principles – economic, political and statistical – about how those rules are founded in individual behaviour, and about how they are best applied in practice. To complete that work is a massive research task; this book can at best give some directions.

In the introduction to his *Philosophy of history*, Hegel wrote that "People and governments have never learned anything from history, or acted on principles deduced from it". Governments and NGOs, however, do seem to have learned from the history of the successes and failures of others in anti-poverty efforts. It is not very likely that the disastrous history of attempts at state and collective farming in Africa and Latin America will be repeated. Policies on credit for the poor are a striking example of multi-phase learning from experience: first, that directed, labelled and heavily subsidized credit "for the poor" was seldom good at reducing poverty or increasing output; second, that this lesson did not imply state (or NGO) withdrawal from credit provision, but did imply more subtle interventions that recognized the realities of rural credit markets, especially their costs.

The whole notion of governments learning lessons from history is perhaps too idealistic, in both the everyday and the philosophical meaning of the word. What happens is part of a process of political competition. Various pressure groups inside and outside government – interest groups as well as groups motivated by a view of the common good – use their power and money, but also their persuasion and influence, to tilt policy, including policy on poverty, in desired directions. As the evidence about past performance of certain sorts of policy accumulates, and to the extent that interpretations of the evidence converge, there are two effects on this process of political competition.

First, the evidence of "history" strengthens the hand of groups arguing for policies proved in several cases to have been cost-effective in reducing poverty elsewhere – policies such as rural employment guarantee schemes – if the rules and circumstances conducive to success can be well defined and shown to be properly applicable in the case under discussion. Such policies become more widely acceptable and attractive. The converse is also true; groups hostile to an allegedly anti-poverty policy become stronger in the debates, if similar policies have proved unsuccessful or cost-ineffective in the past (such as the restriction of agricultural tenancy in the absence of land reform). Such policies become less widely acceptable, and less attractive.

Second – an important and neglected matter – the evidence of "history" shifts people's assessment of which anti-poverty activities are, and which are not, positive-sum. There are three situations: (i) some anti-poverty programmes are not only positive-sum, but in practice often do benefit most of the parties who might otherwise have been disposed to block or divert the schemes; (ii) some anti-poverty programmes are positive-sum, but it is harder, though possible, to achieve sufficient spread of benefits to maintain the political support base; (iii) some types of anti-poverty schemes have proved not to be positive-sum at all, or (although potentially so) in practice to set up irreconcilable fights about distribution. These "lessons of experience" have certainly affected the behaviour of the groups, inside and outside government, that decide on anti-poverty policies.

- Why have some types of anti-poverty policy been revealed, by a number of practical experiences, to be manageable so that they involve potential gains for all politically significant groups affected? This may be because there are no obvious losers; or because gainers are readily persuaded or compelled to compensate losers to a tolerable extent (given the losers' fear of alternatives), yet remain satisfied with their gains; or because of good side-effects (e.g. cost-effective infrastructure useful to many persons other than the employees, if that results from a public works employment programme).

- Some anti-poverty policies which create extra GNP as well, such as PRLR, require politically astute management to steer just enough of those gains as compensation to losers to maintain political progress in the reform, but not so much that the financing of the scheme (or the financial position of beneficiaries or taxpayers, if they must pay) becomes unsustainable.

- A third group of policies against poverty exists, for which the "lessons of experience" have weakened advocacy. This group comprises two types of policies: the zero- (or negative-) sum, and the positive-sum but distributively unsustainable. The first type – including imposed collective and state farming – has been shown to be counter-productive, or at best cost-ineffective, either in reducing poverty or in doing so without harmful side-effects, e.g. on GNP. The second type comprises pro-poor activities whose GNP effects, while positive, cannot be distributed in ways that *either* prevent politically unmanageable dissent from the process, by groups strong enough to disrupt it, *or* prevent harmful side-effects to other poor groups who cannot be readily compensated. The former type is self-explanatory; the latter is illustrated by the impact, on rural farmers (some of them poor) and on their (usually) even poorer employees, of the older types of food subsidy or distribution scheme.

This book should not end by emphasizing difficulties. There has been much success with anti-poverty policy, sometimes in extremely difficult political and administrative circumstances. This is shown in Chapters 4 and 5 for poverty-orientated programmes of credit and of public works employment. Evidence for success is also given, though not discussed fully, in Chapter 6 for some other types of anti-poverty programme. We have also gone some of the way to understanding the rules for success, and the causes of failure. There has been much learning from experience. Great swings of ideology and of financing fashions, especially among aid donors, have made this learning process both sluggish and subject to arbitrary shocks, but the process is real.

Appendix A

Some issues in poverty measurement

The cross-section approach defines a country's "success" against poverty as the attainment of a *low value* either for a **poverty indicator**, or for a **damage indicator** of the harm associated with poverty. The time-series approach defines "success" as *rapid improvement* in indicators of poverty or damage.

Whether a country has enjoyed "success" against poverty, in either sense, can be assessed by comparisons among countries of levels or trends of (1) the poverty or damage indicators as such, or (2) those indicators in comparison with what it would be reasonable to expect, given the resources available and/or other difficulties in improving the indicators. Method (1) compares the well-being of the poor among countries, but not the countries' determination or success in fighting poverty. That is because it is easier to achieve a low indicator, or a high rate of improvement, if resources are ample than if they are scarce. If two countries have the same level (or rate of improvement) of the poverty indicator, but one has GNP per person of $5,000 per year while the other has only $500, then the second country is trying harder, and achieving more, in the fight against poverty. Other indicators of resources, or of vulnerability, could be relevant to evaluating the success of a country's efforts against poverty: given the level of GNP per person, a country has a harder task to reduce poverty (or the damage done by a given amount of poverty) if there is little aid per person, or great climatic variability in agricultural output.

An indicator of poverty or damage is easier to improve if it is very high to begin with, than if it is already low because the easier measures to reduce it have already been taken. It is easier and cheaper to reduce from 80 per cent to 70 per cent the incidence of people who are too poor to eat enough, than to reduce it from 20 per cent to 10 per cent – even, perhaps, from 20 per cent to 17.5 per cent. Similarly, it is harder and costlier to cut infant mortality from 20 to 10 than from 200 to 190 – even perhaps from 200 to 100. This is a very serious objection to Method 1. In Method 2, it may justify using double-log formulations (see footnote 17 in Chapter 3).

How do we identify satisfactory indicators and other relevant variables, and specify the national data sets from which these can be obtained? People are judged to be in PCP if their private consumption (including imputed value of consumption of own produce) falls below a given "poverty line". Given the poverty line and the survey results, the question remains of how one should add up below the line. The overwhelming majority of studies simply count heads below the poverty line and express the total as a proportion of population. This does not take the depth of poverty into account, and other indicators are in principle preferable. One such indicator, taking into account the average depth or "intensity" of poverty as well as the proportions of the poor ("incidence"), is the aggregate poverty gap (i.e. the sum of the gaps between each poor person's income and the poverty line, per head of population). A better indicator (because it also allows for suffering to the poorest that is caused by inequality *among* the poor) is poverty "severity", e.g. as measured by the sum of *squared* poverty gaps [Ravallion 1994; Lipton and Ravallion 1995; Kakwani 1993].[53]

It remains unsatisfactory to use PCP as an indicator of total poverty see Chapter 3, footnote 11). Private consumption understates personal resources in any one period. As for trends, the contribution to the well-being of potentially poor people from resources other than private consumption – common-property hunted and gathered resources – is falling, while that from public expenditure is rising, in most communities. However, these trends need not cancel, and vary greatly over space and time.

What can be done about this? One relevant remedy is to use the food energy method (Chapter 3, footnote 12). Contributions, made to the avoidance of distress, from other sources than private consumption – such as public services, common-property resources, and the degree of security against fluctuations – then appear as intervening variables, helping to determine the extent to which private consumption in fact succeeds in avoiding food poverty. However, the composition and

---

53. The aggregate poverty gap measure – i.e. the per-head cost of eliminating poverty, given perfect targeting – takes account of the average depth of poverty, as well as of the numbers of poor people. The aggregate of *squared* individual poverty gaps is an even better measure of poverty, because it increases with the inequality of income among the poor.

price of food staples varies significantly among groups, even at the same level of private consumption value per head. This variation is especially high among regions with different main food staples, showing different price levels or trends. The above method, therefore, works well only to the extent that national-level measures of food poverty are derived by adding up estimates that had previously been disaggregated by regions, etc., with substantially different levels (of food-bundles, prices and energy intakes, but also perhaps of public and common-property based resources, for the poor). This has been done for Kenya [Greer and Thorbecke 1986] but is rare, though feasible, for other data sets. A second method, tested here, is to present, alongside indicators of the levels and trends in PCP, comparable indicators of the harm done by such poverty – infant or child mortality, or illiteracy, or a human development indicator.

We are forced by the data gaps to accept PCP – and usually incidence at that – rather than more sophisticated indicators of poverty. Most efforts to collate and explain such data, even if sophisticated econometrically, tend (1) to use a very wide range of data, some excellent, but some collected by field or central methods rendering them almost worthless; and/or (2) to combine data that are non-comparable because of different methods used, or in some cases (3) to use data that, while the field methods were good, cannot be used for methodological reasons.[54] The only way to get usable estimates of PCP – let alone to gather more sophisticated information about access to public or common-property resources, or about fluctuations – is through carefully planned and supervised household surveys of consumption per person (or per adult equivalent). In this book we confine ourselves to countries with such estimates.

---

54. Fields [1989] correctly confines himself to data based on 34 developing countries with household surveys or censuses, but uses country-specific poverty lines, so that one cannot compare poverty levels across countries. He also measures both poverty and inequality in terms of inadequacy of expenditure (or even income) per household instead of per person – an unacceptable procedure, because poor households are systematically bigger than others, and because many households with low total income have few members who are not poor. Tabatabai and Fouad [1993] put together data for a very large number of countries – some based on household surveys, some on informed guesses – using different poverty lines, definitions, etc. IFAD [1992] also uses many non-comparable data sets of mixed quality, different definitions of poverty, in many cases no survey base, and often unclear methodology.

Appendix B

Predicted poverty and the outliers

This appendix contains the scatter diagrams and tables required for detailed interpretation of the patterns and deviations discussed in Chapter 3.

Scatter diagram 1 (referring to Eq. 1, Table 2, Chapter 3)

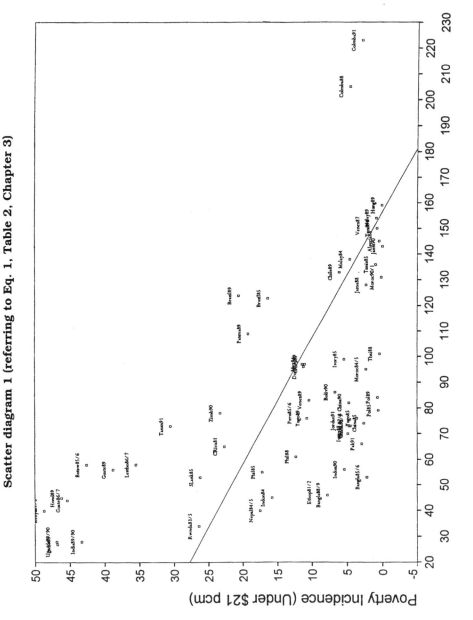

Poverty Incidence (Under $21 pcm)

Real Mean Cons $/capita/mth

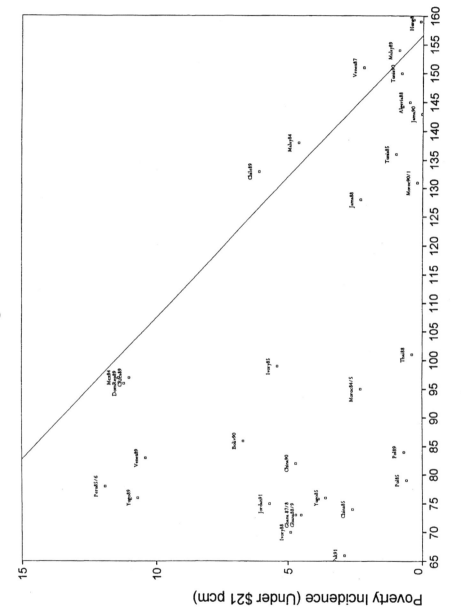

Scatter diagram 1 (inset)

Poverty Incidence (Under $21 pcm)

Real Mean Cons $/capita/mth (INSET 1)

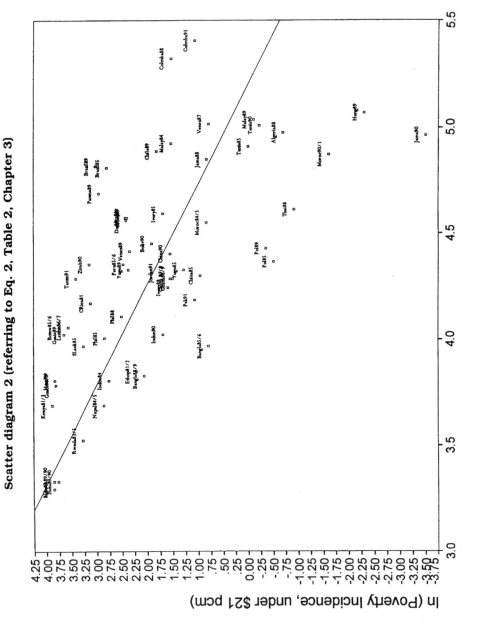

Scatter diagram 2 (referring to Eq. 2, Table 2, Chapter 3)

In (Real Mean Con $/cap/mth)

In (Poverty Incidence, under $21 pcm)

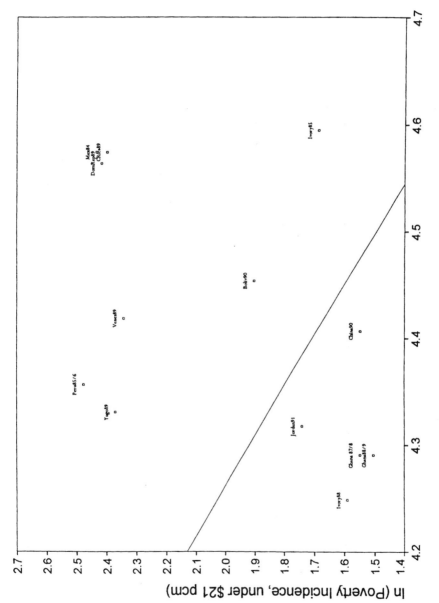

Scatter diagram 2 (inset)

In (Real Mean Con $/cap/mth) (INSET 1)

In (Poverty Incidence, under $21 pcm)

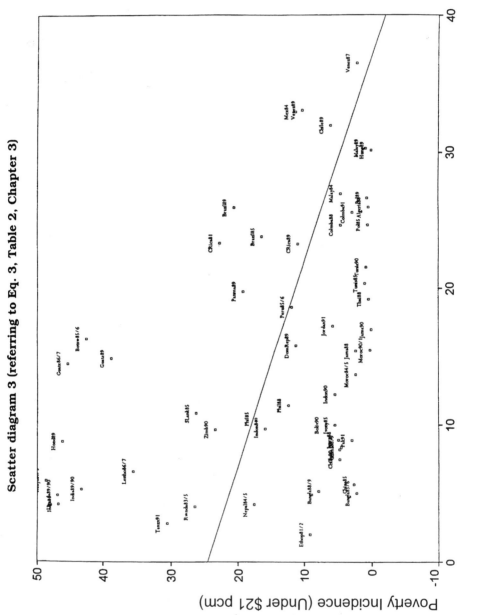

Scatter diagram 3 (referring to Eq. 3, Table 2, Chapter 3)

GNP_ppp/cap(US_ 1987=100)(survey yr est.)

Poverty Incidence (Under $21 pcm)

Scatter diagram 3 (inset)

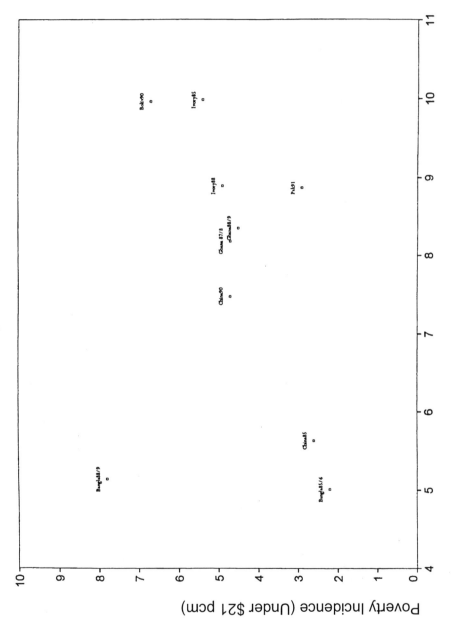

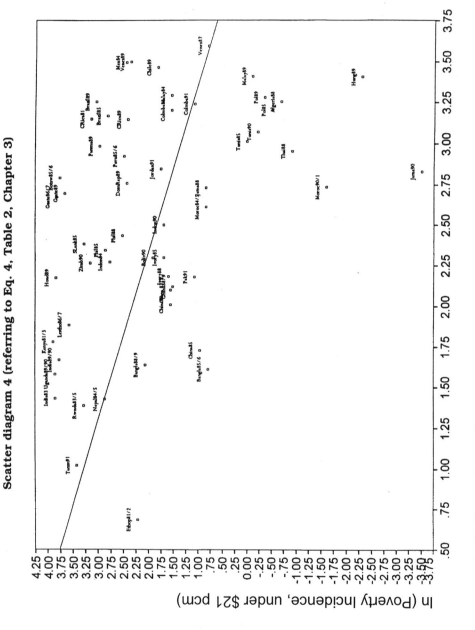

Scatter diagram 4 (referring to Eq. 4, Table 2, Chapter 3)

ln (Poverty Incidence, under $21 pcm)

ln GNP_ppp/cap;US_1987=100;survey yr est.)

Scatter diagram 4 (inset)

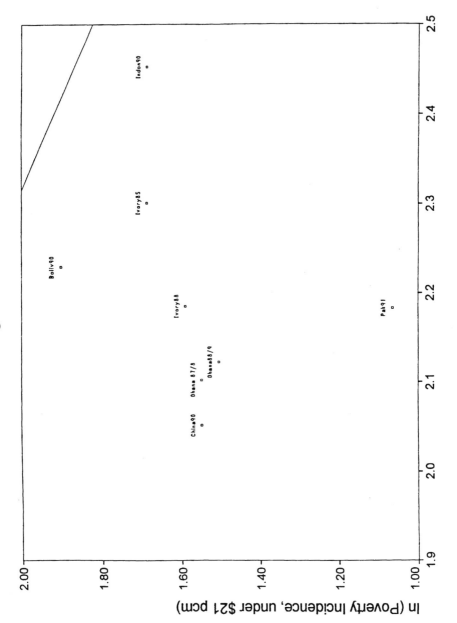

ln (GNP_ppp Capita, US=100, est.) (INSET 1)

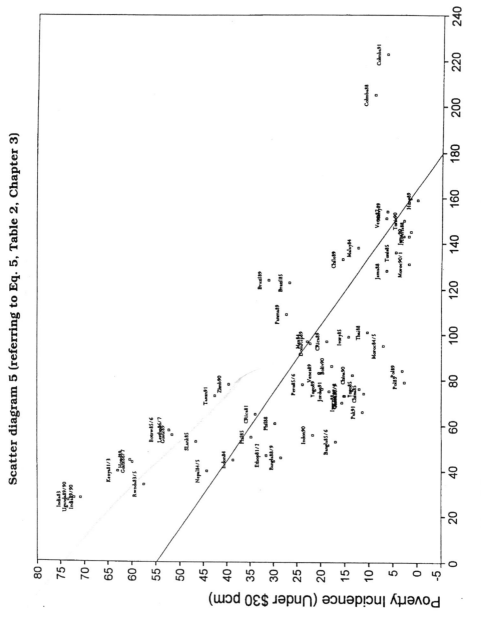

Scatter diagram 5 (referring to Eq. 5, Table 2, Chapter 3)

Poverty Incidence (Under $30 pcm)

Real Mean Cons $/capita/mth

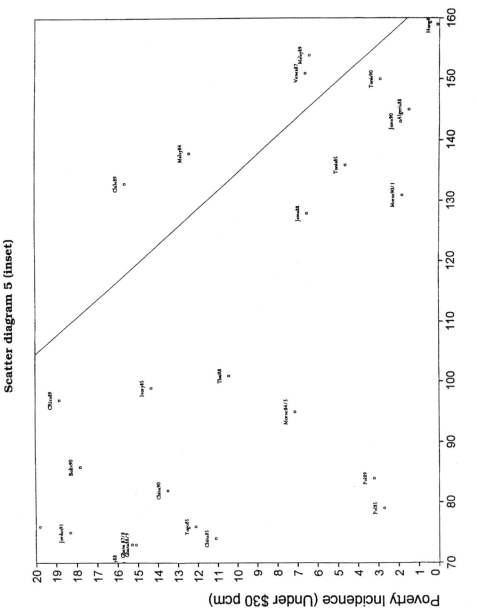

Scatter diagram 5 (inset)

Poverty Incidence (Under $30 pcm)

Real Mean Cons $/capita/mth (INSET 1)

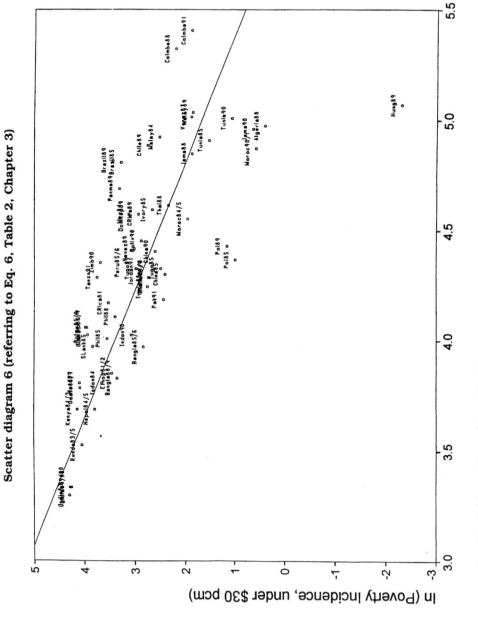

Scatter diagram 6 (referring to Eq. 6, Table 2, Chapter 3)

ln (Poverty Incidence, under $30 pcm)

ln (Real Mean Con, $/cap/mth)

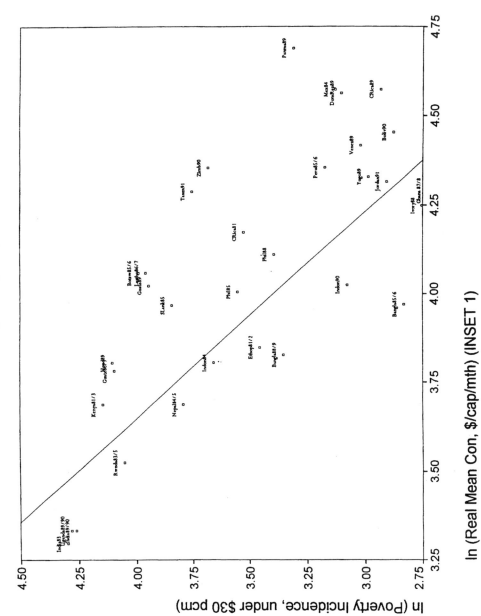

Scatter diagram 6 (inset)

In (Real Mean Con, $/cap/mth) (INSET 1)

In (Poverty Incidence, under $30 pcm)

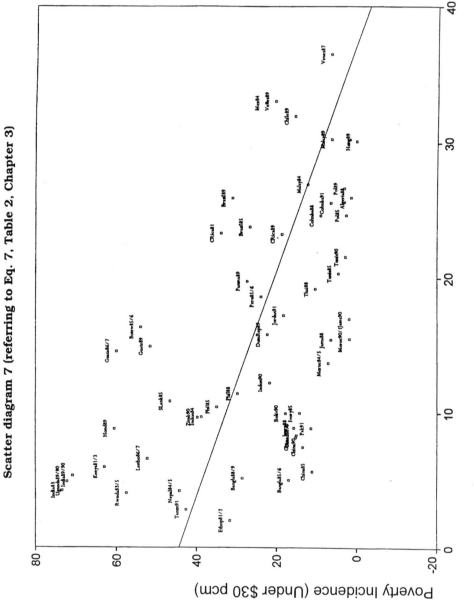

Scatter diagram 7 (referring to Eq. 7, Table 2, Chapter 3)

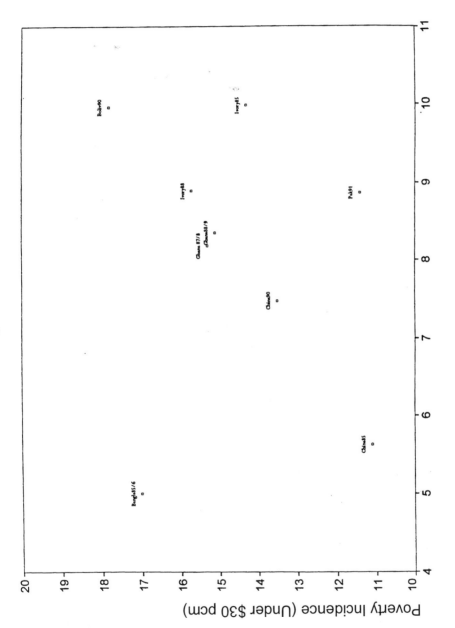

Scatter diagram 7 (inset)

GNP_ppp/cap(US_1987=100)(survey yr est.) (INSET 1)

Poverty Incidence (Under $30 pcm)

Scatter diagram 8 (referring to Eq. 8, Table 2, Chapter 3)

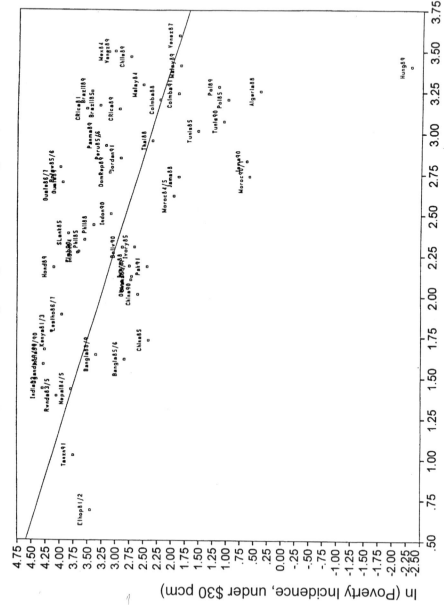

Scatter diagram 8 (inset)

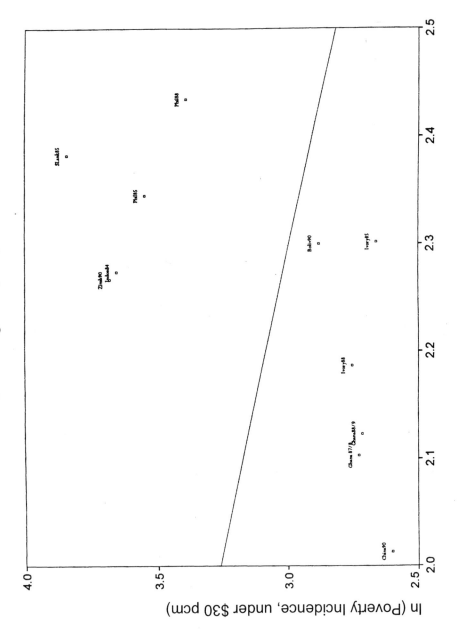

In (GNP_ppp/cap;US_1987=100;survey yr est.) (INSET 1)

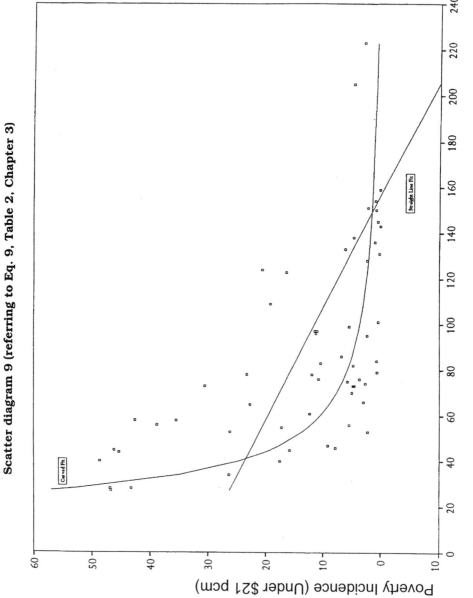

Scatter diagram 9 (referring to Eq. 9, Table 2, Chapter 3)

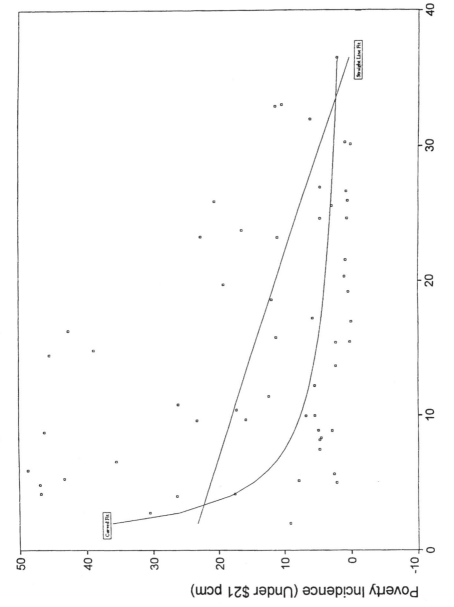

Scatter diagram 10 (referring to Eqs. 3 and 4, Table 2, Chapter 3)

GNP_ppp /capita (US_1987=100) (survey yr est.)

Poverty Incidence (Under $21 pcm)

Scatter diagram 11 (referring to Eqs. 5 and 6, Table 2, Chapter 3)

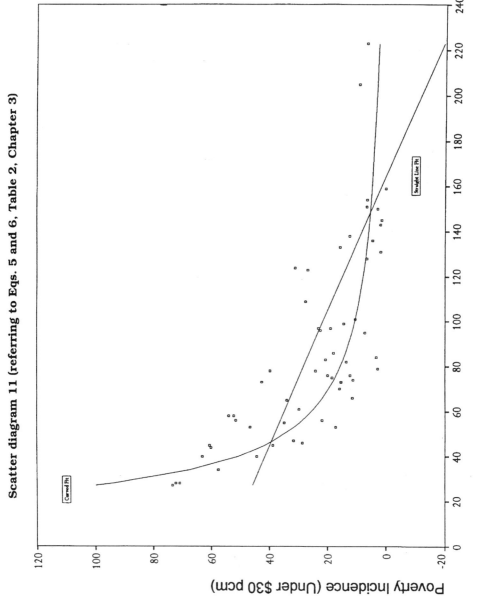

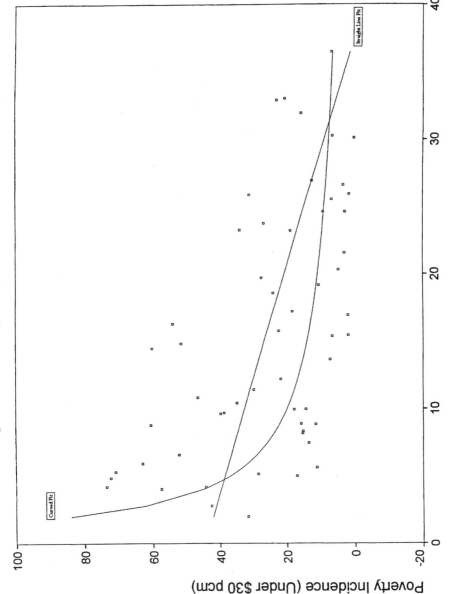

Scatter diagram 12 (referring to Eqs. 7 and 8, Table 2, Chapter 3)

Poverty Incidence (Under $30 pcm)

GNP_ppp /capita (US_ 1987=100)(survey yr est.)

Curved Fit

Straight Line Fit

Appendix B, Table 1. Actual poverty incidence (% popn. below $21 or $30 consumption), straight-line-fit regression estimators (*) of poverty incidence (using consumption and GNP, with neg. estimated values set to zero), and absolute difference (#) between actual and predicted poverty incidence

	(% popn below pov line, $cons/mth, 1985_PPP)		Mean cons $/cap/mth	(S, est'd, US$'87=100)	Poverty estimators from regression eqns. (straight fit)				Actual minus predicted poverty incidence (neg values imply actual PCP better than predicted)			
COUNTRY/Yr	US21	US30	MEANCON	GNP PPP	P 21=31.8-0.2CP *U21Con	21=24.6-0.7GP *U21GNP	30=54.8-0.3CP *U30Con	30=44.4-1.2G *U30GNP	#U21Con	#U21GNP	#U30Con	#U30GNP
Algeria88	0.5	1.5	145	25.93	2.37	7.38	6.58	13.69	-1.87	-6.88	-5.08	-12.19
Bangla85/6	2.2	17	53	5.01	21.05	21.23	37.19	38.49	-18.85	-19.03	-20.19	-21.49
Bangla88/9	7.8	28.5	46	5.15	22.48	21.14	39.52	38.32	-14.68	-13.34	-11.02	-9.82
Boliv90	6.7	17.8	86	9.97	14.35	17.95	26.21	32.61	-7.65	-11.25	-8.41	-14.81
Botsw85/6	42.6	54	58	16.32	20.04	13.74	35.52	25.09	22.56	28.86	18.48	28.91
Brazil85	16.4	26.7	123	23.76	6.84	8.82	13.90	16.27	9.56	7.58	12.80	10.43
Brazil89	20.6	31.1	124	25.90	6.64	7.40	13.56	13.73	13.96	13.20	17.54	17.37
Chile89	6.1	15.6	133	31.97	4.81	3.37	10.57	6.53	1.29	2.73	5.03	9.07
China85	2.6	11.1	74	5.64	16.79	20.82	30.20	37.74	-14.19	-18.22	-19.10	-26.64
China90	4.7	13.5	82	7.48	15.17	19.59	27.54	35.55	-10.47	-14.89	-14.04	-22.05
Colmba88	4.6	9.1	205	24.61	0.00	8.25	0.00	15.26	4.60	-3.65	9.10	-6.16
Colmba91	2.9	6.6	223	25.54	0.00	7.64	0.00	14.16	2.90	-4.74	6.60	-7.56
CRica81	22.7	33.9	65	23.29	18.62	9.13	33.19	16.82	4.08	13.57	0.71	17.08
CRica89	11	18.8	97	23.23	12.12	9.17	22.55	16.90	-1.12	1.83	-3.75	1.90
DomRep89	11.2	22.3	96	15.79	12.32	14.09	22.88	25.71	-1.12	-2.89	-0.58	-3.41
Ethop81/2	9.1	31.6	47	1.98	22.27	23.24	39.18	42.07	-13.17	-14.14	-7.58	-10.47
Ghana 87/8	4.7	15.3	73	8.19	16.99	19.13	30.53	34.72	-12.29	-14.43	-15.23	-19.42
Ghana88/9	4.5	15.1	73	8.36	16.99	19.02	30.53	34.52	-12.49	-14.52	-15.43	-19.42
Guate86/7	45.4	60	44	14.50	22.88	14.95	40.18	27.24	22.52	30.45	19.82	32.76
Guate89	38.8	51.6	56	14.84	20.45	14.72	36.19	26.84	18.35	24.08	15.41	24.76
Hond89	46.2	60.5	45	8.81	22.68	18.71	39.85	33.98	23.52	27.49	20.65	26.52
Hung89	0.1	0.1	159	30.14	0.00	4.59	1.92	8.71	0.10	-4.49	-1.82	-8.61
India83	46.8	73.5	27	4.19	26.33	21.78	45.84	39.46	20.47	25.02	27.66	34.04
India89/90	43.3	70.9	28	5.30	26.13	21.04	45.50	38.14	17.17	22.26	25.40	32.76
Indon84	15.8	38.7	45	9.72	22.68	18.11	39.85	32.91	-6.88	-2.31	-1.15	5.79
Indon90	5.4	21.7	56	12.22	20.45	16.46	36.19	29.95	-15.05	-11.06	-14.49	-8.25

Appendix B, Table 1 *(cont.)*

Ivoire85	5.4	14.3	99	9.99	11.71	17.93	21.88	32.58	-6.31	-12.53	-7.58	-18.28
Ivoire88	4.9	15.7	70	8.90	17.60	18.66	31.53	33.87	-12.70	-13.76	-15.83	-18.17
Jama88	2.3	6.5	128	15.39	5.82	14.36	12.23	26.18	-3.52	-12.06	-5.73	-19.68
Jama90	0.03	1.9	143	16.97	2.78	13.32	7.24	24.32	-2.75	-13.29	-5.34	-22.42
Jordan91	5.7	18.3	75	17.24	16.59	13.13	29.87	23.99	-10.89	-7.43	-11.57	-5.69
Kenya81/3	48.7	63	40	5.94	23.69	20.62	41.51	37.38	25.01	28.08	21.49	25.62
Lestho86/7	35.5	52.3	58	6.60	20.04	20.18	35.52	36.60	15.46	15.32	16.78	15.70
Malay84	4.6	12.4	138	26.95	3.79	6.70	8.91	12.49	0.81	-2.10	3.49	-0.09
Malay89	0.9	6.4	154	30.29	0.54	4.49	3.58	8.53	0.36	-3.59	2.82	-2.13
Mex84	11.4	22.9	97	32.93	12.12	2.74	22.55	5.40	-0.72	8.66	0.35	17.50
Moroc84/5	2.3	7.1	95	13.66	12.53	15.51	23.21	28.24	-10.23	-13.21	-16.11	-21.14
Moroc90/1	0.2	1.8	131	15.45	5.22	14.32	11.24	26.12	-5.02	-14.12	-9.44	-24.32
Nepal84/5	17.5	44.3	40	4.17	23.69	21.79	41.51	39.48	-6.19	-4.29	2.79	4.82
Pak91	2.9	11.4	66	8.87	18.41	18.68	32.86	33.91	-15.51	-15.78	-21.46	-22.51
Panma89	19.2	27.4	109	19.76	9.68	11.46	18.56	21.00	9.52	7.74	8.84	6.40
Peru85/6	11.9	23.9	78	18.62	15.98	12.22	28.87	22.36	-4.08	-0.32	-4.97	1.54
Phil85	17.2	34.8	55	10.44	20.65	17.64	36.52	32.05	-3.45	-0.44	-1.72	2.75
Phil88	12.3	29.7	61	11.41	19.43	16.99	34.53	30.90	-7.13	-4.69	-4.83	-1.20
Pol85	0.6	2.7	79	24.62	15.77	8.24	28.54	15.24	-15.17	-7.64	-25.84	-12.54
Pol89	0.7	3.2	84	26.64	14.76	6.91	26.87	12.86	-14.06	-6.21	-23.67	-9.66
Rwnda83/5	26.4	57.5	34	4.00	24.91	21.90	43.51	39.68	1.49	4.50	13.99	17.82
SLank85	26.2	46.6	53	10.84	21.05	17.37	37.19	31.58	5.15	8.83	9.41	15.02
Tanzn91	30.5	42.6	73	2.78	16.99	22.71	30.53	41.12	13.51	7.79	12.07	1.48
Thai88	0.4	10.4	101	19.20	11.31	11.83	21.22	21.67	-10.91	-11.43	-10.82	-11.27
Tunis85	1	4.6	136	20.35	4.20	11.07	9.57	20.30	-3.20	-10.07	-4.97	-15.70
Tunis90	0.8	2.9	150	21.57	1.36	10.27	4.91	18.87	-0.56	-9.47	-2.01	-15.97
Uganda89/90	46.9	72.3	28	4.86	26.13	21.34	45.50	38.67	20.77	25.56	26.80	33.63
Venez87	2.2	6.6	151	36.50	1.15	0.38	4.58	1.17	1.05	1.82	2.02	5.43
Venez89	10.4	20.5	83	33.05	14.96	2.66	27.21	5.25	-4.56	7.74	-6.71	15.25
Yugo85	3.6	12.1	76	—	16.38	—	29.53	—	-12.78	—	-17.43	—
Yugo89	10.7	19.8	76	—	16.38	—	29.53	—	-5.68	—	-9.73	—
Zimb90	23.3	39.7	78	9.65	15.98	18.16	28.87	32.98	7.32	5.14	10.83	6.72

Appendix B, Table 2. Ranking countries by actual minus predicted poverty incidence
(Under $21 line, straight line fit)

(Countries listed in order of lowest ACTUAL US$21 poverty incidence first)

Lowest = Rank 1

Cons	Cons rank	GNP	GNP rank	COUNTRY/Yr	Actual poverty incidence		Actual minus predicted poverty incidence		RANK by	
					US$21	Rank	#U21Con	#U21GNP	#U21Con	#U21GNP
143	51	16.97	34	Jama90	0.03	1	-2.75	-13.29	29	11
159	56	30.14	51	Hung89	0.1	2	0.10	-4.49	35	26
131	47	15.45	31	Moroc90/1	0.2	3	-5.02	-14.12	23	8
101	42	19.20	37	Thai88	0.4	4	-10.91	-11.43	13	15
145	52	25.93	48	Algeria88	0.5	5	-1.87	-6.88	30	22
79	32	24.62	45	Pol85	0.6	6	-15.17	-7.64	3	20
84	35	26.64	49	Pol89	0.7	7	-14.06	-6.21	7	23
150	53	21.57	40	Tunis90	0.8	8	-0.56	-9.47	34	19
154	55	30.29	52	Malay89	0.9	9	0.36	-3.59	36	29
136	49	20.35	39	Tunis85	1.0	10	-3.20	-10.07	28	18
53	12	5.01	7	Bangla85/6	2.2	11=	-18.85	-19.03	1	1
151	54	36.50	56	Venez87	2.2	11=	1.05	1.82	38	35
95	37	13.66	27	Moroc84/5	2.3	13=	-10.23	-13.21	16	12
128	46	15.39	30	Jama88	2.3	13=	-3.52	-12.06	26	14
74	26	5.64	10	China85	2.6	15	-14.19	-18.22	6	2
66	21	8.87	17	Pak91	2.9	16=	-15.51	-15.78	2	3
223	58	25.54	46	Colmba91	2.9	16=	2.90	-4.74	41	24
76	28	—		Yugo85	3.6	18	-12.78	—	9	—
73	25	8.36	15	Ghana88/9	4.5	19	-12.49	-14.52	11	5
205	57	24.61	44	Colmba88	4.6	20=	4.60	-3.65	43	28
138	50	26.95	50	Malay84	4.6	20=	0.81	-2.10	37	32
82	33	7.48	13	China90	4.7	22=	-10.47	-14.89	15	4
73	24	8.19	14	Ghana 87/8	4.7	22=	-12.29	-14.43	12	6
70	22	8.90	18	Ivoire88	4.9	24	-12.70	-13.76	10	9
99	41	9.99	22	Ivoire85	5.4	25=	-6.31	-12.53	20	13
56	15	12.22	26	Indon90	5.4	25=	-15.05	-11.06	4	17
75	27	17.24	35	Jordan91	5.7	27	-10.89	-7.43	14	21
133	48	31.97	53	Chile89	6.1	28	1.29	2.73	39	37

Appendix B, Table 2 (cont.)

16	17	-11.25	-7.65	29	6.7	**Boliv90**	21	9.97	36	86
10	5	-13.34	-14.68	30	7.8	**Bangla88/9**	8	5.15	10	46
7	8	-14.14	-13.17	31	9.1	**Ethop81/2**	1	1.98	11	47
42	24	7.74	-4.56	32	10.4	**Venez89**	55	33.05	34	83
—	22	—	-5.68	33	10.7	**Yugo89**	—	—	29	76
36	32	1.83	-1.12	34	11.0	**CRica89**	41	23.23	39	97
30	31	-2.89	-1.12	35	11.2	**DomRep89**	32	15.79	38	96
44	33	8.66	-0.72	36	11.4	**Mex84**	54	32.93	40	97
34	25	-0.32	-4.08	37	11.9	**Peru85/6**	36	18.62	31	78
25	18	-4.69	-7.13	38	12.3	**Phil88**	25	11.41	19	61
31	19	-2.31	-6.88	39	15.8	**Indon84**	20	9.72	9	45
40	47	7.58	9.56	40	16.4	**Brazil85**	43	23.76	44	123
33	27	-0.44	-3.45	41	17.2	**Phil85**	23	10.44	14	55
27	21	-4.29	-6.19	42	17.5	**Nepal84/5**	4	4.17	5	40
41	46	7.74	9.52	43	19.2	**Panma89**	38	19.76	43	109
46	49	13.20	13.96	44	20.6	**Brazil89**	47	25.90	45	124
47	42	13.57	4.08	45	22.7	**CRica81**	42	23.29	20	65
39	45	5.14	7.32	46	23.3	**Zimb90**	19	9.65	30	78
45	44	8.83	5.15	47	26.2	**SLank85**	24	10.84	13	53
38	40	4.50	1.49	48	26.4	**Rwnda83/5**	3	4.00	4	34
43	48	7.79	13.51	49	30.5	**Tanzn91**	2	2.78	23	73
48	50	15.32	15.46	50	35.5	**Lestho86/7**	12	6.60	17	58
50	52	24.08	18.35	51	38.8	**Guate89**	29	14.84	16	56
55	56	28.86	22.56	52	42.6	**Botsw85/6**	33	16.32	18	58
49	51	22.26	17.17	53	43.3	**India89/90**	9	5.30	3	28
56	55	30.45	22.52	54	45.4	**Guate86/7**	28	14.50	7	44
53	57	27.49	23.52	55	46.2	**Hond89**	16	8.81	8	45
51	53	25.02	20.47	56	46.8	**India83**	5	4.19	1	27
52	54	25.56	20.77	57	46.9	**Uganda89/90**	6	4.86	2	28
54	58	28.08	25.01	58	48.7	**Kenya81/3**	11	5.94	6	40

Appendix B, Table 3. Ranking countries by actual minus predicted poverty incidence
(Under $30 line, straight line fit)

(Countries listed in order of lowest ACTUAL US$30 poverty incidence first)

Lowest = Rank 1

Cons	Cons rank	GNP	GNP rank	COUNTRY/Yr	Actual poverty incidence		Actual minus predicted poverty incidence		RANK by	
					US$30	Rank	#U30Con	#U30GNP	#U30Con	#U30GNP
159	56	30.14	51	Hung89	0.1	1	-1.82	-8.61	30	22
145	52	25.93	48	Algeria88	1.5	2	-5.08	-12.19	24	17
131	47	15.45	31	Moroc90/1	1.8	3	-9.44	-24.32	17	2
143	51	16.97	34	Jama90	1.9	4	-5.34	-22.42	23	4
79	32	24.62	45	Pol85	2.7	5	-25.84	-12.54	1	16
150	53	21.57	40	Tunis90	2.9	6	-2.01	-15.97	29	13
84	35	26.64	49	Pol89	3.2	7	-23.67	-9.66	2	21
136	49	20.35	39	Tunis85	4.6	8	-4.97	-15.70	25	14
154	55	30.29	52	Malay89	6.4	9	2.82	-2.13	38	28
128	46	15.39	30	Jama88	6.5	10	-5.73	-19.68	22	8
223	58	25.54	46	Colmba91	6.6	11=	6.60	-7.56	41	24
151	54	36.50	56	Venez87	6.6	11=	2.02	5.43	36	36
95	37	13.66	27	Moroc84/5	7.1	13	-16.11	-21.14	7	7
205	57	24.61	44	Colmba88	9.1	14	9.10	-6.16	43	25
101	42	19.20	37	Thai88	10.4	15	-10.82	-11.27	15	18
74	26	5.64	10	China85	11.1	16	-19.10	-26.64	5	1
66	21	8.87	17	Pak91	11.4	17	-21.46	-22.51	3	3
76	28	—	—	Yugo85	12.1	18	-17.43	—	6	—
138	50	26.95	50	Malay84	12.4	19	3.49	-0.09	39	30
82	33	7.48	13	China90	13.5	20	-14.04	-22.05	12	5
99	41	9.99	22	Ivoire85	14.3	21	-7.58	-18.28	20	11
73	25	8.36	15	Ghana88/9	15.1	22	-15.43	-19.42	9	9
73	24	8.19	14	Ghana 87/8	15.3	23	-15.23	-19.42	10	10
133	48	31.97	53	Chile89	15.6	24	5.03	9.07	40	40
70	22	8.90	18	Ivoire88	15.7	25	-15.83	-18.17	8	12
53	12	5.01	7	Bangla85/6	17.0	26	-20.19	-21.49	4	6
86	36	9.97	21	Boliv90	17.8	27	-8.41	-14.81	18	15
75	27	17.24	35	Jordan91	18.3	28	-11.57	-5.69	13	26

Appendix B, Table 3 (cont.)

33	28	1.90	-3.75	29	18.8	CRica89	41	23.23	39	97
—	16	—	-9.73	30	19.8	Yugo89		—	29	76
43	21	15.25	-6.71	31	20.5	Venez89	55	33.05	34	83
23	11	-8.25	-14.49	32	21.7	Indon90	26	12.22	15	56
27	33	-3.41	-0.58	33	22.3	DomRep89	32	15.79	38	96
47	34	17.50	0.35	34	22.9	Mex84	54	32.93	40	97
32	26	1.54	-4.97	35	23.9	Peru85/6	36	18.62	31	78
41	47	10.43	12.80	36	26.7	Brazil85	43	23.76	44	123
38	42	6.40	8.84	37	27.4	Panma89	38	19.76	43	109
20	14	-9.82	-11.02	38	28.5	Bangla88/9	8	5.15	10	46
29	27	-1.20	-4.83	39	29.7	Phil88	25	11.41	19	61
46	51	17.37	17.54	40	31.1	Brazil89	47	25.90	45	124
19	19	-10.47	-7.58	41	31.6	Ethop81/2	1	1.98	11	47
45	35	17.08	0.71	42	33.9	CRica81	42	23.29	20	65
34	31	2.75	-1.72	43	34.8	Phil85	23	10.44	14	55
37	32	5.79	-1.15	44	38.7	Indon84	20	9.72	9	45
39	45	6.72	10.83	45	39.7	Zimb90	19	9.65	30	78
31	46	1.48	12.07	46	42.6	Tanzn91	2	2.78	23	73
35	37	4.82	2.79	47	44.3	Nepal84/5	4	4.17	5	40
42	44	15.02	9.41	48	46.6	SLank85	24	10.84	13	53
49	49	24.76	15.41	49	51.6	Guate89	29	14.84	16	56
44	50	15.70	16.78	50	52.3	Lestho86/7	12	6.60	17	58
52	52	28.91	18.48	51	54.0	Botsw85/6	33	16.32	18	58
48	48	17.82	13.99	52	57.5	Rwnda83/5	3	4.00	4	34
53	53	32.76	19.82	53	60.0	Guate86/7	28	14.50	7	44
51	54	26.52	20.65	54	60.5	Hond89	16	8.81	8	45
50	55	25.62	21.49	55	63.0	Kenya81/3	11	5.94	6	40
54	56	32.76	25.40	56	70.9	India89/90	9	5.30	3	28
55	57	33.63	26.80	57	72.3	Uganda89/90	6	4.86	2	28
56	58	34.04	27.66	58	73.5	India83	5	4.19	1	27

Appendix B, Table 4. Actual poverty incidence (% popn. below $21 or $30 consumption), Rectangular-hyperbolic-fit regression estimators (**) of poverty incidence (using consumption & GNP) (~ signify exponentiation in eqns), and absolute difference (##) between actual and predicted poverty incidence

COUNTRY/Yr	(% popn below pov line, $cons/cap/mth, 1985_PPP) US21	US30	Mean Cons $/cap/mth MEANCON	($, est'd, US$'87=100) GNP_PPP	Poverty estimators from regression eqns (straight fit) P 21=31.8-0.2C **U21Con	P 21=24.6-0.7GP **U21GNP	P 30=54.8-0.3C **U30Con	P 30=44.4-1.2G **U30GNP	Actual minus predicted poverty incidence (neg values imply actual PCP better than predicted) ##U21Con	##U21GNP	##U30Con	##U30GNP
Algeria88	0.5	1.5	145	25.93	1.63	3.01	5.59	8.54	-1.13	-2.51	-4.09	-7.04
Bangla85/6	2.2	17	53	5.01	13.68	14.51	31.42	36.42	-11.48	-12.31	-14.42	-19.42
Bangla88/9	7.8	28.5	46	5.01	18.47	14.51	40.06	36.42	-10.67	-6.71	-11.56	-7.92
Boliv90	6.7	17.8	86	9.30	4.91	8.02	13.70	21.10	1.79	-1.32	4.10	-3.30
Botsw85/6	42.6	54	58	16.32	11.31	4.69	26.92	12.85	31.29	37.91	27.08	41.15
Brazil85	16.4	26.7	123	23.76	2.31	3.27	7.42	9.23	14.09	13.13	19.28	17.47
Brazil89	20.6	31.1	124	25.90	2.27	3.01	7.31	8.55	18.33	17.59	23.79	22.55
Chile89	6.1	15.6	133	31.97	1.95	2.46	6.49	7.10	4.15	3.64	9.11	8.50
China85	2.6	11.1	74	5.64	6.75	12.96	17.73	32.83	-4.15	-10.36	-6.63	-21.73
China90	4.7	13.5	82	7.78	5.44	9.52	14.87	24.69	-0.74	-4.82	-1.37	-11.19
Colmba88	4.6	9.1	205	24.61	.78	3.16	3.09	8.94	3.82	1.44	6.01	0.16
Colmba91	2.9	6.6	223	24.10	.65	3.23	2.67	9.11	2.25	-0.33	3.93	-2.51
CRica81	22.7	33.9	65	23.29	8.89	3.33	22.14	9.39	13.81	19.37	11.76	24.51
CRica89	11	18.8	97	23.23	3.81	3.34	11.14	9.41	7.19	7.66	7.66	9.39
DomRep89	11.2	22.3	96	15.79	3.89	4.83	11.34	13.23	7.31	6.37	10.96	9.07
Ethop81/2	9.1	31.6	47	1.98	17.65	35.19	38.61	82.44	-8.55	-26.09	-7.01	-50.84
Ghana 87/8	4.7	15.3	73	8.19	6.95	9.06	18.15	23.60	-2.25	-4.36	-2.85	-8.30
Ghana88/9	4.5	15.1	73	8.36	6.95	8.89	18.15	23.19	-2.45	-4.39	-3.05	-8.09
Guate86/7	45.4	60	44	14.50	20.29	5.25	43.23	14.26	25.11	40.15	16.77	45.74
Guate89	38.8	51.6	56	14.84	12.18	5.13	28.59	13.97	26.62	33.67	23.01	37.63
Hond89	46.2	60.5	45	8.81	19.35	8.45	41.60	22.13	26.85	37.75	18.90	38.37
Hung89	0.1	0.1	159	30.14	1.34	2.60	4.78	7.48	-1.24	-2.50	-4.68	-7.38
India83	46.8	73.5	27	4.19	57.01	17.22	99.90	42.66	-10.21	29.58	-26.40	30.84
India89/90	43.3	70.9	28	5.12	52.79	14.21	93.86	35.74	-9.49	29.09	-22.96	35.16
Indon84	15.8	38.7	45	9.72	19.35	7.69	41.60	20.30	-3.55	8.11	-2.90	18.40
Indon90	5.4	21.7	56	11.63	12.18	6.48	28.59	17.33	-6.78	-1.08	-6.89	4.37

Appendix B, Table 4 (cont.)

Ivoire85	5.4	14.3	99	9.99	3.65	7.49	10.76	19.81	1.75	-2.09	3.54	-5.51
Ivoire88	4.9	15.7	70	8.90	7.60	8.37	19.50	21.93	-2.70	-3.47	-3.80	-6.23
Jama88	2.3	6.5	128	15.39	2.12	4.96	6.93	13.53	0.18	-2.66	-0.43	-7.03
Jama90	0.03	1.9	143	16.38	1.68	4.67	5.73	12.80	-1.65	-4.64	-3.83	-10.90
Jordan91	5.7	18.3	75	17.36	6.56	4.42	17.32	12.17	-0.86	1.28	0.98	6.13
Kenya81/3	48.7	63	40	5.94	24.82	12.32	50.91	31.34	23.88	36.38	12.09	31.66
Lestho86/7	35.5	52.3	58	6.60	11.31	11.14	26.92	28.56	24.19	24.36	25.38	23.74
Malay84	4.6	12.4	138	26.95	1.81	2.90	6.09	8.26	2.79	1.70	6.31	4.14
Malay89	0.9	6.4	154	30.29	1.43	2.59	5.04	7.45	-0.53	-1.69	1.36	-1.05
Mex84	11.4	22.9	97	32.93	3.81	2.39	11.14	6.92	7.59	9.01	11.76	15.98
Moroc84/5	2.3	7.1	95	13.66	3.98	5.56	11.55	15.03	-1.68	-3.26	-4.45	-7.93
Moroc90/1	0.2	1.8	131	14.80	2.02	5.15	6.66	14.01	-1.82	-4.95	-4.86	-12.21
Nepal84/5	17.5	44.3	40	4.17	24.82	17.29	50.91	42.83	-7.32	0.21	-6.61	1.47
Pak91	2.9	11.4	66	8.87	8.60	8.39	21.57	21.99	-5.70	-5.49	-10.17	-10.59
Panma89	19.2	27.4	109	19.76	2.98	3.90	9.12	10.85	16.22	15.30	18.28	16.55
Peru85/6	11.9	23.9	78	18.62	6.04	4.13	16.20	11.44	5.86	7.77	7.70	12.46
Phil85	17.2	34.8	55	10.44	12.65	7.18	29.49	19.05	4.55	10.02	5.31	15.75
Phil88	12.3	29.7	61	11.41	10.16	6.60	24.69	17.61	2.14	5.70	5.01	12.09
Pol85	0.6	2.7	79	24.62	5.88	3.16	15.85	8.94	-5.28	-2.56	-13.15	-6.24
Pol89	0.7	3.2	84	26.64	5.17	2.93	14.26	8.34	-4.47	-2.23	-11.06	-5.14
Rwnda83/5	26.4	57.5	34	4.00	35.01	17.97	67.28	44.38	-8.61	8.43	-9.78	13.12
SLank85	26.2	46.6	53	10.84	13.68	6.93	31.42	18.44	12.52	19.27	15.18	28.16
Tanzn91	30.5	42.6	73	2.79	6.95	25.36	18.15	60.95	23.55	5.14	24.45	-18.35
Thai88	0.4	10.4	101	19.20	3.50	4.01	10.40	11.13	-3.10	-3.61	0.00	-0.73
Tunis85	1	4.6	136	20.35	1.86	3.79	6.24	10.57	-0.86	-2.79	-1.64	-5.97
Tunis90	0.8	2.9	150	20.68	1.51	3.73	5.28	10.43	-0.71	-2.93	-2.38	-7.53
Uganda89/90	46.9	72.3	28	4.66	52.79	15.53	93.86	38.80	-5.89	31.37	-21.56	33.50
Venez87	2.2	6.6	151	36.50	1.49	2.17	5.22	6.32	0.71	0.03	1.38	0.28
Venez89	10.4	20.5	83	33.05	5.30	2.38	14.56	6.89	5.10	8.02	5.94	13.61
Yugo85	3.6	12.1	76	—	6.38	—	16.93	—	-2.78	—	-4.83	—
Yugo89	10.7	19.8	76	—	6.38	—	16.93	—	4.32	—	2.87	—
Zimb90	23.3	39.7	78	9.47	6.04	7.89	16.20	20.78	17.26	15.41	23.50	18.92

Appendix B, Table 5. Ranking countries by actual minus predicted poverty incidence (Under $21 line, rectangular hyperbolic fit)

(Countries listed in order of lowest ACTUAL US21 poverty incidence first)

Lowest = Rank 1

Cons	Cons rank	GNP	GNP rank	COUNTRY/Yr	Actual poverty incidence		Actual minus predicted poverty incidence		RANK by	
					US21	Rank	##U21Con	##U21GNP	##U21Con	##U21GNP
143	51	16.38	34	Jama90	0.03	1	-1.65	-4.64	22	8
159	56	30.14	51	Hung89	0.1	2	-1.24	-2.50	23	19
131	47	14.80	29	Moroc90/1	0.2	3	-1.82	-4.95	20	6
101	42	19.20	37	Thai88	0.4	4	-3.10	-3.61	15	11
145	52	25.93	48	Algeria88	0.5	5	-1.13	-2.51	24	18
79	32	24.62	46	Pol85	0.6	6	-5.28	-2.56	11	17
84	35	26.64	49	Pol89	0.7	7	-4.47	-2.23	12	20
150	53	20.68	40	Tunis90	0.8	8	-0.71	-2.93	28	14
154	55	30.29	52	Malay89	0.9	9	-0.53	-1.69	29	22
136	49	20.35	39	Tunis85	1	10	-0.86	-2.79	26	15
53	12	5.01	7	Bangla85/6	2.2	11	-11.48	-12.31	1	2
151	54	36.50	56	Venez87	2.2	12	0.71	0.03	31	26
95	37	13.66	27	Moroc84/5	2.3	14	-1.68	-3.26	21	13
128	46	15.39	31	Jama88	2.3	13	0.18	-2.66	30	16
74	26	5.64	10	China85	2.6	15	-4.15	-10.36	13	3
66	21	8.87	17	Pak91	2.9	17	-5.70	-5.49	10	5
223	58	24.10	44	Colmba91	2.9	16	2.25	-0.33	35	25
76	28	—		Yugo85	3.6	18	-2.78	—	16	
73	25	8.36	15	Ghana88/9	4.5	19	-2.45	-4.39	18	9
205	57	24.61	45	Colmba88	4.6	20	3.82	1.44	37	29
138	50	26.95	50	Malay84	4.6	21	2.79	1.70	36	30
82	33	7.78	13	China90	4.7	22	-0.74	-4.82	27	7
73	24	8.19	14	Ghana 87/8	4.7	23	-2.25	-4.36	19	10
70	22	8.90	18	Ivoire88	4.9	24	-2.70	-3.47	17	12
99	41	9.99	22	Ivoire85	5.4	26	1.75	-2.09	32	21
56	15	11.63	26	Indon90	5.4	25	-6.78	-1.08	8	24
75	27	17.36	35	Jordan91	5.7	27	-0.86	1.28	25	28
133	48	31.97	53	Chile89	6.1	28	4.15	3.64	38	31

Appendix B, Table 5 (cont.)

23	33	-1.32	1.79	29	6.7	Boliv90	19	9.30	36	86
4	2	-6.71	-10.67	30	7.8	Bangla88/9	8	5.01	10	46
1	6	-26.09	-8.55	31	9.1	Ethop81/2	1	1.98	11	47
37	41	8.02	5.10	32	10.4	Venez89	55	33.05	34	83
	39	—	4.32	33	10.7	Yugo89		—	29	76
35	43	7.66	7.19	34	11	CRica89	41	23.23	39	97
34	44	6.37	7.31	35	11.2	DomRep89	32	15.79	38	96
40	45	9.01	7.59	36	11.4	Mex84	54	32.93	40	97
36	42	7.77	5.86	37	11.9	Peru85/6	36	18.62	31	78
33	34	5.70	2.14	38	12.3	Phil88	25	11.41	19	61
38	14	8.11	-3.55	39	15.8	Indon84	21	9.72	9	45
42	48	13.13	14.09	40	16.4	Brazil85	43	23.76	44	123
41	40	10.02	4.55	41	17.2	Phil85	23	10.44	14	55
27	7	0.21	-7.32	42	17.5	Nepal84/5	4	4.17	5	40
43	49	15.30	16.22	43	19.2	Panma89	38	19.76	43	109
45	51	17.59	18.33	44	20.6	Brazil89	47	25.90	45	124
47	47	19.37	13.81	45	22.7	CRica81	42	23.29	20	65
44	50	15.41	17.26	46	23.3	Zimb90	20	9.47	30	78
46	46	19.27	12.52	47	26.2	SLank85	24	10.84	13	53
39	5	8.43	-8.61	48	26.4	Rwnda83/5	3	4.00	4	34
32	52	5.14	23.55	49	30.5	Tanzn91	2	2.79	23	73
48	54	24.36	24.19	50	35.5	Lestho86/7	12	6.60	17	58
52	56	33.67	26.62	51	38.8	Guate89	30	14.84	16	56
55	58	37.91	31.29	52	42.6	Botsw85/6	33	16.32	18	58
49	4	29.09	-9.49	53	43.3	India89/90	9	5.12	3	28
56	55	40.15	25.11	54	45.4	Guate86/7	28	14.50	7	44
54	57	37.75	26.85	55	46.2	Hond89	16	8.81	8	45
50	3	29.58	-10.21	56	46.8	India83	5	4.19	1	27
51	9	31.37	-5.89	57	46.9	Uganda89/90	6	4.66	2	28
53	53	36.38	23.88	58	48.7	Kenya81/3	11	5.94	6	40

Appendix B, Table 6. Ranking countries by actual minus predicted poverty incidence (Under $30 line, rectangular hyperbolic fit)

(Countries listed in order of lowest ACTUAL US$30 poverty incidence first)

Lowest = Rank 1

Cons	Cons rank	GNP	GNP rank	COUNTRY/Yr	Actual poverty incidence		Actual minus predicted poverty incidence		RANK by	
					US30	Rank	##U30Con	##U30GNP	##U30Con	##U30GNP
159	56	30.14	51	**Hung89**	0.1	1	-4.68	-7.38	16	14
145	52	25.93	48	**Algeria88**	1.5	2	-4.09	-7.04	18	15
131	47	14.80	29	**Moroc90/1**	1.8	3	-4.86	-12.21	14	5
143	51	16.38	34	**Jama90**	1.9	4	-3.83	-10.90	19	7
79	32	24.62	46	**Pol85**	2.7	5	-13.15	-6.24	5	17
150	53	20.68	40	**Tunis90**	2.9	6	-2.38	-7.53	24	13
84	35	26.64	49	**Pol89**	3.2	7	-11.06	-5.14	7	21
136	49	20.35	39	**Tunis85**	4.6	8	-1.64	-5.97	25	19
154	55	30.29	52	**Malay89**	6.4	9	1.36	-1.05	30	24
128	46	15.39	31	**Jama88**	6.5	10	-0.43	-7.03	27	16
223	58	24.10	44	**Colmba91**	6.6	11	3.93	-2.51	34	23
151	54	36.50	56	**Venez87**	6.6	12	1.38	0.28	31	27
95	37	13.66	27	**Moroc84/5**	7.1	13	-4.45	-7.93	17	11
205	57	24.61	45	**Colmba88**	9.1	14	6.01	0.16	39	26
101	42	19.20	37	**Thai88**	10.4	15	0.00	-0.73	28	25
74	26	5.64	10	**China85**	11.1	16	-6.63	-21.73	12	2
66	21	8.87	17	**Pak91**	11.4	17	-10.17	-10.59	8	8
76	28	—		**Yugo85**	12.1	18	-4.83	—	15	
138	50	26.95	50	**Malay84**	12.4	19	6.31	4.14	40	29
82	33	7.78	13	**China90**	13.5	20	-1.37	-11.19	26	6
99	41	9.99	22	**Ivoire85**	14.3	21	3.54	-5.51	33	20
73	25	8.36	15	**Ghana88/9**	15.1	22	-3.05	-8.09	21	10
73	24	8.19	14	**Ghana 87/8**	15.3	23	-2.85	-8.30	23	9
133	48	31.97	53	**Chile89**	15.6	24	9.11	8.50	43	32
70	22	8.90	18	**Ivoire88**	15.7	25	-3.80	-6.23	20	18
53	12	5.01	7	**Bangla85/6**	17	26	-14.42	-19.42	4	3
86	36	9.30	19	**Boliv90**	17.8	27	4.10	-3.30	35	22
75	27	17.36	35	**Jordan91**	18.3	28	0.98	6.13	29	31

Appendix B, Table 6 (cont.)

						Country				
34	41	9.39	7.66	29	18.8	**CRica89**	41	23.23	39	97
	32	—	2.87	30	19.8	**Yugo89**		—	29	76
38	38	13.61	5.94	31	20.5	**Vene89**	55	33.05	34	83
30	11	4.37	-6.89	32	21.7	**Indon90**	26	11.63	15	56
33	44	9.07	10.96	33	22.3	**DomRep89**	32	15.79	38	96
40	45	15.98	11.76	34	22.9	**Mex84**	54	32.93	40	97
36	42	12.46	7.70	35	23.9	**Peru85/6**	36	18.62	31	78
42	52	17.47	19.28	36	26.7	**Brazil85**	43	23.76	44	123
41	50	16.55	18.28	37	27.4	**Panma89**	38	19.76	43	109
12	6	-7.92	-11.56	38	28.5	**Bangla88/9**	8	5.01	10	46
35	36	12.09	5.01	39	29.7	**Phil88**	25	11.41	19	61
45	55	22.55	23.79	40	31.1	**Brazil89**	47	25.90	45	124
1	10	-50.84	-7.01	41	31.6	**Ethop81/2**	1	1.98	11	47
47	46	24.51	11.76	42	33.9	**CRica81**	42	23.29	20	65
39	37	15.75	5.31	43	34.8	**Phil85**	23	10.44	14	55
43	22	18.40	-2.90	44	38.7	**Indon84**	21	9.72	9	45
44	54	18.92	23.50	45	39.7	**Zimb90**	20	9.47	30	78
4	56	-18.35	24.45	46	42.6	**Tanzn91**	2	2.79	23	73
28	13	1.47	-6.61	47	44.3	**Nepal84/5**	4	4.17	5	40
48	48	28.16	15.18	48	46.6	**SLank85**	24	10.84	13	53
53	53	37.63	23.01	49	51.6	**Guate89**	30	14.84	16	56
46	57	23.74	25.38	50	52.3	**Lestho86/7**	12	6.60	17	58
55	58	41.15	27.08	51	54	**Botsw85/6**	33	16.32	18	58
37	9	13.12	-9.78	52	57.5	**Rwnda83/5**	3	4.00	4	34
56	49	45.74	16.77	53	60	**Guate86/7**	28	14.50	7	44
54	51	38.37	18.90	54	60.5	**Hond89**	16	8.81	8	45
50	47	31.66	12.09	55	63	**Kenya81/3**	11	5.94	6	40
52	2	35.16	-22.96	56	70.9	**India89/90**	9	5.12	3	28
51	3	33.50	-21.56	57	72.3	**Uganda89/90**	6	4.66	2	28
49	1	30.84	-26.40	58	73.5	**India83**	5	4.19	1	27

Table 2B. Positive deviants in
private consumption poverty: Country details

Country	Av. rank	$21 v. $30	Direct v. log-log	Cons. v. GNP	Earlier v. later	Comments
Bangladesh 85/86	2.7	1.2 v. 2.1	–	–	{Varied falls:	All measures for
Bangladesh 88/88	9.1	Each $21 4 to 10 ranks better	log-log 3-8 ranks up [better]	Cons. 2-6 ranks up	{log-log ranks {fall more than {direct; GNP {more than cons.	Bangladesh esp. poverty, seem over-optimistic
Pakistan 1991	5.2	–	Direct 3-8 ranks up	–	–	
Poland 1985 (9)	10.0	$30 ranks better	Direct 4-8 up for cons. No ref. GNP	Cons. 15-19 ranks up direct; 6-14 logs	Falls av. 3 ranks	
Indonesia 1990	16.0	$21 7 ranks up on GNP; 14-21 on cons.	Dir. 7-10 up for cons.	Cons. 9-19 ranks higher	Big rises since 1984, when usually not a positive deviant	
China 1985	5.7	(neg.)	Dir. 7 up for cons., only 1 for GNP	Cons. 4 up dir., 10 up in logs.	{Falls av. 11 {ranks on cons.,	
China 1990	12.9	–	Dir. 12-14 up for cons., only 1-3 for GNP		{3.5 ranks on {GNP	
Côte d'Ivoire 88	12.4	$21 3 to 6 up on GNP	Direct 3-6 up on GNP, 7-12 up on cons.	GNP 2-5 up at $21	{Big improve- {ment 85-8,	
Côte d'Ivoire 85	21.2	–	Direct 12-13 up on cons.; worse on GNP	GNP 7-8 up direct, 10-14 up log-log	{except $30 {pov. on GNP	
Ethiopia 1981-82	8.9	11-12 up direct	Log-log up (2.9) on cons. worse or same on GNP	Same ranking on direct; cons 5-9 better in logs	–	
Ghana 87/8, 88/9	11.9	–	Direct 4 to 12 worse, except once the same	GNP 6-12 ranks up at $21, and log-log at $30	neg.	
India 83, 89-90	39.5	–	Rank is 1-4 on log-log cons.; ll other readings, 41 to 58 (log-log/dir, 21/30 x cons/GNP)		neg.	Rwanda 83-5, Uganda 89-90 show same pattern
Morocco 84-5	13.0	$30 always up, av. 5 ranks	Dir 1-4 up on GNP, 5-10 up on cons.	GNP 4-9 up, except same on "direct $30"	{Rankings down {on cons., up on {GNP	{Sharp {divergence of {GNP farm
Morocco 90-1	11.9	$30 6 up; but same on GNP	Log-log 1-6 ranks up	GNP ranks 8, 2, 6, 5; cons. ranks 23, 17, 20, 14		{cons., 84-85
Jamaica 1988, 90	17.6	$30 3 to 7 up but same on log-log GNP	Log-log up av. 4 in '90; down av. 3 in '88	GNP ranks 11-14 up, but 18-19 for direct cons. in 90	Down for cons., up for GNP; by 8-9 in logs.	
Nepal 1984-5	24.4	$21 av. 5 up, except 16 up on dir. cons.	Log-log up av. 14-24 on cons., 0-7 on GNP	Cons. 15 ranks up on log-log; 6 up on direct	–	
Thailand 1988	17.5	$21 2-3 up dir., 10-14 up in logs	Dir. 7-13 up at $30, no rel. at $21	Dir. cons. 2 ranks up; log-log: cons. 3-4 ranks down	–	

Source: Table 2A, and Appendix B, Tables 1-6.

Appendix C

Analysis of positive deviants

1. Analysis of rankings

Table 2B looks at the top performers in one or more of the eight column rankings of "positive deviance" given in Table 2A.[55] Table 2B ranks these performers, on each of four criteria, in decreasing order with respect to improvement on the expected PCP incidence, given the resources-per-person. Table 2B thus asks four questions.

- Does the country (or country/year combination) do better, relative to regression predictions from the resource base, for the very poor (below $21 at US 1985 PPP per month) or for the poor as a whole (below $30)?

- Does the country appear to be a better performer as compared with the expectations from a linear or a log-log relationship between resources and poverty incidence? (This is a test of the stability of the finding of positive deviance; in addition, if a log-log relationship is preferable, good anti-poverty performance is more telling with regard to it than with regard to a linear regression line.)

- Is anti-PCP performance more "positively deviant" with respect to the prediction (i) from average per-person consumption, or (ii) from average per-person GNP? If success is much more marked on (i) than on (ii), that suggests measures (from incentives for more labour intensity to land reform) tending to distribute private consumption relatively equally between poor and non-poor. If success is much more marked in (ii) than on (i), it suggests state action (out of GNP resources other than private consumption) to enhance the well-being of the poor. (The author is not sure about this interpretation, nor about whether it applies similarly at all levels of average real PCP, consumption and GNP; comments are requested.)

---

55. Table 2A only gives the top 30 country/year combinations. Data for the others may be found in Tables 1-6 in Appendix B.

- Where there are two surveys for the same country, how do they compare?

2. Commentary on countries

Bangladesh, strikingly, ranks clearly highest on the eight scales of "positive deviance" in Table 2A taken together (see Table 2B). The recorded PCP incidence on the source data [Chen et al. 1993] are, however, astonishingly low (e.g. compared with India's, or even Costa Rica's). There must be strong suspicion that the low recorded PCP incidence, and hence the apparent positive deviance, are partly due to problems associated with the conversion of its resources-per-head (and especially those of its poor) into US-PPP dollars [Ravallion 1995: personal communication]. To the extent that this apparently splendid performance can be taken at face value – these are not bad household surveys, and the caveat against rejecting inconvenient findings must be recalled – we should note that (1) it is even stronger in reducing the incidence of ultra-poverty below expected value than for moderate poverty; (2) the deviance from the expected PCP incidence on the direct regression is better than on the log-log regression; (3) also in that year only, relatively equal private consumption – rather than action out of other sources of GNP to enrich the poor – seems mainly responsible for the good performance, which conforms to the general perception of a low degree of land and other inequality [World Bank 1994: Table 30] combined with weak public services; (4) small falls in "positive deviance" from 1985-6 to 1988-9, especially with regard to predictions from mean real GNP, suggest that Bangladesh (while remaining a very strong performer) had fallen further behind other countries in the sample in respect of poverty-oriented state services.

China is another outstanding performer on "positive deviance" overall. However, its PCP incidence falls less far below its predicted value:

- on direct than on log-log regressions;
- relative to mean real consumption than to mean real GNP; and
- above all, in 1990 than in 1985.

In interpreting these data, we should recall that the poverty-reducing effect of the high degree of equality within small areas of China is offset by the poverty-increasing effect of China's high regional *in*equality. Indeed, the proportion of private household income enjoyed by the poorest quintile of persons is only 6.4 per cent, as against 8.8 per cent of private household *consumption* in India, 8.4 per cent in Pakistan and 9.5 per cent in Bangladesh [World Bank 1994: 220].[56] China's degree of positive deviance fell sharply between 1985 and 1990; indeed, on some scales – notably the crucially important scale measuring a country's "PCP distance" from the log-log regression line of PCP on mean private consumption – China was by 1990 not a positive deviant at all. *China's rapid growth meant that poverty incidence nevertheless fell substantially*; the poor may do better under such circumstances than from a high level of, or sharp increase in, "positive deviance". Earlier, however – during agricultural liberalization and land reform, in 1977-84 – China had reduced poverty via rapid growth *and* probably falling inequality, and thus probably rising PCP positive deviance.

Indonesia in 1990 is an interesting case of a country that emerged into strong positive deviance – and also experienced substantial absolute falls in poverty incidence – only during adjustment. It had shown no positive deviance in 1984. By 1990, improvement on the regression lines was especially marked in regard to keeping down the incidence of ultra-poverty (below $21/person/month). In 1990, Indonesia ranked much higher with respect to the improvement of PCP incidence upon the regression predictions from mean consumption, as compared with improvement on regression predictions from mean GNP.

India is statistically fascinating. (Recall that its household survey data, from the National Sample Survey, are among the world's best; and the GNP data are certainly not bad.) India is a huge *negative* deviant – ranked between 41st and 58th (bottom) in both the reported survey years, 1983 and 1989-90 – on six of the eight scales in

---

56. Expenditure is more equally distributed than income when both are correctly recorded. This would mean that the above comparison overstates the extent to which welfare is more unequal in China than in India. However, it is known that in household surveys the relatively rich are much more likely than others to conceal income, and that this is much less true of expenditure. So the contrast in the text may not, after all, greatly overstate the difference in overall inequality between China and India.

Table 2A, in the sense that its PCP incidence is much more than would be expected from its mean real consumption and GNP. Yet on two crucial scales – that predicting the log of PCP incidence from the log of mean consumption per person – India ranks near the top (from first to fourth) in both years, measuring PCP below $21 as well as below $30. A linear rather than a functional form, by failing to allow for heteroscedasticity, is especially severe in its assessments of the "deviance" of countries with very low values of dependent and/or independent variables; so the log-log relationship is likely to be much preferable in this case. The extreme negative deviance of PCP compared to the regression predictions against GNP, even in log-log form – compared with the high positive deviance on this form when regressing against mean consumption – may suggest something about (1) the possible success of public policy in redistributing private consumption expenditures (and in some cases access to land and other assets) to the poor, but also (2) the severe bias against the poor of the impact of most other forms of state expenditure. Of course, such explanations can be valid only if they apply more strongly to the Indian data than to others in the sample.

Moving to West Africa – and given the widespread controversy about the long-delayed, yet allegedly successful and poverty-aware, adjustment process of **Ghana** as compared with **Côte d'Ivoire** – the good, yet similar and rather constant, "positive deviance" of these two countries' PCP incidence is striking.

Appendix D

Comparison of results with those of Anand and Ravallion

Anand and Ravallion [1993: 141, n. 22] regress "80-life expectancy" on real GNP per person, PCP below the $30 cut-off, and real public health spending per person for 22 countries. They find:

$(1AR)$ $log(80 - LE) = -1.08 - 0.28 \ log(G) - 0.21 \ log(PCP\$30) + 0.30 \ log(PH/psn)$
$\qquad\qquad\quad (2.34) \quad (1.34) \qquad (2.36) \qquad\qquad (3.02) \qquad\qquad r^2 = 0.71$

This implies that "once we control for [public health spending per person and PCP at the $30 level] we find that there is no significant partial correlation between life expectancy and average [GNP] across these 22 countries, and the infant mortality rate and under-five mortality [also] behave this way" [ibid.: 141, 143].

Controlling for public education spending when Anand and Ravallion regress *literacy* on GNP and PCP has almost the opposite effect as controlling for public health spending when they regress health variables on GNP and PCP [ibid.: 143, fn 26]:

$(2AR)$ $log(100 - L) = -9.51 + 1.12 \ log(G) - 0.27 \ log(PCP\$30) + 0.33 \ log(PE/psn)$
$\qquad\qquad\quad (1.86) \quad (2.56) \qquad (1.24) \qquad\qquad (1.02) \qquad\qquad r^2 = 0.56$

Thus, the Anand-Ravallion double-logged regressions (for 22 countries) show that, when the interaction with public spending on health is allowed for, illiteracy is strongly associated with real (PPP) GNP per person but not with private consumption poverty incidence at the $30-per-month PCP level; however, once the interaction with public spending on education is allowed for, infant mortality is strongly associated with PCP at $30 but not with real GNP per person. Our double-logged regressions (on 54 to 56 country-year observations, but ignoring public spending) suggest that both infant mortality and illiteracy are associated with real PPP GNP per person; but the link between private consumption poverty and infant mortality (strong in the Anand-Ravallion data) is weak and only marginally significant; whereas the link between PCP and illiteracy (absent in the Anand-Ravallion data once public spending in the sector is allowed for) becomes strong and clearly significant, though the elasticity of illiteracy to PCP is still only one-third as great as to per-person real GNP.

The differences between Anand and Ravallion [1993] and our Table 3 may be due to their success in incorporating data for public spending on health and education, or to our larger sample, or to other factors. In any case, interpretation is not possible until these regressions are replaced by (or used to build and test) causally ordered models. In particular, we need to estimate the possible impact, upon per-person public spending on health and education, of GNP per person (probably strongly positive) and of PCP (arguably: positive in more egalitarian countries, otherwise negative).

Appendix E

New international evidence on resources, poverty reduction and human development

The data set – used in Chapter 3 of this book for international comparisons of (i) real national-accounts GNP per person, (ii) real national-accounts private consumption per person, both at 1985 purchasing power parity (PPP) – was Penn World Tables 5.1. After we had completed Chapter 3, a new data set, PWT 5.6, became available on the Internet for (i). Martin Ravallion used PWT 5.6 to re-estimate, for the most recent nation-wide household survey in each developing and transitional economy with adequate data, (iii) mean survey private consumption, (iv) proportions of persons in poverty, using new $30 and $21 per person per month '1985 PPP' poverty lines as re-estimated from PWT 5.6; he kindly shared his data with us for the work in this Appendix. There were substantial differences between PWT 5.1 and PWT 5.6, mainly in Asia: notably, the estimates of purchasing-power parity in Bangladesh were considerably higher (so that poverty estimates were lower) in the more recent PWT 5.6 calculations than in PWT 5.1, whereas there was a large shift in the opposite direction (lower PPP consumption and GNP, and hence greater estimated $30 and $21 poverty) in China and Pakistan.

These new data offered the chance to test the robustness of – and to update – our estimates, in Chapter 3, of the extent to which (a) international differences in real resources (mean private survey PPP consumption, or mean PPP GNP as a share of the US's) appear to explain international differences in poverty, and (b) international differences in mean real resources and in poverty incidence suffice to explain differences in health and education indicators.

We report the results of enquiry (a) in Table E1, and of enquiry (b) in Table E2.

Table E1 should be read alongside Table 2 on p. 19. As can be seen, the results are qualitatively similar, though, encouragingly, the larger and more reliable PWT 5.6 data set gives consistently higher adjusted r^2. Mean private consumption continues to explain a larger

Table E1. Poverty regressions (selected years 1982-1994)

		Dependent variables			
		Surveyed % of persons with private consumption in 1985 PPP US$ (PWT 5.6) less than:			
		$21 (= P1)		$30 (= P2)	
Explanatory variables per capita	Private consumption (C) 1985 PPP	(1bis) P1= 44.68 (11.11)*	-0.296 C (-7.30)*	(5bis) P2= 62.45 (15.15)*	-0.390 C (-9.39)*
		adj. R-sqr.= 0.511	F = 53.26	adj. R-sqr.= 0.635	F = 88.16
		(2bis) ln_P1= 10.66 (8.14)*	-1.98 ln_C (-6.56)*	(6bis) ln_P2= 9.86 (9.89)*	-1.64 ln_C (-7.16)*
		adj. R-sqr.= 0.467	F = 42.98	adj. R-sqr.= 0.501	F = 51.29
	GNP (=G) 1985 PPP % of US GNP	(3bis) P1= 34.76 (8.33)*	-1.19 G (-4.58)*	(7bis) P2= 50.08 (10.88)*	-1.62 G (-5.66)*
		adj. R-sqr.= 0.285	F = 20.97	adj. R-sqr.= 0.383	F = 32.04
		(4bis) ln_P1= 4.59 (6.29)*	-1.04 ln_G (-3.5)*	(8bis) ln_P2= 5.27 (9.97)*	-1.05 ln_G (-4.92)*
		adj. R-sqr.= 0.190	F = 12.27	adj. R-sqr.= 0.317	F = 24.20

Notes: Figures in brackets are t-statistics; * means significant at 1%.
The sample size is 51 for all regressions, except for regression (4) where it is 49 (Thailand and Hungary have values of $P1 = 0$)
Logs are to base e.

Table E2. Illiteracy and infant mortality regressions

Explanatory variables:
- **G** = GNP/capita % of US GNP 1985 PPP
- **P1** = % below $21 1985 PPP (PWT 5.6) private consumption per month
- **P2** = % below $30 1985 PPP (PWT 5.6) private consumption per month

Dependent variables

Infant mortality (M, per 1,000 live births)

Eq.	Constant	G term	P term	adj. R-sqr.	
(9bis) M=	89.26 (8.80)*	-2.61 G (-5.40)*	+0.41 P1 (1.81)	0.544	F = 30.81
(10bis) ln_M=	5.38 (18.36)*	-0.645 ln_G (-6.51)*	+0.03 ln_P1 (0.69)	0.543	F = 29.56
(11bis) M=	88.78 (6.89)*	-2.46 G (-4.75)*	+0.39 P12 (1.94)	0.548	F = 24.97
(12bis) ln_M=	5.18 (13.92)*	-0.619 ln_G (-5.87)*	+0.07 ln_P2 (1.20)	0.560	F = 32.86

Illiteracy (I, proportion of over-15s)

Eq.	Constant	G term	P term	adj. R-sqr.	
(13bis) I=	47.67 (6.62)*	-1.36 G (-3.95)*	+0.07 P1 (0.42)	0.316	F = 12.56
(14bis) ln_I=	4.72 (8.70)*	-0.669 ln_G (-3.64)*	-0.02 ln_P1 (0.19)	0.226	F = 8.0
(15bis) I=	44.3 (5.20)*	-1.25 G (-3.40)*	+0.11 P2 (0.80)	0.341	F = 13.95
(16bis) ln_I=	4.01 (5.67)*	-0.577 ln_G (-2.89)*	+0.15 ln_P2 (1.37)	0.287	F = 11.06

Notes: Figures in brackets are t-statistics; * means significant at 1%, ** at 5%.
The sample size is 51 for all regressions, except for regressions (10) and (14) where it is 49 (Thailand and Hungary have values of P1 = 0).
Logs are to base e.

share of variance in poverty than does mean GNP. In the log-log equations, the elasticity of poverty to mean GNP remains very close to unity, and to mean private consumption is far higher.

We were able to show that the log-log form is clearly superior to the direct linear form. All the linear relationships between poverty and mean GNP or mean private consumption in Table E1, but none of the log-log relationships, suffer from both incorrect functional form and heteroscedasticity.[57] Conversely, two of the four log-log relationships in Table E1 (equations 4b and 8b) suffer from non-normality of residual errors. Does this matter? In equation 4b, it may. In equation 8b, excluding (or adding dummy variables for) Morocco, Thailand and Hungary cures non-normality, without significantly changing the beta-coefficients or the significance levels. We can thus accept eq. 8b, especially if there is genuinely something about the outliers, in the particular survey year, that renders ln (mean GNP) an especially poor predictor of ln (poverty) at the high-poverty end (or the low-poverty end) *only*. In Thailand and Hungary, reported private consumption poverty is extremely small, even given mean GNP or private consumption; there is reason, especially in Thailand, to expect the purchasing-power of the poor to be over-reported.

Table E2 shows a more mixed impact on the findings of Table 3 (p. 27) of the improved and more recent PWT 5.6 estimates of real per-person resources and poverty. Levels of mean GNP become somewhat more important, but *independently of mean GNP or mean private consumption* the new data suggest that poverty is even less significant, as an influence on the 'misery variables', than in Table 3 suggested. The adjusted r^2 improve slightly with the better data, except for the log-log fit to illiteracy, where the adjusted r^2 declines slightly. Again, the Ramsey RESET test clearly prefers the log-log to the linear functional form: as illiteracy and infant mortality decline, so a greater 'effort' is needed to reduce them further – effort in terms of extra average resources and/or, possibly, their concentration upon the consumption of the poor). Of the log-log equations, all except 12bis

---

57. Ramsey's RESET test of functional form and Bera and Jarque's test for normality were used (see M.H. and B. Pesaran, *Microfit 3.0*, Oxford University Press, 1991). We tested for heteroscedasticity by regressing squared residuals on squared fitted values of the dependent variable (D. Blanchet, 'Estimating the relationship between population growth and aggregate economic growth in LDCs: Methodological problems', in *Consequences of Rapid Population Growth in Developing Countries*, Taylor and Francis, New York, 1988).

have non-normal residual errors; normality is restored by dummy variables for (or removal of) Jamaica and Venezuela, with little effect on the size or significance of the betas.

The central conclusions of Chapter 3 remain. If we accept the preferred log-log relationships, differences among developing countries in the level (growth) of per-person real private consumption is associated with about half of international differences in the level (rate of decline) of private consumption poverty; the elasticity is well over 1.5. Real average GNP has less effect than real average private consumption, though the adjusted r^2 and elasticities are still substantial. Jointly, international differences in real resource variables and poverty are associated with about a quarter of differences in infant mortality, and just over half differences in illiteracy. There are intriguing exceptions to these relationships.

Both these exceptions, and the fact that half or less of the international differences are explained, point to major scope for poverty-specific policies of the sort considered in Chapters 4-6 of this book. Growth is associated with poverty reduction. Growth, and perhaps the reduction of private consumption poverty, are associated with health and literacy. But the associations tell us only about half the story. Even of that 'half', far from all is a simple testimony to better macro-economic policy for growth, important as that is. The associations are two-way: wider access for and advancement of the poor, and better health and literacy, lead to faster growth as well as vice versa. The improved data in Tables E1 and E2 confirm this message.

Bibliography

Aghian, B. 1994. "On the design of a credit agreement with peer-monitoring". Discussion Paper No. 55. London: London School of Economics: STICERD.

Ahmad, E. 1993. "Protecting the vulnerable: Social security and public policy". In Lipton and van der Gaag (eds.)

Alderman, H. 1991. "Food subsidies and the poor". In G.P. Psacharopoulos (ed.), *Essays on poverty, equity and growth*. Oxford: Pergamon Press.

Aleem, J. 1989. "Rural credit policies: A case study in Pakistan". Annapolis: World Bank Conference on Rural Institutions. In Hoff et al.(eds.), 1993.

Anand, S. and R. Kanbur. 1991. "Public policy and basic needs provision: Intervention and achievement in Sri Lanka". In Drèze and Sen (eds.).

Anand, S. and M. Ravallion. 1993. "Human development in poor countries: On the role of private incomes and public services", in *Journal of Economic Perspectives*, Vol. 7, No. 1.

BAAC (Bank for Agriculture and Agricultural Co-operatives, Thailand). 1988. Research Division: Planning Department. "Financial innovations for the rural poor: The BAAC-DAE pilot project". In Quinones (ed.).

Bandyopadhyay, N. 1985. "An evaluation of policies and programmes for the alleviation of rural poverty in India", in Islam (ed.), *Strategies for alleviating poverty in rural Asia*. Bangkok: ILO.

Basu, K. 1981. "Food for work programmes: Beyond roads that get washed away". *Economic and Political Weekly*, January 3-10.

Beaton, G. and H. Ghassemi. 1982. "Supplementary feeding programs for young children in developing countries", in *American Journal of Clinical Nutrition*, Vol. 35 (supplement).

Behrman, J. and A. Deolalikar. 1988. "Health and nutrition". In H. Chenery and T.N. Srinivasan (eds.), *Handbook of development economics: Vol. 1*. Amsterdam: North Holland.

Bell, C. 1989. "Interactions between institutions and informal credit agencies in rural India". In Hoff et al. (eds.), 1993.

——. 1990. "Reforming property rights in land and tenancy", in *World Bank Research Observer*, Vol. 5, No. 2.

Berg, A. 1987. *Malnutrition: What can be done?: Lessons from World Bank experience*. Baltimore: Johns Hopkins.

Berry, A.R. and W.S. Cline. 1979. *Agrarian structure and productivity in developing countries*. Baltimore: Johns Hopkins.

Besley, T. 1995. "Savings, credit and insurance". In J. Behrman and T.N. Srinivasan (eds.), *Handbook of development economics: Vol. 3*. Amsterdam: North Holland.

—— and S. Coate. 1991. *Group lending, repayment incentives and social collateral*. RPDS Discussion Paper No. 152. Princeton: Princeton University, Woodrow Wilson Centre.

—— and R. Kanbur. 1993. "The principles of targeting". In Lipton and van der Gaag (eds.).

Bhende, M., T. Walker, S. Lieberman and J. Venkataraman. 1992. "EGS and the poor: Evidence from longitudinal village studies", in *Economic and Political Weekly*, Vol. 27, No. 13.

Binswanger, H. 1981. "Attitudes towards risk: Theoretical implications of an experiment in South India", in *Economic Journal*, Vol. 91, December.

——, K. Deininger, K. and G. Feder. 1995. "Power, distortions, revolt and reform in agricultural land relations". In J. Behrman and T.N. Srinivasan (eds.), *Handbook of development economics: Vol. 3*. Amsterdam: North Holland.

—— and S.R. Khandker. 1992. *The impact of formal finance on the rural economy of India.* Working Paper 9420. Washington DC.: World Bank (Agriculture and Rural Development Department).

—— and J. von Braun. 1993. "Technological change and commercialization in agriculture: Impact on the poor". In Lipton and van der Gaag (eds.).

Birdsall, N. and E. James. 1993. "Efficiency and equity in social spending: How and why governments misbehave". In Lipton and van der Gaag (eds.).

Boyce, J. 1987. *Agrarian impasse in Bengal: Institutional constraints to technological change.* Oxford: Oxford University Press.

Bryson, J., J. Chudy and J. Pines. 1991. *Food for work: A review of the 1980s with recommendations for the 1990s.* Washington, DC.: USAID.

Carter, N. and D. Mesbah. 1991. "Land reform and the rural poor in Latin America". In Lipton and van der Gaag (eds.).

Chadha, G.K. 1994. *Employment, earnings and poverty: A study of rural India and Indonesia.* London: Sage.

Chambers, R., R. Longhurst and A. Pacey (eds.). 1981. *Seasonal dimensions to rural poverty.* London: Pinter.

Chen, S., G. Datt and M. Ravallion. 1993. "Is poverty increasing in the developing world?" Working Paper 1146. Washington, DC.: World Bank (Policy Research Department).

Chowdhury, A. and M. Mahmood. 1991. "Credit for the rural poor – the case of BRAC in Bangladesh", in *Small Enterprise Development*, Vol. 2, No. 3.

Clay, E. and B. Harriss. 1988. "Emergency measures for food security: How relevant to Africa is the South Asian model?" In D. Curtis, M. Hubbard and A. Shepherd (eds.), *Preventing famine: Policies and prospects for Africa.* London: Routledge.

Copestake, J. 1992. "The integrated rural development programme". In B. Harriss, S. Guhan and R. Cassen (eds.), *Poverty in India.* Bombay: Oxford University Press.

Dandekar, K. 1983. *Employment guarantee scheme: An employment opportunity for women.* Study No. 67. Pune: Gokhale Institute of Politics and Economics.

Dantwala, M. 1989. "Estimates of demand for credit and its role in poverty alleviation", in *Indian Journal of Agricultural Economics*, Vol. 44, No. 4.

Datar, C. 1990. *Maharashtra Employment Guarantee Scheme.* Bombay: Tata Institute of Social Sciences.

David, C. and K. Otsuka, (eds.). 1994. *Modern rice technology and income distribution in Asia.* Boulder, Colorado: Lynne Reinner Publishers.

Deolalikar, A. and R. Gaiha. 1992. "Targeting of rural public works: Are women less likely to participate?" Washington, DC.: International Food Policy Research Institute. Mimeo.

Desai, V. 1975. "A spatial approach to rural unemployment", in *Kurukshetra*, Vol. 1, November 9-11.

de Soto, H. 1989. *The other path.* New York: Harper and Row.

Dev, M. 1994. *Maharashta's employment guarantee scheme: Lessons from long experience.* Ahmedabad: Indira Gandhi Institute of Development Research. Mimeo.

Donovan, W. 1973. *Rural works and employment: Description and preliminary analysis of a land army project in Mysore State, India.* Occasional Paper No. 60. Ithaca, NY: Cornell. Prepared for USAID by the Department of Agricultural Economics, Cornell University.

Drèze, J. 1988. "Social insecurity in India". London: London School of Economics (STICERD). Mimeo.

——. 1990. "Famine prevention in India". In Drèze and Sen, (eds.).

—— and A.K. Sen. 1989. *Hunger and public action.* Oxford: Clarendon.

—— and A.K. Sen (eds.). 1989/1990/1991. *The political economy of hunger [1989 (Vol. I: Entitlements and well-being); 1990 (Vol II: Famine prevention): 1991 (Vol. III: Endemic hunger)].* Oxford: Clarendon.

—— et al. 1992. *Economic mobility and agricultural labour in rural India: A case study.* STICERD Discussion Paper DEP35.

Easter, C. (ed.). 1993. *Strategies for poverty reduction.* London: Commonwealth Secretariat (Food Production and Rural Development Division).

Echeverri-Gent, J. 1988. "The political means of effective development: Comparing public works programmes in Maharashtra and West Bengal". Paper presented at 40th annual meeting of the Association for Asian Studies. San Francisco.

el-Ghonemy, R. 1990. *The political economy of rural poverty.* London: Routledge.

Fernandez, A.P. (n.d.?) 1993. *The Myrada experience.* Bangalore: MYRADA.

Fields, G. 1989. "Changes in poverty and inequality in developing countries", in *World Bank Research Observer*, Vol. 4.

Gaiha, R. 1994. *Design of poverty alleviation strategy in rural areas.* Rome: FAO.

——. 1994a. "Does agricultural growth matter in poverty alleviation?" Delhi: Faculty of Management Studies, University of Delhi. Mimeo.

Galab, S. 1993. "Rural employment programmes: A case for involving voluntary organisations", in *Economic and Political Weekly*, Vol. 28, No. 10.

Getubig, I. 1993. "The role of credit in poverty alleviation: the Asian experience". In M. Bamberger and A. Aziz (eds.), *The design and management of sustainable projects to alleviate poverty in South Asia.* Washington DC.: World Bank (EDI Seminar Series).

Gianchandani, D. 1991. "Summary of discussions". In D. Gianchandani (ed.), *Minimum wages in government sponsored rural employment programmes.* Jaipur: Institute of Development Studies.

Glaessner, P. et al. 1994. *Poverty alleviation and social investment funds: The Latin American experience.* Discussion Paper No. 261. Washington, DC.: World Bank.

Gopal Iyer, K. 1993. "Evaluation of landceiling measures in Bihar". In B.N. Yugandhar and K. Gopal Iyer (eds.), *Land reform in India, Vol.1: Bihar – Institutional constraints.* New Delhi: Sage.

Gopinath, C., G. Asan and V. Dax. 1978. *Pilot intensive rural employment project in Trithala block of Kerala: An evaluation.* Monograph No. 74. Ahmedabad: Centre for Management in Agriculture, Indian Institute of Management.

Greer, J. and E. Thorbecke. 1986. *Food poverty and consumption patterns in Kenya.* Geneva: ILO.

Harriss, B. 1989. "The intra-family distribution of hunger in South Asia". In Drèze and Sen (eds.).

Harvey, C. and S.P. Lewis. 1990. *Policy choice and development performance in Botswana.* Basingstoke: Macmillan.

Hayami, Y., A.R. Quisumbing and L. Adriano. 1990. *Towards an alternative land reform paradigm: A Philippine perspective.* Manila: Ateneo de Manila University Press.

Hazell, P., C. Pomareda and A. Valdes. 1986. *Crop insurance for agricultural development.* Baltimore: Johns Hopkins.

—— and C. Ramasamy, 1991. *The Green Revolution reconsidered.*

Heaver, R. 1989. *Improving family planning, health, and nutrition in India: Experience from some World Bank-assisted programs.* Discussion Paper No. 59. Washington, DC.: World Bank.

Herring, R. and R. Edwards. 1983. "Guaranteeing employment to the rural poor: Social functions and class interests in the employment guarantee scheme in Western India", in *World Development,* Vol. 11, No. 7.

Himmelfarb, G. 1984. *The idea of poverty.* London: Faber.

Hirschman, A. 1971. *A bias for hope : Essays on development and Latin America.* New Haven: Yale University Press.

Hirway, I. 1991. "Poverty alleviation programmes in India: Issues and experience". In Ministry of Foreign Affairs, *Poverty reduction in India*. The Hague.

Hoff, K., A. Braverman and J. Stiglitz (eds.). 1993. *The economics of rural organisation*. New York: Oxford University Press, for World Bank.

Holt, S. and H. Ribe. 1991. *Developing financial institutions for the rural poor and reducing barriers to access for women*. Discussion Paper No. 117. Washington, DC.: World Bank.

Hossain, M. 1988. *Credit for alleviation of rural poverty: The Grameen Bank in Bangladesh*. Research Report No. 55. Washington, DC.: International Food Policy Research Institute.

Howes, M. 1982. "The creation and appropriation of value in irrigated agriculture". In M. Howes and M. Greeley (eds.), *Rural technology, rural institutions and the rural poorest*. Dhaka: CIRDAP/IDS.

Hulme, D. 1989. "The Malawi Mudzi Fund: Daughter of Grameen", in *Journal of International Development*, Vol. 3, No. 4.

Hye, A. 1993. "Design for poverty alleviation programmes in South Asia: Some lessons". In Easter (ed.).

IFAD (International Fund for Agricultural Development). 1992. *The state of world rural poverty*. Rome: IFAD.

ILO (International Labour Office). 1971. *Ceylon: Matching employment opportunities and expectations* (2 vols.). Geneva.

Ishikawa, S. 1968. *Agricultural development in Asian perspective*. Tokyo: Hitotsubashi University.

Jamison, D. and L. Lau. 1982. *Farmer education and farm efficiency*. Baltimore: Johns Hopkins.

Kakwani, N. 1993. "Measuring poverty: Definitions and significance tests with application to the Côte d'Ivoire". In Lipton and van der Gaag (eds.).

Kanbur, R. 1990. *Poverty and development: The Human development report and the World development report"*. Working Paper No. 618. Washington, DC.: World Bank.

Kannan, K. 1993. "Public intervention and poverty alleviation". Trivandrum: Centre for Development Studies. Mimeo.

Kennedy, E. and Peters. 1992. "Household food security and child nutrition: The interaction of income and gender of household head", in *World Development*, Vol. 20.

Khan, A.H. 1974. *Reflections on the Comilla rural development projects*. OLC Paper No. 3. Washington, DC.: Overseas Liaison Committee, American Council on Education.

Khan, A.R. 1977. "Poverty and inequality in rural Bangladesh". In K. Griffin and A. R. Khan (eds.), *Poverty and inequality in rural Asia*. Geneva: ILO.

——. 1990. "Poverty in Bangladesh: Consequence of and a constraint on growth", in *The Bangladesh Development Studies*, Vol. 17, No. 3.

Kumar, S. 1977. *Role of the household economy in determining child nutrition in Kerala*. Occasional Paper No. 95. Ithaca, NY: Cornell University, Division of Nutritional Sciences.

Lanjouw, P. and N. Stern. 1989. "Markets, opportunities and changes in Palanpur 1957-84". In Hoff et al. (eds.), 1993.

Lieberman, S. 1984. "An organisational reconnaissance of the Employment Guarantee Scheme", in *Indian Journal of Public Administration*, Vol. 30, No. 4.

——. 1985. "Field-level perspectives on Maharashtra's employment guarantee scheme", in *Public Administration and Development*, Vol. 5, No. 2.

Lieberman, D.H. 1990. "Special employment programmes in developed and developing countries", in *International Labour Review*, Vol. 129, No. 2.

Lipton, M. 1976. "Urban Bias: Or why rural people stay poor", in *People*, Vol. 3, No. 2.

——. 1983. *Labour and poverty*. Staff Working Paper No. 616. Washington, DC.: World Bank.

——. 1983a. *Poverty, undernutrition and hunger*. Staff Working Paper No. 597. Washington, DC.: World Bank.

——. 1993. "Land reform as commenced business: The evidence against stopping", in *World Development*, April.

——. 1995. "Market, redistributive and proto-reform: Can liberalization help the poor?", in *Asian Development Review*.

—— and M. Lipton. 1993. "Creating rural livelihoods: Some lessons for South Africa from experience elsewhere", in *World Development*, Vol. 21, No. 9.

—— with R. Longhurst. 1989. *New seeds and poor people*. London: Unwin.

——, A. Pain and P. Richards. 1996. *Reaching the poor? Rice research in Sierra Leone and Sri Lanka compared*.

—— and M. Ravallion. 1995. "Poverty and policy". In J. Behrman and T. N. Srinivasan (eds.), *Handbook of development economics: Vol. 3*. Amsterdam: North Holland.

—— and J. Toye. 1991. *Does aid work in India?* London: Routledge.

—— and J. van der Gaag (eds.). 1993. *Including the poor*. Baltimore: Johns Hopkins for World Bank/IFPRI.

Matin, I. 1994. "Group credit contract: Towards a better understanding". Brighton: University of Sussex. Mimeo.

McGregor, J.A. 1988. "Credit and the rural poor: The changing policy environment in Bangladesh", in *Public Administration and Development*, Vol. 8, No. 4.

——. 1994. "Government failures and NGO successes: Credit, banking and the poor in rural Bangladesh 1970-90". In T. Lloyd and B. Morrissey (eds.), *Poverty, inequality and rural development*. Basingstoke: Macmillan.

Mishra, P. 1994. "The comprehensive crop insurance scheme in India 1985-91: A study of its working with special reference to Gujarat". DPhil (unpub.). Brighton: University of Sussex.

Morris, M.D. and M. McAlpin. 1982. *Measuring the condition of India's poor: The Physical Quality of Life Index.* New Delhi: Promilla.

Narain, D. and S. Roy. 1980. *Impact of irrigation and labour availability on multiple cropping: A case study of India.* Research Report No. 20. Washington, DC.: IFPRI.

OASS (Organisation for Applied Socioeconomic Systems). 1985. *National Rural Employment Programme, Haryana: Impact evaluation.* New Delhi, October.

Olson, M. 1982. *The rise and decline of nations: Economic growth, stagflation and social rigidities.* New Haven: Yale University Press.

Ostrom, E. 1990. *Governing the commons.* Cambridge: Cambridge University Press.

Parikh, K. and T.N. Srinivasan. 1993. "Poverty alleviation policies in India". In Lipton and van der Gaag (eds.).

Paul, S. 1991. "Poverty alleviation programs: A case-study of IRDP". Campbelltown: University of Western Sydney, Macarthur. Mimeo.

PEO (Programme Evaluation Organisation). 1980. *Joint evaluation report on the Employment Guarantee Scheme in Maharashtra.* New Delhi: Planning Commission.

Pope, A. 1733. *Essay on man.* London: Methuen, 1950.

Psacharopoulos, G. 1981. "Returns to education: An updated international comparison". Reprint Series, No. 210. Washington, DC.: World Bank.

Quinones, B.R. (ed.). 1988. *Financial innovations for the rural poor: The Asian experience.* Bangkok: Asian & Pacific Regional Agricultural Credit Association.

Rao, C. H. H., S. K. Ray and K. Subbarao. 1988. *Unstable agriculture and droughts.* Delhi: Vikas.

Ravallion, M. 1990. *Reaching the poor through rural public employment.* Discussion Paper No. 94. Washington, DC.: World Bank.

——. 1991. "Employment guarantee schemes: Are they a good idea?", in *Indian Economic Journal.*

——. 1994. *Poverty comparisons.* Chur, Switzerland: Harwood.

—— and G. Datt. 1994. "Growth and poverty in rural India". Washington, DC.: World Bank. Mimeo.

——, G. Datt and S. Chaudhuri. 1993. "Does Maharashta's Employment Guarantee Scheme guarantee employment?", in *Economic Development and Cultural Change*, Vol. 42, No. 2.

—— and B. Sen. 1994. "Impacts on rural poverty of land-based targeting: Further results for Bangladesh", in *World Development*, Vol. 22, No. 6.

Reserve Bank of India. 1989. *A review of the agricultural credit system in India.* Bombay.

Robbins, L. 1930. "The elasticity of supply of labour in terms of effort", in *Economica*, Vol. 10.

Rodgers, G. 1973. "Effects of public works on rural poverty: some case studies from the Kosi area of Bihar", in *Economic and Political Weekly*, Vol. 8, Nos. 4-6.

Rosenzweig, M. and P. Schultz. 1982. "Market opportunities, genetic endowment and intra-family resource distribution: Child survival in rural India", in *American Economic Review*, Vol. 72, No. 4, pp. 803-15.

Rowlingson, K. 1994. *Moneylenders and their customers.* London: Institute of Policy Studies.

Rugarabamu, G. 1993. "Resources and the sustainability of poverty alleviation programmes". In Easter (ed.).

Sahn, D. (ed.). 1989. *Seasonal variability in Third World agriculture.* Baltimore: Johns Hopkins.

—— and J. Arulpragasam. 1993. "Land tenure, dualism and poverty in Malawi". In Lipton and van der Gaag (eds.).

Schultz, T.P. 1988. "Education, investments and returns". In H. Chenery and T. N. Srinivasan (eds.), *Handbook of development economics: Vol. 1.* Amsterdam: North Holland.

Sen, A.K. 1980. *Levels of poverty: Policy and change".* Staff Working Paper No. 401. Washington, DC.: World Bank.

——. 1981. *Poverty and famines: An essay on entitlement and deprivation.* Oxford: Clarendon.

——. 1985. "Rights and capabilities". In T. Honderich (ed.), *Ethics and objectivity.* London: Routledge.

Siamwalla, A. et al. 1989. *"The Thai rural credit system: A description and elements of a theory".* In Hoff et al. (eds.), 1993.

Singh, B. 1985. *Agrarian structure, technical change and poverty.* New Delhi: Agricole.

Singh, R. and P. Hazell. 1993. "Rural poverty in the semi-arid tropics of India", in *Economic and Political Weekly*, Vol. 28, Agriculture Supplement.

Stiglitz, J. 1989. "Peer monitoring and credit markets". In Hoff et al. (eds.), 1993.

—— and A. Weiss. 1981. "Credit rationing in markets with imperfect information", in *American Economic Review*, Vol. 71.

Tabatabai, H. and M. Fouad. 1993. *The incidence of poverty in developing countries: An ILO compendium of data.* Geneva: ILO.

Taylor, C. et al. 1978. "The Narangwal experiment on interactions of nutrition and infections: 1. Project design and effects upon growth", in *Indian Journal of Medical Research*, Vol. 68 (Supplement), December.

Tendler, J. 1993. *New lessons from old projects: The workings of rural development in North-east Brazil.* Operations Evaluation Study. Washington, DC.: World Bank.

Thiesenhusen, W. (ed.). 1989. *Searching for agrarian reform in Latin America.* Boston: Unwin Hyman.

—— and J. Melmed-Sanjak. 1990. "Brazil's agrarian structure: Changes from 1970 through 1980", in *World Development*, Vol. 18, No. 3.

Tyler, G., R. el-Ghonemy and Y. Couvreur. 1993. "Alleviating rural poverty through agricultural growth", in *Journal of Development Studies*, Vol. 29, No. 2.

Udry, C. 1989. "Rural credit in Northern Nigeria". In Hoff et al. (eds.), 1993.

UNDP. 1991. *Human development report.* New York: Oxford University Press.

UNDP. 1994. *Human development report.* New York: Oxford University Press.

UNDP. 1995. *Human development report.* New York: Oxford University Press.

Vyas, V. 1976. "Structural change in agriculture and the small farm sector", in *Economic and Political Weekly*, Vol. 11, No. 1-2, January 10.

Walker, T. and J. Ryan. 1990. *Village and household economies in India's semi-arid tropics.* Baltimore: Johns Hopkins.

Wiggins, S. and B. Rogaly. 1989. "Providing rural credit in South India", in *Public Administration and Development*, Vol. 9.

Wood, G. 1984. "Provision of irrigation assets by the landless", in *Agricultural Administration*, Vol. 17, No. 2.

World Bank. 1976. *Public works programmes in developing countries: A comparative analysis.* Staff Working Paper No. 224. Prepared by S. J. Burki, D. G. Davies, R. H. Hook and J. W. Thomas (edited by R.V. Weaving). Washington, DC.

——. 1990. *World development report.* New York: Oxford University Press.

——. 1991. *Gender and poverty in India.* World Bank Country Study. Washington, DC.

——. 1994. *World development report.* New York: Oxford University Press.

——. 1994a. *Implementing the World Bank's strategy for reducing poverty and hunger.* Washington, DC.

DATE DUE